Trees, Shrubs, and Vines
for Attracting Birds

RICHARD M. DEGRAAF AND GRETCHIN M. WITMAN

DRAWINGS BY ABIGAIL RORER

TREES, SHRUBS, and VINES

A MANUAL FOR THE NORTHEAST

VINES

for Attracting Birds

University of Massachusetts Press   Amherst, 1979

To George H. Harrison and Jonathan Czar
who roused our interests in these things

Library of Congress Catalog Card Number 78-19698
ISBN 0-87023-266-5
Designed by Mary Mendell
Library of Congress Cataloging in Publication Data
DeGraaf, Richard M
Trees, shrubs, and vines for attracting birds.
Bibliography: p.
Includes index.
1. Birds, Attracting of. 2. Woody plants—
Northeastern States. 3. Landscape gardening—
Northeastern States. 4. Birds—Northern States.
I. Witman, Gretchin M., 1949-   joint author.
II. Title.
QL676.5.D38   639'.97'82974   78-19698
ISBN 0-87023-266-5

This volume is a contribution of the Urban Forestry
Research Unit of the Northeastern Forest Experiment
Station—U.S. Forest Service.

Short Contents

PREFACE ix

INTRODUCTION xi

TREES 1

SHRUBS 79

VINES 159

APPENDIX 171

SOURCES 181

GLOSSARY 186

INDEX 188

Contents

Preface   ix
Introduction   xi

TREES

Balsam Fir   2
Boxelder   3
Norway Maple   4
Red Maple   5
Silver Maple   6
Sugar Maple   6
Downy Serviceberry   9
Shadblow Serviceberry   10
Smooth Serviceberry   11
Sweet Birch   12
Yellow Birch   12
Paper Birch   15
Gray Birch   16
American Hornbeam   18
Pignut Hickory   19
Shagbark Hickory   21
Mockernut Hickory   22
Common Hackberry   23
Flowering Dogwood   24
Common Persimmon   26
American Beech   28
White Ash   29
Black Ash   30
Green Ash   31
American Holly   32

Butternut   34
Eastern Black Walnut   34
Eastern Red Cedar   36
Eastern Larch   38
American Sweetgum   39
Yellow-poplar   41
Common Apple   42
Crabapple   42
White Mulberry   45
Red Mulberry   46
Black Tupelo   48
American Hop-hornbeam   49
White Spruce   50
Colorado Spruce   51
Red Spruce   52
Red Pine   53
Pitch Pine   54
Eastern White Pine   56
Scotch Pine   59
Eastern Cottonwood   59
Bigtooth Aspen   60
Quaking Aspen   61
Pin Cherry   62
Black Cherry   63
Common Chokecherry   65
White Oak   66
Scarlet Oak   68
Pin Oak   69
Northern Red Oak   69
Black Oak   70
Black Willow   71
Common Sassafras   72
American Mountain-ash   73
Northern White Cedar   74
Eastern Hemlock   76
American Elm   77

SHRUBS

Speckled Alder   80

Smooth Alder   81

Bartram Serviceberry   82

Devil's Walkingstick   83

Common Bearberry   84

Red Chokeberry   85

Black Chokeberry   86

Japanese Barberry   87

European Barberry   88

Eastern Chinkapin   88

Common Buttonbush   90

Sweetfern   91

Alternate-leaf Dogwood   91

Silky Dogwood   93

Bunchberry   94

Gray Dogwood   95

Red-osier Dogwood   96

American Hazel   98

Beaked Filbert   100

Hawthorns   100

Russian Olive   103

Autumn Olive   104

Huckleberries   106

Black Huckleberry   106

Box Huckleberry   106

Dwarf Huckleberry   107

Dangleberry   108

Witch-hazel   109

Shrubby St. Johnswort   110

Inkberry   111

Smooth Winterberry   112

Common Winterberry   113

Common Juniper   115

Common Spicebush   116

Honeysuckles   118

Northern Bayberry   121

Scarlet Firethorn   122

Alderleaf Buckthorn   123

Common Buckthorn   124

Glossy Buckthorn   124

Flameleaf Sumac   125

Smooth Sumac   126

Staghorn Sumac   127

American Black Currant   129

Pasture Gooseberry   130

Roses   131

Brambles   134

Pussy Willow   136

Prairie Willow   137

Purpleosier Willow   137

American Elder   138

Scarlet Elder   140

Narrowleaf Meadowsweet   142

Broadleaf Meadowsweet   142

Hardhack   143

Common Snowberry   144

Coralberry   145

Canada Yew   146

Lowbush Blueberry   148

Highbush Blueberry   148

Mapleleaf Viburnum   151

Hobblebush   152

Witherod   153

Southern/Northern Arrowwood   154

Nannyberry   155

American Cranberrybush   157

VINES

Heartleaf Ampelopsis   160
Common Trumpetcreeper   161
American Bittersweet   162
Common Moonseed   163
Virginia Creeper   164
Cat Greenbrier   165
Common Greenbrier   166
Poison Ivy   167
Grapes   168

APPENDIX

Plant Hardiness Zone Map   172
Flowering and Fruiting Periods of Trees,
    Shrubs, Vines   173
Street Trees That are Valuable for Birds   178
Plants That will Grow in Dry, Sandy Soils   178
Plants That Withstand City Conditions   179
Some Salt-tolerant Plants   180
Sources   181
Glossary   186
Index   188

Preface

This book is a guide to woody plants—trees, shrubs, and vines—that are useful for attracting birds in the northeastern United States and adjacent Canada. It is a guide for landscape architects, gardeners, homeowners—for anyone interested in landscaping and in creating a rich and diverse bird habitat. Habitat provision is especially important today, because its loss is the greatest threat to wildlife; with each new shopping center, highway, or subdivision, more wildlife habitat is destroyed.

Interest in birdwatching or "birding"—the term preferred by its adherents—has increased greatly in recent years. Most birders do more than merely watch; they feed and study birds, even landscape their yards to attract a variety of birds and so observe them more closely.

This volume is intended as an aid in selecting woody plants that offer birds food, nest sites, and protection from predators or from the elements.

Trees, shrubs, and vines are the major vegetation that determines the vegetative character of residential landscapes and, to a large extent, of the bird life these landscapes contain. Careful selection and arrangement of that vegetation can produce a landscape that is both visually attractive and alive with the year-round sounds and colors of birds.

This book brings together plant descriptions, ranges, flowering and fruiting periods, landscape values, site requirements, and propagation methods for 162 plant species that provide food, cover, and/or nest sites. The introduction provides some of the principles involved in landscaping for birds and gives some sample planting designs. The remainder of the book is divided into three sections: trees, shrubs, and vines, listed alphabetically by genus. Common names vary for many of the plants listed, especially for shrubs; some names are quite local.

This is not a complete guide to attracting birds. A good review of the basic principles of habitat provision is included in *Songbirds in Your Garden* by John K. Terres (New York: Thomas Y. Crowell, 1953). The following books are also valuable supplements: John V. Dennis has provided *A Complete Guide to Bird Feeding* (New York: Knopf, 1976). Both Verne E. Davison, *Attracting Birds: From the Prairies to the Atlantic* (New York: Thomas Y. Crowell, 1967) and Alexander Martin et al., *American Wildlife and Plants* (New York: Dover Publications, 1951) are guides to the food habits of birds.

No one reference proved adequate for current scientific plant names. We relied primarily upon two works: *Standardized Plants Names,* prepared by the editorial committee of the American Joint Committee on Horticultural Nomenclature, 2nd ed. (Harrisburg, Pa.: J. Horace McFarland Co., 1942), and *A Field Guide to Trees and Shrubs* by G. A. Petrides (Boston: Houghton Mifflin Co., 1972).

Birds are listed in taxonomic order by common names in the *A.O.U. Checklist of North American Birds,* 5th ed. (Baltimore: American Ornithologists' Union, Lord Baltimore Press, 1957), with updates from Tate and Kibbe, *American Birds* 28:747–53, 1974.

We gratefully acknowledge those who helped in various ways: Harry E. Ahles of the Botany Department, University of Massachusetts, thoroughly reviewed the text for botanical accuracy, particularly the plant descriptions and taxonomy; Robert W. Franzen, biologist, Henry J. Ritzer, resource conservationist, Soil Conservation Service, and Edward R. Ladd, biologist, U.S. Fish and Wildlife Service, critically reviewed the manuscript and made many useful suggestions; Katherine Freygang conducted the preliminary library research and contributed much to the book's format.

A great amount of work went into typing manuscript drafts, revisions, and checking details. For their truly willing and cheerful help, we thank Cheryl Bellows, Valerie McCarthy, and Gloria Kennelly. Dr. Brian R. Payne, former leader of the Urban Forest Research Unit, U.S. Forest Service, enthusiastically supported our work from the beginning. Without his help, this book would not have been published.

Finally, we thank Abigail Rorer for preparing the book's illustrations, and Leone Stein, director, Richard Martin, editor, and Mary Mendell, designer, University of Massachusetts Press, for their capable editorial assistance.

1 Line Short

Introduction

The idea of planting residential grounds to attract wildlife has undergone a resurgence of interest in recent years. The original efforts were probably the bird gardens of nineteenth-century England. There, knowledgeable amateur ornithologists provided the habitat requirements of many birds when planting the grounds of their homes and estates. They were rewarded with a wealth of bird life to enjoy and study.

Published accounts of techniques to attract birds to American homes began to appear in the 1930s, although people surely had been employing them earlier. The basic idea is simple: provide food, water, and shelter, and birds will take advantage of the habitat created. The key is to select plants that are of value to birds. Some plants, of course, are more valuable than others. Many common ornamentals—shrubs such as forsythias (*Forsythia* spp.) and hydrangeas (*Hydrangea* spp.), or trees such as eastern redbud (*Cercis canadensis*)—are rarely used by birds. While such plants may be used occasionally for their visual effects, often plants similar in form but of real value to birds can be substituted for purely ornamental varieties. Thus, American cranberrybush (*Viburnum trilobum*), silky dogwood (*Cornus amomum*) and downy serviceberry (*Amelanchier arborea*) might be used instead of those ornamentals cited above.

Today, a great variety of planting materials is available from nurseries and garden centers. Many are exotics. Others may be sterile cultivars of otherwise fruit-bearing plants. And, while the wildlife value of some exotics such as autumn olive (*Eleagnus umbellata*) or white mulberry (*Morus alba*) cannot be denied, many native species are excellent for attracting wildlife. The serviceberries (*Amelanchier* spp.), American mountain-ash (*Sorbus americana*), common winterberry (*Ilex verticillata*) and many others are too rarely available commercially. Most of the plants included in this book can be either transplanted from the wild or propagated vegetatively.

Designing a landscape is not a simple task, even for small areas or yards. Careful planning and consideration of individual plant characteristics are required. Keep in mind the eventual size of mature trees. It is common to see older houses virtually hidden by towering blue spruces or other conifers planted by the front steps. These trees looked attractive as foundation plantings when they were small, but they eventually darken windows and make house maintenance extremely difficult.

Large evergreens such as hemlock, spruce, and pine are best kept to the sides and rear of the grounds, preferably on the north side to prevent shading of the yard and to reduce winter winds. Place smaller trees in front of this green backdrop. One can hardly choose a better small tree than flowering dogwood (*Cornus florida*) for year-round beauty and for attracting birds. Several planted in a small grove are especially attractive; not only are the spring flower clusters striking, but the red berries that ripen in late summer and early fall are readily eaten by almost a hundred kinds of birds, especially robins.

Face the border with a lower layer of fruit-bearing deciduous and evergreen shrubs. This arrangement combines good landscape design with good wildlife management. The resulting series of plant layers, from large and small trees and shrubs, creates a variety of nest sites and a diverse habitat attractive to many kinds of birds.

Plant selection is just one consideration. The landscape must have elements to unify it with the house—the grounds then become an extension of a home's interior. Attractive views from windows are important in all seasons, but particularly in winter when much time is spent indoors.

The scale of the plantings must suit the size of the house and grounds—tall trees and shrubs are needed to balance tall buildings. Likewise, the shape of the grounds must be considered. Irregular angles in property boundaries can become inviting enclosures with the use of hedges or masses of shrubs. Deep, odd corners can be left in a natural state to allow such plants as sumacs (*Rhus* spp.) or even poison ivy (*Toxicodendron radicans*) to grow. Both of these plants produce fruits that are quite valuable as bird food.

Exposure is important. Many plants require full sun—junipers (*Juniperus* spp.) and roses (*Rosa* spp.), for example. Use shade-tolerant plants in the cool shade of buildings and tall trees. Place wind-sensitive plants and those that are near the northern limits of their ranges in areas protected from winter winds. Use the included USDA map of plant hardiness zones to help determine which plants can withstand winter cold in your area. The hardiness zones, based on average minimum winter temperatures, generally represent the most northern zone in which a plant will grow in unprotected locations.

A plan is needed to take account of all the factors that must be considered when designing a landscape. The importance of a detailed scale drawing or sketch—showing all permanent features, as well as the plantings to be retained—cannot be overemphasized.

The sample plan shown illustrates some of the principles of planting to attract birds; it can be adapted to suit many situations. This plan and the accompanying list provide a selection of plants that are hardy throughout the Northeast and that provide food, cover, and nest sites for a variety of birds.

Notice the positions of the trees and shrubs and the massed plantings shown in the plan. This arrangement will result in an unobstructed view from the windows or terrace, and will eventually form an effective green wall which will afford privacy and show off flowering and fruiting trees and shrubs.

Massed plantings and thick borders of shrubs and vines provide both security for nests and shelter from the elements and from predators.

Evergreen trees such as hemlock (*Tsuga canadensis*) and white pine (*Pinus strobus*) are used by robins, wood thrushes, bluejays, grackles, and others for nesting; the seeds are eaten by pine siskins, pine grosbeaks, and crossbills. Colorado (*Picea pungens*) and white (*P. glauca*) spruces are used by nesting mourning doves, chipping sparrows, and mockingbirds.

Among deciduous trees, sugar maples (*Acer saccharum*) are used for nesting by robins, orioles, goldfinches, and red-eyed vireos. Others that provide fruit for birds are mountain-ashes (*Sorbus* spp.), serviceberries, white mulberry (*Morus alba*), and pin cherry (*Prunus pensylvanica*). These are all small trees that produce a profusion of fruits preferred by many birds. Two additional small trees to consider are the box elder (*Acer neguno*) and Washington hawthorn (*Crataegus phaenopyrum*). Some consider the box elder a less than ideal ornamental tree, but the winged seeds are a favorite food of wintering evening grosbeaks. The Washington hawthorn's thorny branches and dense foliage make it a favorite nesting tree for catbirds, brown thrashers, mockingbirds, and robins, among others. Its red fruits persist throughout the winter and so provide a good supply of emergency food. This tree is a fine upright ornamental; it is especially beautiful after its leaves fall, when its red fruits contrast with the gray branches. Another advantage of Washington hawthorn is its resistance to infection by cedar-hawthorn rust.

Many bird species live quite close to the ground, and so are dependent on shrubs for food, nest sites, and cover. Song sparrows, for example, feed on seeds on the ground, nest on or within a yard of the ground, and when frightened, usually fly close to the ground to the nearest thicket. Many birds seem to live more underfoot than in the tree-

LARGE TREES
1. American Beech
2. Northern Red Oak
3. White Oak
4. Sugar Maple
5. Eastern White Pine
6. White Spruce
7. Eastern Hemlock

SMALL TREES
8. American Mountain-ash
9. Flowering Dogwood
10. Washington Hawthorn

LARGE SHRUBS
11. Common Winterberry
12. Amur Honeysuckle
13. Autumn Olive
14. American Cranberrybush
15. American Elder

SMALL SHRUBS
16. American Blackberry
17. Silky Dogwood
18. Red-osier Dogwood
19. Tatarian Honeysuckle
20. Common Snowberry
21. Japanese Barberry
22. Your favorite ornamental—
    Pyracantha, Yew, Juniper, etc.

tops. What shrubs are most useful in meeting their year-round needs? In wet areas, consider planting a few clumps of elderberry (*Sambucus* spp.). Elderberry provides a showy flower display in summer after most other shrubs have bloomed, and the heavy panicles of dark purple berries attract many kinds of birds: among them, chipping and song sparrows, indigo buntings, cardinals, catbirds, and bluebirds.

Other deciduous shrubs that provide fleshy fruits are gray dogwood (*Cornus racemosa*), arrowwood (*Viburnum dentatum* or *V. recognitum*), amur (*Lonicera maacki*) and tatarian honeysuckles (*L. tatarica*), highbush blueberry (*Vaccinium corymbosum*), and American cranberrybush. Also consider red-osier dogwood (*Cornus stolonifera*), alternate-leaf dogwood (*C. alternifolia*), and common winterberry.

Several exotics are proven bird attractors—Russian olive (*Eleagnus angustifolia*), autumn olive, and multiflora rose (*Rosa multiflora*). These plants grow in almost any soil and produce fruit in abundance. The multiflora rose retains its fruit all winter and is one of the best plants for providing protection and nest sites for song sparrows, mockingbirds, catbirds, and brown thrashers. Multiflora rose grows to a thick, often climbing mass. Of course the wilder it grows, the more cover and fruit it produces, but plant it only where it can be controlled. Incidentally, this rose was heavily planted in the 1950s along highway medians, and many ornithologists now believe it was the most important factor in enabling mockingbirds to increase their range northward. Mockingbirds certainly use it for nesting; and in Northeast winters they are rarely found far from this fruit-bearing rose.

Some evergreen shrubs should complement most plantings. Junipers provide food and protection from predators and the weather; they are fine nest sites for chipping sparrows. Yews (*Taxus* spp.) are used by nesting mockingbirds, chipping and song sparrows, and robins; they produce fleshy red berries that are eaten by several species.

The main body of this book presents the bird habitat values of many trees, shrubs, and vines from which to choose when landscaping to attract birds. Scattered specimen plants, especially the smaller trees and shrubs, are less attractive to birds for nesting and escape cover than are massed plants. Also give thought to planting both coniferous and deciduous trees of varying mature heights in order to provide as many layers of vegetation as is possible. Your efforts will be rewarded anew each year with an increased variety of birds as the plantings mature.

TREES

BALSAM FIR

Abies balsamea (L.) Mill.
PINACEAE

Description. Balsam fir, familiar as the traditional Christmas tree, is a small or medium-sized evergreen tree, 40 to 60 feet tall. It is the most symmetrical of northeastern trees. Balsam fir is used for nesting by many bird species—especially robins and mourning doves—for their first nest of the season, which is commonly built before hardwoods produce leaves. Balsam fir seed is readily eaten by boreal and black-capped chickadees, purple finches, and both red and white-winged crossbills.

Bark. Gray, filled with resin blisters.

Leaves. Fragrant, flat needles, ⅜- to 1¼ inches long, whitish beneath, with a broad circular base, arranged spirally, but often appear in flat rows on either side of the branch.

Flowers. Inconspicuous, male and female flowers (sporophylls) occur separately on the same plant.

Cones. Upright, 2 to 4 inches long, dark purple. Mature the first season after flowering. Seed production may begin on trees fifteen years old (U.S. Forest Service 1965), with good crops occurring at two- to four-year intervals.

Flowering period. May to June.

Fruiting period. Late August to early September (seeds ripen). Cones disintegrate by dropping scales.

Habitat. Occurs in cool, moist locations on high ground as well as in swamps, and from sea level to 5,000 feet where average annual rainfall is equal to or greater than 30 inches, and average temperatures are equal to or less than 70° F. (U.S. Forest Service 1965).

Range. Newfoundland south in the mountains to Virginia, west to Minnesota and Iowa.

Hardiness zone. 4.

Landscape notes. Balsam fir is useful for landscaping in the cooler, moister sections of the Northeast, but does not do well elsewhere. It can be made attractive by selective pruning

when young, but it cannot tolerate heavy pruning. The tree is the preferred evergreen for Christmas use because of its long-lasting needles and strong fragrance. Balsam fir is sensitive to smoke and pollution and does poorly in cities.

Propagation. Trees may be propagated from seeds and cuttings. Fresh seeds should be collected and sown in the fall on moist, shaded mineral soil, or stratified and sown in spring. Stratification at 40° F. for one to three months improves germination. Dried seeds may be stored for a year or more in sealed containers kept at 36°–39° F. Seeds sown in the fall generally germinate the following spring (Hartmann and Kester 1968; U.S. Forest Service 1948).

Birds That Use Balsam Fir

	Food	Cover	Nesting
Spruce grouse*	S	X	
Ruffed grouse	S	X	
Mourning dove		X	X
Long-eared owl	S	X	
Yellow-bellied sapsucker	sap	X	
Blue jay	S	X	X
Gray jay	S	X	X
Black-capped chickadee	S	X	
Boreal chickadee*	S	X	
White-breasted nuthatch	S	X	
Red-breasted nuthatch		X	X[1]
American robin		X	X
Swainson's thrush		X	X
Black-throated Blue warbler		X	X
Evening grosbeak*	S	X	X
Purple finch*	S	X	X
Pine grosbeak*	S	X	X
Red crossbill*	S	X	X
White-winged crossbill*	S	X	X

Note: *preferred food; [1]Uses pitch in nest building; S, seeds.
Sources: McKenny 1939; Davison 1967; Martin et al. 1951; Headstrom 1970; Petrides 1972.

BOXELDER
Acer negundo L.
ACERACEAE

Description. The boxelder is moderately tall—50 to 75 feet—and has a trunk diameter of 2 to 4 feet. Its distribution is widespread. Its seeds are a preferred food of the evening grosbeak and purple finch. Another common name is ashleaf maple.

Bark. Light brown, furrowed with shallow fissures and low ridges.

Twigs. Purplish-green or green, shiny, covered with whitish powder.

Leaves. Opposite, compound, 4 to 10 inches long, 3 to 7 (occasionally 9) leaflets, each with lobes and coarsely toothed margins, light green above, paler beneath. Autumn color: pale yellow.

Flowers. Yellow-green, male and female flowers occur on separate plants, before the leaves.

Fruits. Flat, one-seeded samaras, green ripening to brown. Good seed crops occur nearly every year.

Flowering period. March to mid-May.

Fruiting period. August to October, persistent to early spring.

Habitat. Prefers rich, moist soils but will grow on poor sites. Tolerates sun or partial shade, cold, and drought.

Range. Nova Scotia south to Florida, west to Alberta and California.

Hardiness zone. 2.

Landscape notes. Boxelder is the least attractive of the large maples for landscaping due to its irregular, bushy crown, but it may be the hardiest because it is best able to withstand unfavorable conditions. The seeds are important winter food for evening grosbeaks. The tree grows rapidly, often sprouting about the base, and is short-lived. It is commonly used for shelter belts in the prairie states.

Propagation. Seeds may be collected as they ripen and sown immediately in drills ¼- to 1 inch deep, or broadcast. They may be sown in spring if stratified in sand for ninety days at 41° F., or anytime thereafter up to eighteen months if stored in sealed containers at 41° F. Seedbeds should contain moist mineral soil. Seeds sown in late fall should be covered with a layer of mulch until germination begins (U.S. Forest Service 1948). Boxelder can also be propagated from softwood cuttings or by division (U.S. Forest Service 1948).

Birds That Use Boxelder
(See Maples)

	Food	Cover	Nesting
Ring-necked pheasant	S		
Yellow warbler		X	X
Evening grosbeak*	S	X	
Purple finch	S		X[1]
Pine grosbeak	S		

Note: *preferred food; [1]occasionally used for nest sites by songbirds; S, seeds.
Sources: McKenny 1939; Davison 1967; Dugmore 1904; Barnes 1973.

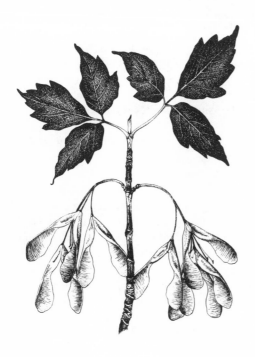

Boxelder

NORWAY MAPLE
Acer platanoides L.
ACERACEAE

Description. The Norway maple grows 40 to 70 feet tall. It has been widely planted as a street tree in residential areas.
Bark. Dark gray, tight with shallow fissures and ridges.
Leaves. Opposite, simple, 2 to 8 inches across, palmate with 7 lobes, surfaces dark green, broken leaf stalk exudes milky fluid. Autumn colors: green until late, turning yellow briefly before dropping.
Flowers. Small, yellow, forming in clusters before the leaves unfold.
Fruits. Paired, widely divergent samaras, forming in dense clusters.
Flowering period. April to June.
Fruiting period. September to November.
Habitat. Although of European origin, the tree is planted widely in the United States and occasionally spreads by gravity and wind to fields and woodlands. Does well on a variety of soils.
Range. Throughout the Northeast.
Hardiness zone. 4.
Landscape notes. An excellent shade producer, this tree is popular along rural, suburban, and urban streets and lawns for its bright yellow flowers in spring, long leaf period, and yellow fall foliage. Trees grow to about 15 feet in ten years.
Propagation. There are many varieties of Norway maple, some of which are propagated from seeds and others from cuttings. Seeds may be sown in rich mineral soil as soon as they ripen, or stratified in sand for three to four months at 41° F. and sown in spring. Seeds may be stored for one year at 41° F. with about 20 percent loss of germination (U.S. Forest Service 1948). They may be broadcast or sown in drills ¼- to 1 inch deep and should be kept moist. Fall-sown seeds should be lightly mulched until they germinate. Seedlings may be transplanted when

they are one year old (U.S. Forest Service 1948).

Bird uses. See Maples.

RED MAPLE
Acer rubrum L.
ACERACEAE

Description. The red maple is generally a moderate-sized tree, about 50 to 70 feet tall. It can achieve great size, however, with a trunk diameter exceeding 3 feet. Another common name is swamp maple.

Bark. Light gray and smooth on young trunks, becoming rough with plates and fissures on older trees.

Twigs. Dark red, shiny.

Leaves. Opposite, simple, 2 to 6 inches across, palmate with 3 (occasionally 5) toothed lobes, light green above, pale beneath. Autumn colors: scarlet or crimson.

Flowers. Bright red, appearing before the leaves. They are among the first trees to flower in spring.

Fruits. Bright-red, paired samaras, ¾-inch long, forming in clusters. Good seed crops occur almost every year.

Flowering period. February to May.

Fruiting period. March to July.

Habitat. Grows in low wet meadows, swamps, and along rivers and streams. Also mixes with white pines and hardwoods in northern forests.

Range. Newfoundland south to Florida, west to Texas.

Hardiness zone. 4.

Landscape notes. This fairly handsome shade tree has outstanding autumn colors. It is useful on wet and dry soils. Generally less symmetrical in outline and faster growing than the sugar maple, the red maple often grows 2 feet per year. These trees are hardy and may live 150 years.

Propagation. Ripe seeds may be collected from trees or the ground. They may be stored in sealed containers for one to two years without significant loss of viability. For best results, seeds should be sown soon after collection or stratified in sand for sixty to seventy-five days at 41° F. and sown in spring. Good germination and seedling development occurs in moist mineral soil rich in organic matter. Seeds may be broadcast or sown in drills ¼- to 1 inch deep and kept constantly moist. Seedlings may be transplanted when 6 to 12 inches tall (U.S. Forest Service 1948).

Birds That Use Red Maple
(See Maples)

	Food	Cover	Nesting
Bobwhite	S		
Yellow-bellied sapsucker	sap		
American robin		X	X
Prairie warbler		X	X
Cardinal	S		
Evening grosbeak	S, BD		
Pine grosbeak	S		
American goldfinch		X	X

Note: S, seeds; BD, buds.
Sources: McKenny 1939; Allen 1934; Rushmore 1969.

SILVER MAPLE
Acer saccharinum L.
ACERACEAE

Description. The silver maple is a fast-growing, short-lived tree, and its wood is relatively weak. It can grow 60 to 80 feet tall. The buds are readily eaten by evening grosbeaks. Other common names are soft maple, river maple, and white maple.
Bark. Silver-gray with thin, vertical, rectangular, flaky plates.
Twigs. Reddish-brown, give off an unpleasant odor when bruised.
Leaves. Opposite, single, 2 to 10 inches long, palmate with 5 deeply cut lobes, pale green above, silvery below. Autumn colors: yellow, red, orange, and green.
Flowers. Greenish or reddish forming in clusters before the leaves develop.
Fruits. Paired, winged seeds, 1½ to 2 inches long, green to red. Forest trees begin bearing fruits when thirty-five to forty years old. Those grown in the open bear sooner (U.S. Forest Service 1965).
Flowering period. February to May.
Fruiting period. April to June.
Habitat. Damp, bottomland soils. Commonly found along ponds and watercourses. Able to withstand several weeks of flooding without apparent injury.
Range. New Brunswick south to northwest Florida, west to Minnesota and Oklahoma.
Hardiness zone. 4.
Landscape notes. Wild and cultivated varieties of silver maples are attractive for yards and parks with moist soils. They are not recommended for street planting because the brittle branches are easily broken by storms. The variety *wieri* is popular for its cut leaves and ability to grow in dry, clay soils. These trees are hardy, grow rapidly—reaching 26 feet in ten years—and bear fruits when thirty-five to forty years old.
Propagation. Trees may be propagated from ripe seeds gathered from the plant or the ground. They may be sown immediately, or stored without excessive drying in cool, moist air (32°–50° F.), they should keep for at least one year without significant loss of viability. Seeds that are sown upon ripening should germinate immediately. Best seed growth occurs in beds of mineral soil with high organic content. They may be broadcast or sown in drills ¼- to 1 inch deep (U.S. Forest Service 1948).

Birds That Use Silver Maple
(See Maples)

	Food	Cover	Nesting
Bobwhite	S		
Northern oriole		X	X
Cardinal	S		
Evening grosbeak	S, BD		
Pine grosbeak	S		
American goldfinch		X	X

Note: S, seeds; BD, buds.
Source: McKenny 1939.

SUGAR MAPLE
Acer saccharum Marsh.
ACERACEAE

Description. The sugar maple is a stately tree which, when open-grown, has a spreading, rounded crown with a fine branching pattern. It can grow 60 to 100 feet tall, with a trunk diameter of 3 to 4 feet. Other common names are rock maple and hard maple.
Bark. Gray, brown, rough and furrowed on mature trees.
Twigs. Reddish-brown, shiny.
Leaves. Opposite, simple, 3 to 5 inches in diameter, palmate with 5 lobes, margins without teeth, bright green above, pale below. Autumn colors: golden yellow with splashes of red and orange.
Flowers. Small, bright yellow, appearing with the leaves.

Sugar Maple

Fruits. U-shaped, formed by two, joined, parallel winged seeds or samaras. Light fruit production begins on forest trees when they are about forty years old, with good crops appearing every three to seven years and light crops in intervening years (U.S. Forest Service 1948 and 1965).

Flowering period. April to June.

Fruiting period. June to October, ripen mid-September to October, persistent through December.

Habitat. Prefers rich, deep, moist soils of upland forests and fields but tolerates more sterile conditions. Best development occurs on loam soils with pH range of 5.5 to 7.3 (U.S. Forest Service 1965).

Range. Quebec south to the mountains of northern Georgia, west to Manitoba and Texas (variety *barbatum* to northern Florida).

Hardiness zone. 4.

Landscape notes. Sugar maple is commonly used as an ornamental for its attractive shape, dense summer shade, and colorful autumn leaves. It is a common forest and roadside tree, particularly in rural New England where cool temperatures and clean air prevail. It is adversely affected by road salt and air pollution. The sap of the sugar maple is the source of maple syrup and sugar. Trees are hardy, moderate to slow-growing, and may live for 200 to 300 years. They grow about one foot per year for the first thirty to forty years (U.S. Forest Service 1965).

Propagation. Trees may be grown from ripe seeds that are planted in the fall, or stratified and planted in spring. Seeds should be stratified in sand or peat for two to three months at 36°–41° F., and sown ¼- to 1 inch deep in mineral soil containing plenty of organic matter. Germination usually occurs within a few weeks. Fall-sown seeds should be mulched to protect them from freezing (U.S. Forest Service 1948). Seeds may be stored for at least one year in open or airtight containers at 36°–40° F. (U.S. Forest Service 1948).

Birds That Use Sugar Maple
(See Maples)

	Food	Cover	Nesting
Bobwhite	S		
American robin		X	X
Red-eyed vireo		X	X
Northern oriole			X
Cardinal	S		
Evening grosbeak	S, BD		
Rose-breasted grosbeak	S	X	X
Pine grosbeak	S		
American goldfinch		X	X

Note: S, seeds; BD, buds.
Sources: McKenny 1939; Davison 1967.

Birds That Use Maples

	Food	Cover	Nesting
Turkey	S		
Ruffed grouse	S		
Bobwhite	S		
Red-bellied woodpecker		X	X (cavity)
Yellow-bellied sapsucker	sap		
Carolina chickadee	S (red maple)		
American robin	S	X	X
Starling		X	X (cavity)
Red-eyed vireo		X	X (saplings)
Northern oriole		X	X
Cardinal	S		
Rose-breasted grosbeak*	S	X	X
Evening grosbeak*	S	X	X
Purple finch*	S		
Pine grosbeak*	S		
Pine siskin	S		
American goldfinch	S	X	X
Song sparrow	S		

Note: *preferred food; S, seeds
Sources: McKenny 1939; Davison 1967; Martin et al. 1951.

DOWNY SERVICEBERRY

Amelanchier arborea (Michx. f.) Fern.

ROSACEAE

Description. A small tree or large shrub, downy serviceberry is similar to Allegany and shadblow serviceberries, but with fine white hairs on the undersides of the leaves. It grows 20 to 40 feet tall, and can have a stem diameter of 8 to 16 inches. The fruits of serviceberries ripen early and are preferred by many birds, among them the mockingbird, rufous-sided towhee, cardinal, rose-breasted grosbeak, northern oriole, robin, wood thrush, scarlet tanager, brown thrasher, catbird, and ruffed grouse (Davison 1967:211). Other common names are juneberry and shadbush.

Bark. Light gray, smooth.

Leaves. Alternate, simple, 1½ to 4 inches long, broadly elliptic to obovate with rounded to heart-shaped bases, long tips, finely toothed, lower surfaces densely hairy. Autumn colors: yellow and red.

Flowers. White, forming in spreading or drooping clusters.

Fruits. Sweet, purple pomes, ⅓-inch diameter, juicy. Good fruit crops are borne nearly every year.

Flowering period. March to June.

Fruiting period. June to August.

Habitat. Lowland, moist, rich soils and drier uplands in woods and open sites.

Range. Quebec south to Florida, west to Minnesota and Texas.

Hardiness zone. 3.

Landscape notes. This is an excellent tree for the small yard or as a filler in naturalistic compositions. It grows well in sun or shade. However, flower and fruit production is greater on trees grown in full sun.

Propagation. Trees may be grown from seeds that are extracted from ripe fruits by maceration or left to dry within the pulp. For best results, seeds should be sown immediately, ¼-inch deep in nursery soil, and mulched lightly to prevent drying in summer and freezing in winter. Germination should occur the following spring, at which time the mulch should be removed and the seedlings given half shade for one year. For later sowing, seeds may be stored for at least one year at 41° F., or stratified in peat at 33°–41° F. for 90 to 120 days in order to overcome embryo dormancy. Other methods of propagation include taking cuttings in spring or fall and digging root suckers (U.S. Forest Service 1948). Seedlings may be transplanted when one year old, and field planted when two or three years old.

Birds That Use Downy Serviceberry
(See Serviceberries)

	Food	Cover	Nesting
Ruffed grouse*	F		
Common flicker	F		
Hairy woodpecker*	F		
Eastern kingbird*	F		
Gray catbird*	F		
Mockingbird*	F		
Brown thrasher*	F		
American robin*	F		
Wood thrush*	F		
Hermit thrush*	F		
Veery*	F		
Cedar waxwing*	F		
Red-eyed vireo*	F		
Common grackle	F		
Northern oriole*	F		
Scarlet tanager*	F		
Rufous-sided towhee*	F		
Cardinal*	F		
Rose-breasted grosbeak*	F		

Note: *preferred food; F, fruit.
Source: Davison 1967.

SHADBLOW SERVICEBERRY
Amelanchier canadensis (L.) Medic.
ROSACEAE

Description. Shadblow serviceberry is a large shrub or small tree, occasionally growing to 25 feet. Fruits are readily taken by many birds. Another common name is oblongleaf juneberry.
Bark. Gray, with distinct vertical lines.
Leaves. Alternate, simple, 1½ to 2½ inches long, oblong-elliptic to oblong-ovate, finely toothed, dull green. Autumn colors: deep orange to rusty red.
Flowers. Delicate, white, long-petaled blossoms that form in dense racemes.
Fruits. Dark purple, about ⅓-inch long, applelike, sweet, often used in pies and jellies. Good fruit crops are borne nearly every year.
Flowering period. March to June.
Fruiting period. June to August.
Habitat. Commonly grows along margins of woodlands, in swamps and thickets.
Range. Southwest Quebec to Georgia.
Hardiness zone. 5.
Landscape notes. Shadblow serviceberry usually grows in alderlike clumps from several upright trunks, or in the form of small trees with delicate, airy crowns. It is the most abundant eastern species and, therefore, the most available for propagating or transplanting. Useful as a specimen or as an understory tree in cool moist woodlands. Blossoms and fruits are striking when plants are positioned in front of a darker background of evergreens. Much admired since colonial times, these plants are hardy and grow rapidly.
Propagation. See Downy Serviceberry.

Shadblow Serviceberry

Birds That Use Shadblow Serviceberry
(See Serviceberries)

	Food	Cover	Nesting
Ruffed grouse	F		
Mourning dove	F		
Common flicker	F		
Red-headed woodpecker	F		
Hairy woodpecker	F		
Downy woodpecker	F		
Eastern kingbird	F	X	X
Eastern phoebe	F		
Blue jay	F		
Tufted titmouse	F		
Brown thrasher	F		
American robin	F	X	X
Wood thrush	F	X	X
Hermit thrush	F	X	
Swainson's thrush	F	X	
Eastern bluebird	F		
Cedar waxwing	F		
Red-eyed vireo	F		
American redstart	F		
Red-winged blackbird	F		
Northern oriole	F		
Scarlet tanager	F		
Cardinal	F		
Rose-breasted grosbeak	F		
Northern junco	F		
Song sparrow	F		

Note: F, fruit.
Source: McKenny 1939.

SMOOTH SERVICEBERRY
Amelanchier laevis Wieg.
ROSACEAE

Description. This serviceberry is a small tree, 15 to 30 feet tall, with a trunk diameter of 6 to 12 inches. The fruits are a choice food of the catbird, rose-breasted grosbeak, northern oriole, brown thrasher, and cedar waxwing (Davison 1967:210). Other common names are Allegany serviceberry, juneberry, and shadbush.
Bark. Light gray with shallow fissures.

Leaves. Alternate, simple, 1½ to 2½ inches long, ovate or obovate with rounded to heart-shaped bases, margins finely toothed, surfaces hairless. Autumn color: reddish-bronze.
Flowers. White, forming in spreading or drooping clusters.
Fruits. Sweet, juicy, purple or black pomes, ¼-inch in diameter.
Flowering period. March to June.
Fruiting period. June to August.
Habitat. Occurs in damp or dry, slightly to moderately acid soils of woodlands and open sites.
Range. Newfoundland south to Georgia, west to Minnesota and Kansas.
Hardiness zone. 5.
Landscape notes. Smooth serviceberry is attractive in bloom with its delicate and airy drooping flowers. It is useful alone as a specimen or as an understory or woodland border tree, and is attractive along ponds with wooded backgrounds.
Propagation. See Downy Serviceberry.

Birds That Use Smooth Serviceberry
(See Serviceberries)

	Food	Cover	Nesting
Ruffed grouse	F		
Mourning dove	F		
Eastern kingbird	F		
Eastern phoebe	F		
Gray catbird*	F		
Brown thrasher*	F		
American robin*	F		
Eastern bluebird	F		
Cedar waxwing*	F		
Red-eyed vireo	F		
American redstart	F		
Red-winged blackbird	F		
Northern oriole*	F		
Scarlet tanager	F		
Rose-breasted grosbeak*	F		
American goldfinch*	F		
Northern junco	F		
Song sparrow	F		

Note: *preferred food; F, fruit.
Sources: McKenny 1939; Davison 1967.

SWEET BIRCH
Betula lenta L.
BETULACEAE

Description. Sweet or black birch is a medium-sized tree, about 50 or 60 feet tall. In the forest, it occurs scattered among other tree species, and typically develops a long clear trunk, 1 to 2 feet in diameter. The seeds are preferred by many bird species. Other common names are cherry birch and mountain mahogany.

Bark. Black or reddish-brown with horizontal lenticels on young trees. Sweet and aromatic due to the presence of wintergreen oil in the inner bark.

Leaves. Alternate, simple, 1 to 6 inches long, ovate, often with heart-shaped bases, margins single-toothed. Autumn color: golden yellow.

Flowers. Inconspicuous on male and female catkins.

Fruits. Small and winged, contained in a strobile. Good crops are borne every one to two years. Light crops occur during intervening years.

Flowering period. April to May.

Fruiting period. August to November, persistent to winter.

Habitat. Abundant in moist, well-drained soils of northeastern woodlands. Also on rocky terrain where its roots grow close to the surface and reach into crevasses. Commonly found near evergreens and stands of mixed hardwoods.

Range. Quebec south to the mountains of northern Georgia, west to Ohio.

Hardiness zone. 4.

Landscape notes. Sweet birch is an attractive lawn or border tree in pure clumps or mixed with other species. It is all too infrequently used. Hardy, with a moderate to rapid growth rate, sweet birch may live for 200 years.

Propagation. Trees can be grown from collected seeds. Seeds can be removed from the small cones and dried and stored in airtight jars for one year at 40° F., or stratified over winter. Stratify seeds in sand or peat for 42 to 70 days at 32°–41° F. Young seedlings should be given partial shade for the first two or three years of growth (U.S. Forest Service 1948).

Birds That Use Sweet Birch
(See Birches)

	Food	Cover	Nesting
Green-winged teal	S		
Wood duck	S		
Bufflehead	S		
Red-shouldered hawk		X	X
Turkey	S		
Ruffed grouse*	S, BD		
Ring-necked pheasant	S		
Great blue heron	S		
Yellow-bellied sapsucker	sap	X	X (cavity)
Blue jay	S	X	
Tufted titmouse	S	X	
Pine siskin*	S	X	
American goldfinch*	S, BD	X	
Northern junco	S		

Note: *preferred food; S, seeds; BD, buds.
Sources: McKenny 1939; Petrides 1972.

YELLOW BIRCH
Betula alleghaniensis Britt.
BETULACEAE

Description. Yellow birch, so typical of the northern hardwood forest, is a moderate-sized tree, 60 to 70 feet tall, with an irregularly rounded crown. It is a preferred nest tree of red-shouldered hawks, and its seeds are eaten by many bird species.

Bark. Thin, shiny, golden to bronze and peeling on young trunks, thicker, red-brown and platelike on mature trunks.

Twigs. Thin, brown, with strong wintergreen flavor.

Leaves. Alternate, simple, 3 to 4½-inches long, 1½ to 2 inches wide, ovate with bases rounded or slightly heart-shaped, margins doubly toothed. Autumn color: yellow.

Flowers. Inconspicuous, male and female flowers occur on separate catkins on same

[12]

plant before the leaves appear.

Fruits. Short, woody, erect cones containing many small winged seeds. Seed production begins on forest trees about forty years old. A prolific seeder.

Flowering period. Mid-April to late May.

Fruiting period. August to October, persistent to winter.

Habitat. Prefers cool moist conditions. Seedlings grow best in the shade of taller trees and are often found growing in association with beech and maple, or hemlock.

Range. Newfoundland south to the mountains of Georgia, west to Manitoba and Iowa.

Hardiness zone. 4.

Landscape notes. The slender, graceful habit of the yellow birch is attractive in all locations favorable to its growth. Trees planted in the open develop a low, widespreading crown. They are hardy, slow-growing and long-lived, occasionally surviving for 300 years.

Propagation. Trees may be propagated from collected seed. Seeds should be stratified at 32°–40° F. for several months (Harlow and Harrar 1969). Seedlings should be given light shade for the first two or three years after germination (U.S. Forest Service 1948).

Birds That Use Yellow Birch
(See Birches)

	Food	Cover	Nesting
Green-winged teal	S		
Wood duck	S		
Bufflehead	S		
Red-shouldered hawk		X	X
Turkey	S		
Ruffed grouse*	S, BD		
Ring-necked pheasant	S		
Great blue heron	S		
Yellow-bellied sapsucker	sap	X	X (cavity)
Blue jay	S		
Tufted titmouse	S		
Pine siskin*	S		
American goldfinch*	S, BD		
Northern junco	S		

Note: *preferred food; S, seeds; BD, buds.
Sources: McKenny 1939; Petrides 1972.

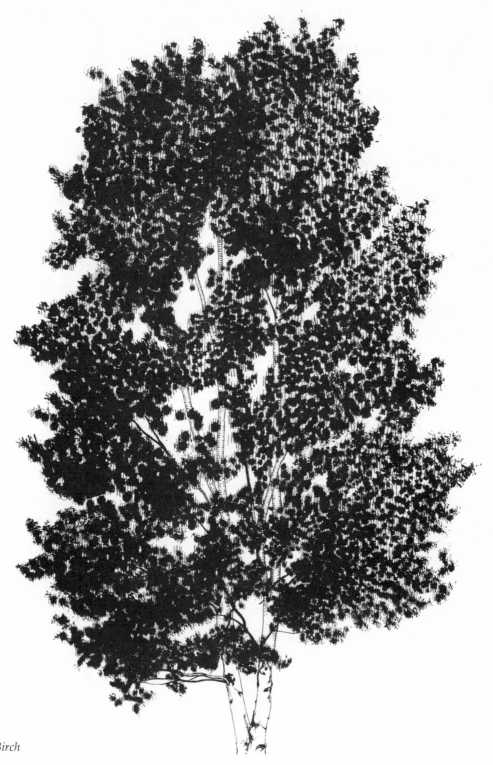

Paper Birch

PAPER BIRCH

Betula papyrifera Marsh.
BETULACEAE

Description. The paper or white birch is sometimes called the "lady of the woods" because of its spectacular white bark and graceful form. It is relatively short-lived, and grows 50 to 80 feet tall. The American goldfinch is one of many birds that relishes the seeds. Another common name is canoe birch.

Bark. Shiny brown when young, turning creamy white with age, separates from trunk in thin, papery strips.

Twigs. Reddish-brown, slender, and flexible.

Leaves. Alternate, simple, 2 to 3 inches long, ovate, margins doubly toothed, leaf tips pointed, medium to dark green and smooth above, pale yellowish-green with or without fine hairs beneath. Autumn color: golden-yellow.

Flowers. Inconspicuous on catkins. Male catkins ¾- to 1¼ inches long, usually forming in twos or threes. Female catkins 1 to 1¼ inches long, solitary.

Fruits. Small, stalked cones, 1 to 1½ inches long, containing many small, flat, two-winged nutlets. Good seed crops occur periodically, with light crops occurring during intervening years.

Flowering period. Mid-April to early June.

Fruiting period. August to September, persistent to winter.

Habitat. Occurs in cool, moist areas of the Northeast. Occasionally found in pure stands, but more often seen scattered throughout mixed (coniferous-hardwood) forests. Occurs on north-facing slopes in the southern parts of its range.

Range. Newfoundland south to North Carolina, west to Iowa.

Hardiness zone. 2.

Landscape notes. One of our best native ornamental trees, paper birch is very popular as a yard tree for its white, showy bark and handsome, airy crown. Branching occurs closer to the ground on trees grown in the open than on those in forests or clumps. Trees are hardy and grow rapidly, but are short-lived with a normal life span of less than eighty years. They are subject to light damage by the bronze birch borer (Harlow and Harrar 1969; Wyman 1951). Trees do not do well in lower elevations south of New York State (Lemmon 1952).

Propagation. Plants may be propagated from ripe seeds collected directly from the small cones. Seeds may be stored for 18 months at room temperature in air containing 1 percent moisture. Seeds may be sown in fall, or stratified in sand or peat for 60 to 75 days at 41° F. In both cases, they should germinate in the spring (U.S. Forest Service 1948).

Birds That Use Paper Birch
(See Birches)

	Food	Cover	Nesting
Green-winged teal	S		
Wood duck	S		
Bufflehead	S		
Turkey	S		
Ruffed grouse*	S		
Ring-necked pheasant	S		
Great blue heron	S		
Yellow-bellied sapsucker	sap	X	X (cavity)
Downy woodpecker		X	X (cavity)
Blue jay	S	X	
Black-capped chickadee	S	X	X (cavity)
Tufted titmouse	S	X	
Pine siskin*	S	X	
American goldfinch*	S	X	
Northern junco	S		

Note: *preferred food; S, seeds.
Sources: McKenny 1939; Petrides 1972; Headstrom 1970.

GRAY BIRCH

Betula populifolia Marsh.
BETULACEAE

Description. Gray birch is a short-lived tree
that invades old fields and burned areas. It
retains its dead lower branches, often has
several stems, and grows to 30 feet. Other
common names are poverty birch, fire birch,
and old-field birch.
Bark. Grayish-white with many dark horizontal marks, nonpeeling.
Twigs. Dark gray, thin and wiry.
Leaves. Alternate, simple, 1 to 4 inches long,
triangular, doubly toothed with long, pointed
tips and short petioles. Autumn color: yellow.
Flowers. Inconspicuous on short catkins.
Fruits. Small, thin-winged, flat nutlets forming inside ascending, cylindrical cones. Heavy
crops occur periodically.
Flowering period. Mid-April to May (before the
leaves).
Fruiting period. Early September to mid-Octo-
ber, persistent into winter.
Habitat. Sterile, dry-to-wet soils, usually in
open, sunny locations. Commonly found on
wastelands and rocky slopes.
Range. Quebec south to North Carolina, west
to Indiana.
Hardiness zone. 5.
Landscape notes. This graceful delicate tree
grows from a single trunk or from multiple
trunks dividing at the base. Its short branches
form a narrow crown which extends nearly to
the ground on trees growing in the open.
Prolific seeding often results in extensive
stands which may periodically require selective tree removal. The tree is hardy, grows
rapidly, and is especially well-suited for dry,
rocky soils. As the tree grows, sprouts and
dead lower branches must be removed.
Propagation. Trees may be grown from seed or
transplanted. Seeds may be collected from the
cones when ripe and sown immediately, or
stratified in sand or peat for sixty to ninety
days at 32°–50° F. Seeds may be stored at
room temperature in air with 5 percent mois-

ture for up to eighteen months with only slight loss of viability. Seeds may be broadcast on top of snow or on the ground and covered with 1/16-inch of nursery soil (U.S. Forest Service 1948). Germination usually occurs in four to six weeks. Plants should be given partial shade during the first two to three months of growth (U.S. Forest Service 1948).

Birds That Use Gray Birch
(See Birches)

	Food	Cover	Nesting
Green-winged teal	S		
Wood duck	S		
Bufflehead	S		
Turkey	S		
Ring-necked pheasant	S		
Great blue heron	S		
American woodcock		X	
Yellow-bellied sapsucker	sap		
Blue jay	S		
Black-capped chickadee	S	X	X (cavity)
Tufted titmouse	S		
Common redpoll	S		
Pine siskin	S		
American goldfinch	S		
Northern junco	S		

Note: S, seeds.
Sources: McKenny 1939; Headstrom 1970; Petrides 1972; Terres 1968.

Birds That Use Birches

	Food	Cover	Nesting
Green-winged teal	S		
Wood duck	S		
Bufflehead	S		
Goshawk		X	X
Turkey	S		
Ruffed grouse*	S, BD, CK		
Ring-necked pheasant	S		
Great blue heron	S		
American woodcock		X	
Yellow-bellied sapsucker	sap	X	X (cavity)
Hairy woodpecker		X	X (cavity)
Downy woodpecker		X	X (cavity)
Blue jay	S		
Black-capped chickadee	S	X	X (cavity)
Tufted titmouse	S	X	X (cavity)
White-breasted nuthatch	S	X	X (cavity)
Red-breasted nuthatch*	S		
Cedar waxwing	S		
Solitary vireo		X	X[1]
White-eyed vireo			X[1]
Philadelphia vireo			X[1]
Black-throated green warbler			X[1]
American redstart			X[1]
Northern oriole		X	X
Scarlet tanager			X[1]
Cardinal	S		
Rose-breasted grosbeak	S		
Purple finch*	S, BD		
Common redpoll*	S		
Pine siskin*	S		
American goldfinch*	S, BD		
Red crossbill*	S, BD		
White-winged crossbill			X[1]
Northern junco	S		
Tree sparrow	S		
Fox sparrow*	S		

Note: *preferred food; [1]uses gray or white birch bark for nest material; S, seeds; BD, buds; CK, catkins.
Sources: McKenny 1939; Martin et al. 1951; Davison 1967; Headstrom 1970; Langille 1884; Collins 1965; Forbush and May 1939.

AMERICAN HORNBEAM
Carpinus caroliniana Walt.
BETULACEAE

Description. American hornbeam is a small
tree, usually less than 20 feet tall, with several
leaning trunks. It is commonly found in wet
spots in the forest where it occasionally grows
to 45 feet. The seed is preferred by ruffed
grouse. Other common names are bluebeech,
water beech, ironwood, and musclewood.
Bark. Dark bluish-gray, smooth or twisted,
fluted trunks resembling muscles.
Twigs. Brown, with or without fine hairs.
Leaves. Alternate, simple, 1 to 5 inches long,
elliptic with doubly toothed margins. Autumn
colors: yellow, orange, red, or tan.
Flowers. Inconspicuous, green on male and female catkins forming on separate trees.
Fruits. Small, hard nutlets attached to three-
lobed, leafy bracts, somewhat persistent.
Good seed crops are produced every three
to five years, with light crops occurring dur-
ing intervening years.
Flowering period. April to June.
Fruiting period. August to October.
Habitat. Rich upland forests and bottomlands.
Tolerates many soil types in sun or shade.
Commonly occurs as an understory tree in
hardwood forests.
Range. Southeastern Canada south to Florida,
west to eastern Minnesota and Texas.
Hardiness zone. 2.
Landscape notes. Hornbeam develops an attractive form when grown in the open, and has
interesting "muscle" trunks and pendulous
fruits. It is useful as a small shade tree in
yards or as an understory plant in woodlots.
It tolerates pruning and requires little care.
Trees are hardy in the Northeast, grow slowly
and are relatively short-lived, seldom living
longer than 150 years (Robinson 1960). Heavy
fruiting occurs when trees are about fifteen
years old (U.S. Forest Service 1948).
Propagation. Seed should be picked directly
from the tree when ripe (light greenish-gray),
and then dried. The seeds should be sepa-

rated from their wings before they are sown. They may be fall-sown, or stratified in sand or peat for 100 to 120 days at 35°–45° F. and sown in spring (U.S. Forest Service 1948). Soil should be kept moist and partially shaded until seedlings become established (U.S. Forest Service 1948). Seedlings are difficult to transplant. Therefore, for best results select small plants, 1 to 2 feet tall, and take a large root ball to avoid root disturbance.

Birds That Use American Hornbeam

	Food	Cover	Nesting[1]
Mallard	F		
Wood duck	F		
Turkey	F		
Ruffed grouse*	F, BD, CK		
Bobwhite	F, BD, CK		
Ring-necked pheasant	F, BD, CK		
American woodcock		X	
Yellow-rumped warbler	F		
Cardinal*	F		
Evening grosbeak*	F		
American goldfinch*	F		

Note: *preferred food; [1]used for nesting by several songbirds; F, fruit; BD, buds; CK, catkins.
Sources: Martin et al. 1951; Davison 1967; McKenny 1939; Petrides 1972.

PIGNUT HICKORY
Carya glabra (Mill.) Sweet
JUGLANDACEAE

Description. Pignut hickory is a handsome tree, 50 to 70 feet tall. When grown in the open, it makes a fine shade tree with an oblong crown. Squirrels and chipmunks eat the nuts, as do bobwhite, ring-necked pheasant, and turkey.
Bark. Smooth on young trees, develops rounded ridges with age.

Twigs. Slender, reddish-brown, without hairs.
Leaves. Alternate, compound with 5 (occasionally 7) leaflets, leaf length 8 to 12 inches, surfaces dark green above, paler beneath, hairless. Autumn colors: yellow to gold.
Flowers. Inconspicuous, on female spikes and male catkins.
Fruits. Nuts, about 1 inch in diameter, not ribbed, covered with thin husks which split halfway to bases, sweet or slightly astringent. Heavy fruiting begins on trees about thirty years old (U.S. Forest Service 1965). Heavy crops usually occur every one or two years.
Flowering period. April to June.
Fruiting period. September to October, persistent to December.
Habitat. Grows in upland heavy clays or well-drained bottomlands. Commonly found on dry hillsides in association with oaks.
Range. Southern New Hampshire south to Florida, west to Michigan and Kansas.
Hardiness zone. 5.
Landscape notes. This is a handsome lawn and border species, attractive singly or in groves. Its bark does not peel like shagbark hickory. Fallen nuts are sometimes regarded as a nuisance on manicured lawns. Pignut hickory is hardy and slow-growing.
Propagation. Trees may be propagated from seeds that are stratified in sand or peat for 90 to 120 days at 32°–45° F. Seeds may be stored dry in airtight containers for one year at 41° F. Such seed need only be stratified for 30 to 60 days (U.S. Forest Service 1948). Trees may be transplanted when very young. Place two or three plants in the same area for maximum fertilization and fruit production.
Bird uses. See Hickories.

Shagbark Hickory

SHAGBARK HICKORY
Carya ovata (Mill.) K. Koch
JUGLANDACEAE

Description. This is probably the best-known hickory because of the distinctive bark on the clear, straight trunk. It grows 70 to 80 feet tall.

Bark. Smooth on young stems, breaking up and peeling away from trunk in vertical strips on older trees, giving them a shaggy appearance.

Twigs. Stout, grayish-brown to reddish-brown with large terminal buds ½- to ¾-inch long.

Leaves. Alternate, compound with 5 (sometimes 7) leaflets, leaf length 10 to 14 inches, surfaces without hairs. Autumn colors: yellow to gold.

Flowers. Inconspicuous on male catkins and female spikes.

Fruits. Sweet, edible nuts, 1⅜ to 3 inches long, covered with a thick yellowish husk which splits to the base. Trees begin to fruit heavily when about forty years old (U.S. Forest Service 1965). Good crops occur at one- to three-year intervals.

Flowering period. April to June.

Fruiting period. September to October, persistent to December.

Habitat. Prefers light, well-drained loams of alluvial origin that are deep and moist, but often grows on dry upland slopes in the Northeast in association with oaks. Prefers full or partial sunlight.

Range. Quebec south to northwestern Florida, west to Texas and Minnesota.

Hardiness zone. 5.

Landscape notes. This is a handsome yard, park, and woodland tree. Varieties have been developed for high nut production. Trees usually produce large crops of seeds every other year. Yields from open-grown trees may exceed two bushels per tree (Harlow and Harrar 1969). Trees are hardy and grow at a moderate rate—about 12 feet in ten years. Trees are long-lived, surviving for 250 to 300 years.

Propagation. Trees may be grown from seeds stratified in sand or peat for 90 to 150 days at 35°–45° F. If seeds have been stored in airtight containers at 41° F. for one year, the stratification period may be reduced to 30 to 60 days with good results (U.S. Forest Service 1948). Trees may be transplanted when very young before the taproot becomes too large. For maximum pollination and fruiting, place several trees together so that when mature, they will form a grove.

Bird uses. See Hickories.

MOCKERNUT HICKORY
Carya tomentosa Nutt.
JUGLANDACEAE

Description. A more southern hickory, mockernut is common on dry, upland slopes. It is a small tree, 40 to 50 feet tall, which is generally considered maximum height. It is frequently found with sassafras and black locust (Harlow and Harrar 1969).

Bark. Gray, tight with low ridges and shallow fissures.

Twigs. Stout, reddish-brown or gray.

Leaves. Alternate, compound with 7 or 9 (occasionally 5) leaflets, 2 to 3 inches long, leaf length 9 to 14 inches, upper surface dark yellow-green and smooth, lower surface pale yellow-green and woolly with fine hairs, fragrant when crushed. Autumn colors: yellow or russet.

Flowers. Inconspicuous on male catkins and female spikes.

Fruits. Sweet, edible nuts, 1½ to 2 inches long, round to oval shaped, covered by thick husks, not splitting to the base. Trees bear prolific fruits when about twenty-five years old (U.S. Forest Service 1965). Good crops occur every two to three years.

Flowering period. April to May.

Fruiting period. September to October, persistent to December.

Habitat. Grows in a variety of soils from dry and sandy to moist and rich. Likes sun or partial shade. More commonly found in upland woodlands than on bottomlands of alluvial origin.

Range. Southern New Hampshire south to northern Florida, west to eastern Texas.

Hardiness zone. 5.

Landscape notes. These trees are handsome in all seasons. Autumn colors are very attractive, especially when contrasting with the reds of maples. The trees are hardy, slow growing, and may live for 250 to 300 years.

Propagation. Seeds may be stored for three to five years in closed containers, chilled to 41° F., and maintained in 90 percent humidity. They may be stratified over winter in either a sand or peat mixture or in sandy loam at 35°–45° F. (U.S. Forest Service 1948). Stratified seeds may be planted in drills and covered with ¾- to 1½-inches of soil in the spring. The beds should be mulched until all seeds have germinated. Seedlings will grow in full sunlight (U.S. Forest Service 1948). Young trees may be transplanted with good results if moved before the taproot becomes too large.

Bird uses. See Hickories.

Birds That Use Hickories

	Food[1]	Cover	Nesting
Mallard	F		
Wood duck	F		
Turkey	F		
Bobwhite	F		
Ring-necked pheasant	F		
Red-bellied woodpecker*	F		
Yellow-bellied sapsucker	sap		
Blue jay	F		
Common crow	F		
Carolina chickadee*	F		
Tufted titmouse*	F	X	
White-breasted nuthatch*	F		
Brown creeper		X	X[2]
Yellow-rumped warbler*	F		
Pine warbler*	F		
Cardinal*	F		
Rose-breasted grosbeak	F		
Pine grosbeak	F		
Rufous-sided towhee*	F		
Field sparrow*	F		

Note: *preferred food; F, fruit; [1]many of these birds readily consume the meats of hickory nuts, often after the nuts have been opened by squirrels or other mammals, or have split naturally; [2]nests under bark of shagbark hickory.

Sources: Martin et al. 1951; Davison 1967.

COMMON HACKBERRY
Celtis occidentalis L.
ULMACEAE

Description. Hackberry is a small tree, 30 to 50 feet tall. Like sweet birch, it only occurs scattered among other tree species. Hackberry grows in a variety of sites, but best growth occurs in alkaline soils. Many wildlife species relish the sweet berries, particularly members of the thrush family. The fruits are especially valuable to birds because they often persist into winter. Other common names are sugarberry and false elm.

Bark. Light grayish-brown, smooth on young trees, becoming rough and warty with age.

Twigs. Reddish-brown, slender, smooth.

Leaves. Alternate, simple, 3 to 7 inches long, ovate with uneven bases, coarse teeth, and pointed tips. Autumn color: pale yellow.

Flowers. Greenish, appearing with or soon after the leaves, sexes separate on same plant.

Fruits. Round or oval drupes, ¼- to ⅓-inch diameter, dark red or purple, dry, sweet, edible. Sometimes called sugarberries.

Flowering period. April to May.

Fruiting period. September to November, often persistent into winter.

Habitat. Prefers moist, alluvial, and calcareous soils but does well in many soils, moist or dry. Grows in open places and mixed hardwood forests where it is an occasional rather than a common species.

Range. Central New England south to North Carolina, west to Idaho and Kansas.

Hardiness zone. 5.

Landscape notes. Hackberry resembles the American elm but is shorter and less arching. Lower branches occur high on the trunk, a characteristic desirable for street-side trees. Trees are often planted in rows for windbreaks or singly as specimens. Trees are subject to witches-broom, a disease causing abnormal and somewhat unsightly growths of twigs on the branches. These growths do not affect the tree's value to wildlife. Hardy, moderately long-lived (150 to 200 years), and slow growing, hackberry grows to about 14 feet in ten years.

Propagation. Plants are usually propagated by hardwood cuttings taken in winter, but may be grown from seed, layers, and grafts. When fruits turn purple, they may be collected by hand from the trees and sown immediately, or they may be dried and stored in sealed containers at 41° F. for several years. It is not necessary to separate the seeds from the pulp. Fall-sown seeds should germinate in spring. Germination may be hastened by stratifying seeds in moist sand for sixty to ninety days at 41° F. (Mahlstede and Haber 1957; U.S. Forest Service 1948).

Birds That Use Common Hackberry

	Food	Cover	Nesting[1]
Turkey*	F		
Bobwhite	F		
Ring-necked pheasant	F		
Rock dove	F		
Common flicker*	F		
Pileated woodpecker	F		
Yellow-bellied sapsucker*	sap		
Eastern phoebe	F		
Common crow	F		
Fish crow	F		
Tufted titmouse	F		
Mockingbird*	F		
Gray catbird	F		
Brown thrasher	F		
American robin*	F		
Hermit thrush	F		
Swainson's thrush*	F		
Eastern bluebird*	F		
Cedar waxwing	F		
Starling*	F		
Common grackle	F		
Cardinal*	F		
Evening grosbeak	F		
Rufous-sided towhee	F		
Fox sparrow	F		

Note: *preferred food; F, fruit; [1]frequently used for nesting by many bird species.

Sources: McKenny 1951; Davison 1967; Martin et al. 1951.

FLOWERING DOGWOOD

Cornus florida L.
CORNACEAE

Description. Flowering dogwood is a small tree, rarely over 40 feet tall. It prefers rich, moist sites, and occurs as an understory plant in hardwood forests. It is a widely used landscape plant because of its ornamental value in all seasons. The fruits are eaten by over 100 species of birds. Other common names are American dogwood and white dogwood.

Bark. Brown to gray or black, deeply checked with rectangular blocks.

Twigs. Greenish, reddish, or purple.

Leaves. Opposite, simple, 2 to 5 inches long, elliptic or wedge-shaped, dark green above and pale beneath with prominent parallel veins. Autumn colors: rose to scarlet and violet.

Flowers. Small, yellowish, in a central cluster, surrounded by 4 showy white, petallike bracts.

Fruits. Scarlet, oval drupes forming in clusters of 2 to 5.

Flowering period. March to June.

Fruiting period. August to November.

Habitat. Usually found in rich, moist, light, well-drained soils of forest borders, on south or west-facing slopes, or near streams. Found in abundance in soils with a pH range of 6 to 7, in sun or shade.

Range. Southwestern Maine, southern New Hampshire and Vermont south to Florida, west to Michigan and eastern Texas.

Hardiness zone. 5.

Landscape notes. Flowering dogwood is one of our finest native ornamentals. Its delicate horizontal branches are attractive from the time the first blossoms unfold in spring, preceding the leaves, until the last fruits disappear in autumn. It is slow growing, long-lived, and hardy throughout its range, though not as common in New England and the northern states as it is to the south. Fallen leaves decompose rapidly and enrich the surrounding soil with calcium. Plants withstand temperature extremes of 115° F. to −30° F., but do not tolerate excessive drought (U.S. Forest Service 1965).

Propagation. Trees may be purchased from nurseries or propagated from seeds, layering, cuttings, and grafting. Seeds should be collected when ripe and sown immediately, or stratified in moist sand or peat moss for 3½ to 4 months at 41° F. to break dormancy. They should be sown ¼- to ½-inch deep in rich nursery soil. Seeds lose their viability rapidly in storage (U.S. Forest Service 1948). Fall-sown seeds should be planted while seed coats are soft, and then should be covered with a thick layer of mulch to prevent freezing (Heit 1968). Mulch should be removed when first signs of germination appear. Seedlings and young trees usually show relatively rapid growth in height (U.S. Forest Service 1965), but flowering and fruiting may be delayed for six years (Spinner and Ostrum 1945).

Softwood cuttings taken immediately after plants bloom will root and harden off before winter. Terminal shoot tips should be cut to 3-inch lengths, leaving two to four leaves and their bases dipped into root-inducing hormone and inserted 1¼ inches deep in sand. In early August, they should be moved to a cold frame (Pease 1953). Grafting can be done in winter or early spring. Scions ¼-inch in diameter and 8 to 12 inches long with three or four sets of buds should be removed from new growth and side grafted onto healthy stock (Coggeshall 1960).

Flowering Dogwood

Birds That Use Flowering Dogwood

	Food	Cover	Nesting[1]
Turkey*	F		
Ruffed grouse	F		
Bobwhite*	F		
Common flicker*	F		
Pileated woodpecker*	F		
Red-bellied woodpecker*	F		
Red-headed woodpecker*	F		
Yellow-bellied sapsucker*	F, sap		
Hairy woodpecker*	F		
Downy woodpecker	F		
Eastern kingbird	F		
Common crow	F		
Mockingbird*	F		
Gray catbird	F		
Brown thrasher*	F		
American robin*	F		X
Wood thrush*	F		
Hermit thrush*	F		
Swainson's thrush*	F		
Gray-cheeked thrush*	F		
Eastern bluebird*	F		
Cedar waxwing*	F		
Starling*	F		
Red-eyed vireo	F		
Warbling vireo	F		
Yellow-rumped warbler*	F		
Pine warbler	F		
House sparrow	F		
Common grackle	F		
Summer tanager*	F		
Cardinal*	F		
Rose-breasted grosbeak	F		
Evening grosbeak*	F		
Purple finch	F		
Pine grosbeak*	F		
White-throated sparrow	F		
Song sparrow	F		

Note: *preferred food; F, fruit; [1]occasionally used by songbirds for nesting.
Sources: McKenny 1939; Davison 1967; Petrides 1972.

COMMON PERSIMMON

Diospyros virginiana L.

EBENACEAE

Description. Common persimmon is a small tree, 30 to 50 feet tall. The ripe fruit is preferred by mockingbirds, catbirds, and cedar waxwings, among others.

Bark. Dark, thick, deeply cut into small square blocks.

Twigs. Slender with slight zig-zag.

Leaves. Alternate, simple, 2 to 5 inches, elliptic, without teeth, shiny. Autumn color: yellow.

Flowers. Greenish-yellow, tubular, less than one inch long, male and female on separate plants.

Fruits. Rounded, orange to yellowish-green berries, about 1½ inches in diameter, containing 3 to 8 large seeds. Occasional fruiting may occur when trees are about ten years old. Good crops occur about every two years.

Flowering period. March to June.

Fruiting period. September to November.

Habitat. Commonly grows on moist bottomlands and in old fields and roadsides where soils are light and deep.

Range. Southern Connecticut south to Florida, west to Kansas and Texas.

Hardiness zone. 5.

Landscape notes. Persimmon is of minor ornamental value but is esteemed in some areas for its fruits which are sold locally to make jams and jellies. Trees may begin bearing when only 6 or 8 feet tall (Lemmon 1952). The Japanese species, *D. kaki,* is widely planted in the South; it may be adaptable north to southern New England.

Propagation. Common persimmon may be propagated by seed, root cuttings, and grafting. Seeds should be collected from ripe fruits and cleaned of pulp. After a day or two of air-drying, they may be sown outside in plowed beds, ½- to ¾-inch deep and covered with mulch for the winter. Or they may be stratified for two to three months in sand or peat at 50° F., and sown in spring (U.S. For-

Common Persimmon

est Service 1948). Seeds should be kept moist until germination begins. Seedlings should be transplanted from bed to field before their first winter because they develop strong tap-roots which would make later transplanting difficult (U.S. Forest Service 1948).

Birds That Use Common Persimmon

	Food	Cover	Nesting
Mallard	F		
Turkey	F		
Bobwhite	F		
Pileated woodpecker	F		
Yellow-bellied sapsucker	F		
Mockingbird*	F		
Gray catbird*	F		
American robin*	F		
Eastern bluebird	F		
Cedar waxwing*	F		
Yellow-rumped warbler	F		

Note: *preferred food; F, fruit.
Sources: McKenny 1939; Davison 1967; Martin et al. 1951.

AMERICAN BEECH
Fagus grandifolia Ehrh.
FAGACEAE

Description. This distinctive tree is very shade tolerant. When nut crops are abundant, the trees are alive with wildlife—both birds and mammals.
Bark. Light gray, thin, very smooth. Does not change as tree grows older.
Twigs. Smooth and slender, often zig-zag with slender, sharply pointed buds.
Leaves. Alternate, simple, 2½ to 6 inches long, 1 to 2½ inches wide, elliptic with coarsely toothed margins and parallel veins. Autumn colors: vary from shades of yellow to orange and bronze.
Flowers. Male flowers form in rounded heads. Female flowers form on spikes. Both are inconspicuous and occur after the leaves have developed.
Fruits. Small nuts ½- to ¾-inch long, covered with a four-parted bur. Nuts usually occur in pairs and are sweet and edible. Forest trees begin producing abundant fruits when about forty years old (U.S. Forest Service 1965). Good fruit crops occur every two or three years.
Flowering period. April to May.
Fruiting period. September to November.
Habitat. Grows in a variety of soils having adequate loam and moisture. Commonly found in cool, moist locations in eastern woodlands.
Range. Nova Scotia south to northern Florida, west to eastern Wisconsin and Texas.
Hardiness zone. 4.
Landscape notes. This is a beautiful grove or specimen tree. When grown in the open, it develops a low, wide-spreading crown supported by a thick trunk. Trees are hardy, slow growing and long-lived. Dense shade and shallow fibrous root systems which deplete the surface soil of nutrients create inhospitable conditions for grass and other vegetation growing directly beneath the tree. Suckers grow abundantly from the roots.

Propagation. Beech can be propagated by seed or grafting. Seeds may be sown in the season they ripen for spring germination, or they may be stratified for three months at 40° F. for earlier germination (U.S. Forest Service 1948). Young nursery trees should be root-pruned often to prevent growth of a single taproot which makes later transplanting difficult (Hartmann and Kester 1968).

Birds That Use American Beech

	Food	Cover	Nesting
Black duck*	F		
Wood duck*	F		
Turkey*	F		
Spruce grouse	F		
Ruffed grouse*	F		
Bobwhite*	F		
Ring-necked pheasant	F		
Common flicker*	F		
Pileated woodpecker*	F		
Red-bellied woodpecker*	F		
Red-headed woodpecker*	F		
Yellow-bellied sapsucker	sap		
Hairy woodpecker	F		
Downy woodpecker	F		
Blue jay*	F		
Common crow*	F		
Black-capped chickadee	F		
Tufted titmouse*	F		
White-breasted nuthatch*	F		
Red-winged blackbird	F		
Rusty blackbird	F		
Common grackle*	F		
Purple finch	F, BD		
Red crossbill	F		
White-throated sparrow*	FL		

Note: *preferred food; F, fruit; BD, buds, FL, flowers.
Sources: McKenny 1939; Davison 1967; Martin et al. 1951.

WHITE ASH
Fraxinus americana L.
OLEACEAE

Description. White ash is our most common ash. The winged seeds are a preferred food of evening grosbeaks and purple finches, and are eaten by bobwhites, cardinals, and others. White ash can grow up to 100 feet tall, with a trunk diameter of 4 feet.
Bark. Gray, close, with furrows and ridges forming narrow diamond-shaped areas.
Twigs. Dark green to gray-green, shiny, speckled with lenticels.
Leaves. Opposite, compound, 8 to 12 inches long, with 7 (occasionally 11 or 13) 3- to 5-inch, elliptical leaflets, margins serrate, surfaces dark green above, paler beneath. Autumn colors: green, yellow, and purple.
Flowers. Inconspicuous, male and female flowers form on separate plants, before the leaves.
Fruits. Winged seeds or samaras, 1 to 2 inches long, ¼-inch wide. Trees bear good crops every three to five years.
Flowering period. April to June.
Fruiting period. September to November, persistent to early winter.
Habitat. Grows in a variety of soils but prefers those that are deep, moist, and rich with a pH range of 5.0 to 7.5 (U.S. Forest Service 1965). Common in uplands growing with basswood, beech, and red maple.
Range. Southern Quebec south to Florida, west to Minnesota and eastern Texas.
Hardiness zone. 4.
Landscape notes. White ash is a handsome, symmetrical tree for lawns, woodlands, streets, and parks. It grows vigorously in a variety of soils, produces plenty of shade, and is seldom attacked by insects. It is hardy, grows to approximately 20 feet in ten years, and is moderately long-lived. Flowering and fruiting may begin on open-grown trees 3 to 4 inches in diameter (U.S. Forest Service 1965).

Propagation. Trees are usually propagated by seed. Seeds may be collected in the fall or early winter and sown immediately, stratified and sown in spring, or stored for future use. Stratification in sand or peat for sixty or ninety days at 41° F. is common practice and gives good results. Seeds may be broadcast, or sown in drills ¼- to ½-inch deep. Fall-sown seeds should be protected from freezing by a layer of mulch, to be removed upon germination (U.S. Forest Service 1948).

Birds That Use White Ash
(See Ashes)

	Food	Cover	Nesting
Bobwhite	S		
Wood duck	S		
Red-winged blackbird*	S		
Rusty blackbird	S		
Cardinal	S		
Evening grosbeak*	S		
Purple finch*	S		
Pine grosbeak*	S		

Note: *preferred food; S, seeds.
Sources: Davison 1967; McKenny 1939; Collins 1965.

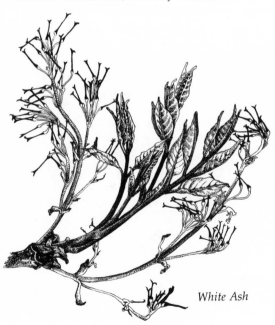

White Ash

BLACK ASH
Fraxinus nigra Marsh.
OLEACEAE

Description. Black ash is of moderate value to wildlife. The open branching pattern is not conducive to bird nesting, but evening and pine grosbeaks and cardinals readily eat the seeds. It grows 40 to 70 feet tall, with a diameter of 1 to 2 feet.
Bark. Gray, with shallow fissures and scaly plates.
Twigs. Gray, hairless.
Leaves. Opposite, compound, 12 to 16 inches long with 7 to 13 oblong to lanceolate, toothed, unstalked leaflets. Autumn color: yellow.
Flowers. Inconspicuous, sexes form on separate trees in clusters, before the leaves.
Fruits. Winged seeds, 1 to 2 inches long, blunt at both ends.
Flowering period. April to May.
Fruiting period. June to September, persistent through winter.
Habitat. Commonly occurs along river banks, stream banks and swamp borders in association with northern white cedars and red maples.
Range. Newfoundland south to Virginia, west to Manitoba and Iowa.
Hardiness zone. 2.
Landscape notes. Not as widely used in landscaping as white and other ashes.
Propagation. Black ash is usually propagated from seeds sown in spring and summer and covered with mulch until they germinate the following spring. Seeds may be stratified soon after collection by a two-stage process: they should be kept at 68° F. for two to three months, followed by cooling to 41° F. for two to three months. Seeds are usually sown in drills ½- to ¾-inch deep in nursery soil and should be partially shaded the first summer (U.S. Forest Service 1948).
Bird uses. See Ashes.

GREEN ASH

Fraxinus pennsylvanica Marsh.
OLEACEAE

Description. Green ash is the most widely distributed of American ashes (Harlow and Harrar 1969). It is a small tree—30 to 50 feet tall, with a diameter to 20 inches—which grows in wet areas. Heavy seed crops are produced, hence its wildlife value. The variety *F. p. subintegerrima* (Vahl.) Fern. is the common cultivated form. Other common names are Darlington ash and red ash.

Bark. Similar to white ash but not as thick.

Twigs. Greenish-brown, smooth or covered with fine hairs.

Leaves. Opposite, compound, 6 to 9 inches long with 7 to 9 leaflets, 3 to 4 inches long, margins with or without teeth, yellowish-green above, paler beneath. Autumn colors: yellow to purple.

Flowers. Inconspicuous, male and female flowers form on separate trees.

Fruits. Winged seeds or samaras, 1 to 2 inches long, about ¼-inch wide, forming in clusters. Fruits usually appear when trees are about twenty years old.

Flowering period. April to May.

Fruiting period. September to October, persistent through winter.

Habitat. Usually found in river valleys and moist bottomlands, but will grow on dry, sterile soils.

Range. Quebec south to Georgia, west to Saskatchewan and Texas.

Hardiness zone. 2.

Landscape notes. These trees develop the best form east of the Appalachian Mountains. Extremely hardy, they are commonly used in landscaping because of their handsome form and dense foliage. They grow rapidly—up to 26 feet in ten years—and develop well in sun or partial shade.

Propagation. Seeds should be collected when ripe and sown in fall, or stratified and sown in spring. Fall-sown seeds should be protected from freezing with a layer of mulch, to be removed upon germination. Spring-sown seeds should be stratified over winter for two to three months at 41° F. Green ash seeds store well in sealed containers when their moisture content is maintained at 7.3 percent. Seeds should be sown in drills ¼- to ½-inch deep or broadcast (U.S. Forest Service 1948). Experience shows that up to 20 percent of seedlings may be poorly formed. It may be more practical to propagate trees by budding onto well-formed plants of clones (Wyman 1951).

Bird uses. See Ashes.

Birds That Use Ashes

	Food	Cover	Nesting
Wood duck*	S		
Turkey	S		
Bobwhite*	S		
Mourning dove		X	X
Yellow-bellied sapsucker	sap		
Red-winged blackbird*	S		
Rusty blackbird	S		
Cardinal*	S		
Evening grosbeak*	S	X	X
Purple finch*	S		
Pine grosbeak*	S		

Note: *preferred food; S, seeds.
Sources: McKenny 1939; Davison 1967; Collins 1965; Martin et al. 1951.

AMERICAN HOLLY
Ilex opaca Ait.
AQUIFOLIACEAE

Description. This is the largest native holly. It grows 40 to 50 feet tall and has a spread of 10 to 20 feet. Its fruit is consumed by many bird species, and it is a preferred nest site of cardinals, catbirds, and mockingbirds. Another common name is Christmas holly.

Bark. Young branches slightly downy.

Leaves. Alternate, simple, 2 to 4 inches long, elliptic to ovate, margins with coarse spiny teeth, stiff and leathery, dull dark green above, yellowish beneath.

Flowers. Inconspicuous, greenish to white blossoms, male and female flowers form on separate plants, female solitary, male in clusters.

Fruits. Scarlet red drupes, 1/3-inch in diameter, persistent.

Flowering period. May to June.

Fruiting period. August, persistent to June.

Habitat. Prefers light, moist, rich or sandy soils in partial or deep shade. Will not grow in dry, unprotected areas.

Range. Massachusetts south along the coast to Florida, inland as far west as Missouri and Oklahoma.

Hardiness zone. 6.

Landscape notes. A highly ornamental tree, its horizontal branches form an attractive pyramidal crown which extends nearly to the ground. Its crown is dense in youth, becoming more open with age. This holly makes an excellent hedge or border planting as well as a fine specimen tree. The berry-laden boughs are used extensively for Christmas decorations. Plants are not fully hardy in northern New England, are difficult to transplant, and grow slowly. The compact shape makes it suitable for planting fairly close to buildings for accent in corners or near main entrances. North of zone 6, American holly should be planted in protected areas.

Propagation. Fruits may be hand-collected when ripe and separated from the seeds by maceration. Seeds may be sown immediately by broadcasting or drilling and covered with 1/8-inch of soil. They should be protected with mulch during winters prior to germination. For later sowing, they should be dried and stored in airtight containers at low refrigerator temperatures, or stratified in sand for thirty days at 75°–80° F. Germination takes one to three years. Plants may also be propagated by layering, cuttings, and grafting (U.S. Forest Service 1948).

Birds That Use American Holly
(See Hollies)

	Food	Cover	Nesting
Turkey	F		
Bobwhite	F	X	
Common flicker	F		
Red-bellied woodpecker	F		
Yellow-bellied sapsucker	sap		
Mockingbird*	F	X	X
Gray catbird	F	X	X
Brown thrasher	F	X	
American robin	F	X	X
Hermit thrush	F	X	
Eastern bluebird*	F		
Cedar waxwing*	F	X	
Cardinal	F	X	X

Note: *preferred food; F, fruit.
Sources: McKenny 1939; Davison 1967.

American Holly

BUTTERNUT
Juglans cinerea L.
JUGLANDACEAE

Description. The butternut tree is sometimes used as a nest site by the broad-winged hawk (Davison 1967:167). Its nut meat is a favorite food of chickadees, nuthatches, red-bellied woodpeckers, and Carolina wrens. It grows 40 to 60 feet tall, with a diameter of 1 to 2 feet. Other common names are white walnut and oilnut.
Bark. Light gray with flat ridges separated by deep fissures.
Twigs. Greenish-gray to brown with chambered pith.
Leaves. Alternate, compound, with 11 to 17 leaflets each 3 to 4 inches long, leaf length 15 to 30 inches, yellow-green and wrinkled above, pale and downy below. Autumn color: briefly yellow-green before dropping.
Flowers. Inconspicuous.
Fruits. Oblong, hard nuts, 1½ to 2 inches in diameter forming singly or in clusters of two or three. Each nut is covered with a thick sticky husk. Seeds are sweet, oily, and edible. Heavy fruiting begins when trees are about twenty years old (U.S. Forest Service 1965). Good crops occur every two or three years.
Flowering period. April to June.
Fruiting period. September to November.
Habitat. Grows on moist, rich loams and dry, rocky soils. Does not occur naturally in pure stands but is scattered throughout woodlands mixed with hardwood species (Harlow and Harrar 1969).
Range. New Brunswick south to Georgia, west to Minnesota and Mississippi.
Hardiness zone. 4.
Landscape notes. This is a fast-growing tree for yard and park borders where there is ample room for the crown to spread. Fallen nuts may be a nuisance on lawns. Plants are hardy but short-lived, with few trees surviving beyond seventy-five years.
Propagation. See Eastern Black Walnut.

Birds That Use Butternut

	Food[1]	Cover	Nesting
Broad-winged hawk		X	X
Red-bellied woodpecker*	F		
Black-capped chickadee*	F		
Carolina chickadee*	F		
Tufted titmouse*	F		
White-breasted nuthatch*	F		
Red-breasted nuthatch*	F		
Brown-headed nuthatch*	F		
Carolina wren*	F		
Yellow-rumped warbler*	F		
Pine warbler*	F		
Purple finch*	F		
Field sparrow*	F		

Note: *preferred food; F, fruit; [1]most of the above birds usually consume the meats of butternuts after they have been opened by squirrels or chipmunks, or have split naturally.
Sources: Davison 1967; Martin et al. 1951.

EASTERN BLACK WALNUT
Juglans nigra L.
JUGLANDACEAE

Description. Black walnut is a handsome tree which produces very valuable wood. The nut meats are preferred by gray squirrels and by many birds. It grows 70 to 90 feet, with a diameter of 2 to 3 feet.
Bark. Dark brown to grayish-black with ridges and fissures forming diamond-shaped patterns.
Twigs. Orange-brown with chambered piths.
Leaves. Alternate, compound, with 7 to 17 narrow leaflets, 3 to 3½ inches long, margins toothed, end leaflet often lacking, leaf length 12 to 24 inches, upper surface dark green and smooth, lower surfaces pale green and

Eastern Black Walnut

slightly hairy. Autumn color: yellow shortly before falling.

Flowers. Female flowers inconspicuous, male flowers on catkins, both occurring on same plant.

Fruits. Large, spherical nuts, 1½ to 2 inches in diameter, forming singly or in clusters of two or three, covered with a one-piece husk. Seeds are sweet, oily, and edible. Tree begins abundant fruit production when about twelve years old (U.S. Forest Service 1965).

Flowering period. April to June.

Fruiting period. September to November.

Habitat. Prefers deep, rich bottomland and good garden soils. Grows poorly on dry, sandy sites.

Range. Western Massachusetts south to northwestern Florida, west to Minnesota and Texas.

Hardiness zone. 5.

Landscape notes. This excellent specimen tree for yards and parks is especially handsome when planted in the open where the crown can develop to maximum proportions. Trees reach maturity at 150 years of age, may live for 250 years (Harlow and Harrar 1969), and produce large crops of fruit at irregular intervals. Trees are hardy to southern New England. Young trees grow rapidly on good soil, reaching 16 feet in ten years. The handsome stature of this tree should offset any inconveniences that may be caused by its fallen fruits, but trees should be planted away from buildings, walks, and driveways. The roots of black walnut produce a material that may be toxic to other plants, so trees should be somewhat isolated (Wyman 1951).

Propagation. Trees may be propagated from seeds, by grafting in spring and budding in summer. Fruits may be collected from the ground in autumn and the husks removed while green. They should either be sown in fall or stratified over winter in moist sand or peat at 33°–50° F. for 60 to 120 days. Fall-sown seeds usually germinate the following spring. Recommended sowing depth is 1 to 2 inches (U.S. Forest Service 1948).

Birds That Use Eastern Black Walnut

	Food[1]	Cover	Nesting[2]
Pileated woodpecker*	F		
Red-bellied woodpecker*	F		
Downy woodpecker*	F		
Blue jay*	F		
Common crow*	F		
Carolina chickadee*	F		
Tufted titmouse*	F		
Brown-headed nuthatch*	F		
Carolina wren*	F		
Gray catbird*	F		
Ruby-crowned kinglet*	F		
Yellow-rumped warbler*	F		
Pine warbler*	F		
Northern oriole	F	X	X
Cardinal*	F		
Northern junco*	F		
Field sparrow	F		
White-crowned sparrow*	F		
Song sparrow*	F		

Note: *preferred food; F, fruit; [1]most of the above birds consume walnut meats after the nuts have been opened by mammals or have split naturally; [2]occasional nest site of songbirds.
Sources: Davison 1967; Dugmore 1904; Martin et al. 1951.

EASTERN RED CEDAR
Juniperus virginiana L.
PINACEAE

Description. Eastern red cedar commonly invades old fields in the middle Atlantic states. It can reach good size—50 feet, with a 1- to 2-foot diameter—but is usually shorter north of Pennsylvania. It is used as a nest site by several birds, and the fruits are preferred by many more. The tree is spread by birds dropping seed. Often a line of red cedars will be seen through an old field, or across the dunes on the coast. These are evidence that a fence or wire was once present where the birds perched and dropped seed.

Bark. Reddish-brown or gray and fibrous.

Leaves. Two forms: juvenile leaves are long, awl-shaped, and sharply pointed; adult leaves are shorter, scalelike, and blunt. Length varies from 1/6- to 3/4-inch. Leaves form in pairs in four rows along four-sided branchlets.

Flowers. Inconspicuous sporophylls, male and female form on separate plants.

Fruits. Two-seeded, borne in round, hard, berrylike cones, whitish to blackish-green, ¼-inch diameter, persistent. Heavy fruiting may occur every second or third year (Wyman 1951) with light crops occurring during intervening years.

Flowering period. March to May.

Fruiting period. September to November, persistent until March.

Habitat. Grows on many kinds of soil, but does best in light loam of limestone origin. Pure and mixed stands are commonly found on very poor soils.

Range. New England south to Georgia, west to Minnesota and Texas.

Hardiness zone. 2.

Landscape notes. Red cedar is commonly cultivated in yards and parks. It is useful for screening purposes, as a windbreak, and as a background for showy plants. It is tolerant of pruning and is sometimes used in topiary work. Red cedar is occasionally affected by rusts that can be transmitted to apples, quinces, hawthorns, and mountain-ashes. It is best to plant red cedar away from these trees (Terres 1968). Trees are very hardy, grow slowly, and may live for 300 years. They develop best when grown in the open.

Propagation. Plants may be grown from seeds or cuttings. Fruits should be collected when ripe and seeds separated from the pulp by soaking in a lye solution (one teaspoon per gallon of water) for two days, followed by maceration and another day of soaking (U.S. Forest Service 1948). Seeds may be sown in fall, or stratified in sand or peat for 100 to 120 days at 41° F. over winter and sown in

Eastern Red Cedar

spring. They are usually sown in drills and should be covered with ¼-inch soil, mulched until they germinate and kept moist (U.S. Forest Service 1948). Plants are usually propagated by either hardwood or softwood cuttings.

Birds That Use Eastern Red Cedar

	Food	Cover	Nesting
Turkey	F	X	
Ruffed grouse	F	X	
Bobwhite	F	X	
Ring-necked pheasant	F	X	
Mourning dove	F		
Screech owl		X	
Common flicker	F		
Yellow-bellied sapsucker*	sap		
Eastern kingbird	F		
Eastern phoebe	F		
Alder flycatcher	F		
Tree swallow	F		
Common crow	F		
Fish crow	F		
Mockingbird*	F	X	X
Gray catbird	F	X	
Brown thrasher	F	X	X
American robin*	F	X	X
Hermit thrush	F		
Swainson's thrush	F		
Eastern bluebird*	F	X	
Cedar waxwing*	F	X	X
Starling	F		
Yellow-rumped warbler*	F	X	
Common grackle		X	X
Cardinal	F	X	X
Evening grosbeak*	F	X	
Purple finch*	F	X	
Pine grosbeak*	F	X	
White-winged crossbill	F	X	
Chipping sparrow		X	X
Fox sparrow	F	X	
Song sparrow		X	X

Note: *preferred food; F, fruit.
Sources: National Wildlife Fed. 1974; McKenny 1939; Martin et al. 1951; Davison 1967.

EASTERN LARCH
Larix laricina (Du Roi) K. Koch.
PINACEAE

Description. Eastern larch is a frequent nest site, and its seed is a preferred food of crossbills and purple finches. Spruce grouse feed on the buds and leaves (Davison 1967:218). Also known as tamarack and hackmatack, this tree grows 40 to 80 feet tall, with a diameter of 1 to 2 feet.
Bark. Gray to reddish-brown and scaly.
Twigs. Brownish-gray.
Leaves. Deciduous, soft, linear, ¾- to 1¼-inches long, flat, bright bluish-green in summer and briefly yellow before falling in September and November.
Flowers. Inconspicuous, both sexes occur on same plant.
Fruits. Borne in small cones, ½- to ¾-inch long, erect, oblong to oval in shape. Heavy fruiting occurs when trees are about forty years old. Good seed crops occur at five- or six-year intervals.
Flowering period. May.
Fruiting period. August to September.
Habitat. Prefers bogs or wet soils in open sunny meadows.
Range. Northern Canada south to West Virginia, west to Minnesota.
Hardiness zone. 1.
Landscape notes. This delicate tree is attractive in groups or alone. Eastern larch grows rapidly at first, and slows after forty or fifty years. It reaches maturity when 100 or more years old, and may survive for 200 years or more. Hardy on moist sites, it will develop well on any good garden soil.
Propagation. Larch grows well from seeds either sown in fall or stratified and sown in spring. The recommended stratification period is one to two months at 40° F. Softwood cuttings may be taken in late summer, treated with root-inducing hormone, and placed in sand. They should periodically be given light mist (Hartmann and Kester 1968).

[38]

Birds That Use Eastern Larch

	Food	Cover	Nesting
Spruce grouse*	BD, S, L		
Ruffed grouse	BD, S, L		
Ring-necked pheasant	S		
Blue jay		X	X
American robin		X	X
Purple finch*	S	X	
Pine siskin	S	X	
Red crossbill*	S	X	
White-winged crossbill*	S	X	

Note: *preferred food; BD, buds; S, seeds; L, leaves.

Sources: McKenny 1939; Davison 1967; Martin et al. 1951; Petrides 1972.

Eastern Larch

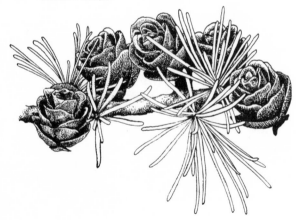

AMERICAN SWEETGUM
Liquidambar styraciflua L.
HAMAMELIDACEAE

Description. Sweetgum is a stately tree—50 to 120 feet tall. It is common in the mid-Atlantic states, and occurs on moist sites. The seeds are preferred by many sparrows and finches, as well as by the turkey, mourning dove, and bobwhite. Other common names are red gum and starleaf gum.

Bark. Grayish-brown with deep fissures and rounded flaky ridges.

Twigs. Greenish-brown, shiny, aromatic.

Leaves. Alternate, simple, 5 to 8 inches long, star-shaped with 5 or 7 pointed lobes, margins with fine teeth, fragrant when crushed. Autumn colors: brilliant shades of purple, red, orange, and yellow on the same tree.

Flowers. Occur in rounded clusters, sexes separate on same plant.

Fruits. Woody rounded heads, 1 to 1½ inches in diameter, containing many capsules which hold two small winged seeds. Heavy seed production begins on trees twenty to thirty years old (U.S. Forest Service 1965). Heavy crops are borne every three years.

Flowering period. March to May.

Fruiting period. September to November.

Habitat. Swamps and bottomlands where soils are rich and moist, but does well on drier soils.

Range. Southern Connecticut south to Florida, west to Oklahoma and Illinois.

Hardiness zone. 6.

Landscape notes. Sweetgum is often planted as an ornamental for its attractive star-shaped leaves that are glossy green in summer and brilliantly colored in autumn. It is a good producer of shade and is suitable for formal landscapes. The tree is moderately hardy throughout its range, long-lived, grows 1 to 2 feet per year, and is salt tolerant. The flower buds are sensitive to cold and are often killed by frost. Best growth occurs south of Massachusetts. Trees are highly resistant to disease and insect damage (U.S. Forest Service 1965). *Propagation.* Trees may be grown from seeds or cuttings. Fruits should be collected before they release their seeds and then air-dried for two weeks, at which time seeds may be shaken out. Seeds that are stratified in moist sand for thirty to ninety days at 41° F. and sown in spring germinate better than those sown in fall. They should be sown in moist, rich soil receiving plenty of sunlight (U.S. Forest Service 1948).

Birds That Use American Sweetgum

	Food	Cover	Nesting
Mallard	S		
Turkey*	S		
Bobwhite*	S		
Rock dove*	S		
Mourning dove*	S		
Yellow-bellied sapsucker	S		
Black-capped chickadee	S		
Carolina chickadee	S		
Carolina wren	S		
Starling*	S		
Red-winged blackbird	S		
Cardinal*	S		
Evening grosbeak*	S		
Purple finch*	S		
Common redpoll*	S		
Pine siskin*	S		
American goldfinch*	S		
Rufous-sided towhee	S		
Northern junco*	S		
White-crowned sparrow	S		
White-throated sparrow*	S		

Note: *preferred food; S, seeds.
Sources: Martin et al. 1951; Davison 1967.

American Sweetgum

YELLOW-POPLAR

Liriodendron tulipifera L.
MAGNOLIACEAE

Description. Yellow-poplar is the tallest North American hardwood tree—over 150 feet. It is essentially a southern and southeastern tree, frequently used by birds for nesting. The nectar is readily sought by the ruby-throated hummingbird, and the seeds are eaten by several sparrows and finches. Other common names are tuliptree and whitewood.

Bark. Dark gray, thick, and rough with vertical ridges and fissures.

Twigs. Reddish-brown, moderately stout.

Leaves. Alternate, simple, 6 to 10 inches long, mostly four-lobed with notched tips, surfaces smooth, margins without teeth. Autumn color: golden yellow.

Flowers. Light greenish with an orange base, tulip-shaped blossoms, 1½ to 2 inches across, showy.

Fruits. Upright, conelike structures, 2½ to 3 inches long, containing many four-angled, whitish, winged seeds. Trees fruit heavily at irregular intervals after they are fifteen years old.

Flowering period. April to June.

Fruiting period. September to November, persistent until January.

Habitat. Best growth occurs in rich, moist but well-drained soils of moderate depth. The tree is common in eastern woodlands where it is found most often in the company of other hardwoods (Harlow and Harrar 1969).

Range. Southern Vermont south to Florida, west to Michigan and Louisiana.

Hardiness zone. 5.

Landscape notes. This is a beautiful ornamental tree with large showy flowers and attractive four-lobed leaves. It grows very rapidly on good sites, where it may attain heights of 120 feet in fifty years. In the open it develops a magnificent, wide-spreading crown which provides excellent shade. Yellow poplar is hardy in its range, withstands temperature extremes from −20° to 100° F., and may live for 300 years. Its comparative resistance to smoke makes it a good choice for street plantings.

Propagation. Trees may be grown from seed, stem cuttings, and root cuttings. Good germination usually results from seeds stratified outdoors over winter, or indoors for two months in moist peat at 32° F. (night) and 50° F. (day). Seeds should be sown in drills ¼-inch deep in good nursery soil. Seedlings should be given shade for two months after germination. Young trees are difficult to transplant and should be balled and burlapped to minimize root disturbance (U.S. Forest Service 1948; Hartmann and Kester 1968).

Birds That Use Yellow Poplar

	Food	Cover	Nesting[1]
Bobwhite	S		
Ruby-throated hummingbird*	N		
Yellow-bellied sapsucker	sap		
Carolina chickadee	S		
Red-winged blackbird	S		
Cardinal*	S		
Evening grosbeak	S		
Purple finch*	S		
Pine grosbeak	S		
American goldfinch	S		

Note: *preferred food; [1]often used for nesting by songbirds; S, seeds, N, nectar.

Sources: Davison 1967; Martin et al. 1951; Barnes 1973.

COMMON APPLE
Malus pumila, Mill.
ROSACEAE

Description. The common apple is a preferred nest site of many species—robin, great crested flycatcher, and red-eyed vireo, among others (DeGraaf et al. 1975). The fruits are eaten by many birds. Grosbeaks (evening and pine) also eat the buds, to the dismay of orchardists. This tree grows 20 to 30 feet tall.
Bark. Grayish-brown, scaly.
Leaves. Alternate, simple, 1 to 4 inches long, elliptic to ovate with whitish hair below, rounded teeth. Autumn color: greenish-brown.
Flowers. Showy pinkish or white blossoms, usually 1 to 2 inches in diameter, fragrant.
Fruits. Yellowish to red, rounded pomes, over ¾-inch in diameter, containing several small seeds.
Flowering period. April to June.
Fruiting period. September to November.
Habitat. Native to Europe. Brought to the United States in colonial times, it has escaped from gardens and is naturalized in some areas. Prefers clay-loam soils but will grow on a wide variety of sites.
Range. Grows throughout temperate areas of the United States.
Hardiness zone. 4.
Landscape notes. Common apple is the original source of most of our cultivated apples. Besides its sweet fruits, it produces lovely, fragrant flowers in spring, and provides shade in summer. Plants are mostly hardy, grow rapidly, and have a moderate life span. They are susceptible to insect attack and fungus diseases which may require control measures. Apple trees are frequent hosts of the fall webworm, but the defoliating larvae seldom, if ever, harm the tree.
Propagation. Apples are propagated by seeds, budding, or grafting onto hardy rootstocks. Seeds should be separated from ripe fruits and dried for storage, or stratified in peat for seventy-five days at 41° F. Seeds stored in airtight containers held at temperatures just above freezing will keep for at least two and a half years. Stratified seeds may be sown in spring in drills and covered with ¼-inch of nursery soil. Most commercial varieties are produced by grafting or budding (U.S. Forest Service 1948). For an excellent discussion of grafting techniques, see Wyman (1977:456–59).
Bird uses. See Apples.

CRABAPPLE
Malus spp.
ROSACEAE

Description. Crabapples are generally less than 30 feet tall and are among the most commonly planted ornamental flowering and fruiting trees.
Bark. On young stems, smooth, reddish to red-brown to gray; on older stems, scaly, becoming gray-brown.
Leaves. May be long and thin, stoutly oval, or lobed.
Flowers. Flower colors vary from white to dark purplish-red, with many intermediate shades of pink and red. Flowering usually occurs in May and most trees have fragrant blossoms.
Fruits. Vary in size from ¼-inch to 2 inches in diameter, and are dark red to yellow or green. They generally are most colorful in September and October, and drop to the ground in the months following. A few varieties retain their fruits throughout the winter, adding touches of color to the landscape and providing food for wildlife.
Habitat. Malus species grow best in clay-loam soils but tolerate a wide variety of soil types. They prefer a temperate climate.
Landscape notes. Crabapples are widely used for landscaping in parks, along streets, and on private grounds. Hundreds of species and varieties exist, many of which are available commercially and suit nearly every planting need. Some are small and moundlike; others

are columnar, having weeping branches, and grow to 50 feet. Many are extremely hardy. Edible varieties are economically important in colder regions of the country where common apples cannot survive. All crabapples may be affected by scale insects and borers, and a few by rusts and fire blight. Infestations may be controlled by occasional spraying and pruning (Wyman 1951).

Propagation. Most crabapples are propagated by vegetative means because few reproduce true to seed. Common nursery practices include root grafting, whip and tongue grafting, and T-budding seedlings. T-budding in the fall is the preferred method of propagation. Also, seedling root-stalks may be grafted onto older *Malus* trees, changing the trees' varieties (Hartmann and Kester 1968).

Bird uses. See Apples.

Japanese Flowering Crabapple

Birds That Use Apples

	Food	Cover	Nesting
Ruffed grouse*	F		
Bobwhite	F, S, BD		
Ring-necked pheasant*	F, S, BD		
Ruby-throated hummingbird	N	X	X
Red-bellied woodpecker*	F, S		
Red-headed woodpecker*	F, S		
Yellow-bellied sapsucker*	sap, F, S		
Hairy woodpecker	F, S		
Downy woodpecker	F, S		
Great crested flycatcher		X	X (cavity)
Eastern kingbird			X
Blue jay	F, S	X	X
Gray jay	F		
Common crow	F		
Tufted titmouse	F		
Mockingbird	F	X	X
Gray catbird*	F	X	X
American robin*	F	X	X
Eastern bluebird		X	X (cavity)
Cedar waxwing*	FL, F		
Starling*	F, S		X (cavity)
Red-eyed vireo		X	X
Common grackle	F		
Orchard oriole	F	X	X
Northern oriole	F, S	X	X
Cardinal	F		X
Evening grosbeak*	F, BD		
Purple finch*	F, S, FL		
Pine grosbeak	F, BD, S		
Red crossbill	S		
Rufous-sided towhee	F, S		

Note: *preferred food; F, fruit; S, seeds; BD, buds; FL, flowers.
Sources: Davison 1967; Martin et al. 1951.

Some Recommended Crabapples

Species	Height	Flower		Fruit		Fruiting schedule	Range
		Period	Color	Period	Color		
Siberian Crabapple* *Malus baccata*	to 50'	early May	white, single, fragrant	Autumn, persistent to March	red or yellow ⅜" dia.	bears annually	Hardy in NE U.S. Intro. from NE Asia. Hardiness zone: 2.
Bobwhite Crabapple *Malus "Bob White"*	to 20'	early May	buds pink, flowers white	Autumn, persistent to April	pale yellow to dull brown ⅜"–½" dia.	bears in alternate years	Hardy in NE U.S., except in NE Vermont, N New Hampshire, and cent. and N Maine. Hardiness zone: 5.
Dorothea Crabapple *Malus "Dorothea"*	to 25'	mid-May	pink and white, semi-double	Autumn, persistent to March or April	yellow ½" dia.	bears annually	Hardy in NE U.S., except in NE Vermont, N New Hampshire, and cent. and N Maine. Hardiness zone: 5.
Tea Crabapple* *Malus hupehensis*	to 24'	early May	buds pink, flowers white, single	Autumn, persistent to mid-February	greenish-yellow to red ⅜" dia.	bears in alternate years	Hardy in NE U.S., except in NE Vermont, N New Hampshire, and cent. and N Maine. Intro. from China. Hardiness zone: 5.
Japanese Flowering Crabapple* *Malus floribunda*	to 30'	early May	buds pink, flowers white, fragrant	Autumn, persistent to March	yellow and red ⅜" dia.	bears annually	Hardy in NE U.S., except in NE Vermont, N New Hampshire, and cent. and N Maine. Intro. from Japan. Hardiness zone: 5.
Sargent Crabapple* *Malus sargentii*	to 8'	mid-May	white	Autumn, persistent to Feb. and March	red ¼" dia.	bears annually	Hardy in NE U.S., except in NE Vermont, N New Hampshire, and cent. and N Maine. Intro. from Japan. Hardiness zone: 5.

*Introduced.
Sources: Smith 1973; Wyman 1951.

WHITE MULBERRY
Morus alba L.
MORACEAE

Description. White mulberry, introduced from Asia, has become naturalized throughout the eastern United States. It is a small tree, 30 to 60 feet tall. The fruits are preferred by a great variety of birds. Another common name is Russian mulberry.

Bark. Yellowish-brown.

Leaves. Alternate, simple, smooth and shiny, variable sizes and shapes, smaller than those of red mulberry, coarsely toothed. Autumn color: yellow.

Flowers. Green on pendant spikes, sexes occur on same or separate plants.

Fruits. Fleshy, white, pink, or purplish-violet multiple fruits shaped like blackberries, bland to slightly sweet. Fruiting may begin when trees are about five years old (U.S. Forest Service 1948).

Flowering period. May.

Fruiting period. July to August.

Habitat. Prefers rich moist soils but grows in sand, clay, or other very poor soils.

Range. Maine south to Florida, west to Texas.

Hardiness zone. 5.

Landscape notes. A useful tree for windbreaks and lawns, white mulberry is attractive for its ornamental leaves and fruits. Trees are hardy, grow rapidly, produce abundant shade, and are pleasant to sit under except when in fruit. They should be planted away from playgrounds, sidewalks, and patios.

Propagation. There are several varieties of white mulberry, some of which are hardier or more drought-resistant than others. One should collect seeds or cuttings from trees having characteristics most suitable to the planting locality.

Seeds may be extracted by soaking the fruits in water for twenty-four hours and then mashing the fruits. When clean, seeds should be air-dried in shade. Seeds sown in fall should germinate in spring. Germination may be hastened by stratifying the seeds in moist sand for sixty days at 68° F. (night) and 86° F. (day). Seeds may be broadcast or sown in drills and covered with ¼-inch of nursery soil. They should be lightly mulched until they germinate. Spring-sown seeds should germinate in two weeks. Seedlings should be given light shade for the first two weeks of growth and may be moved to the field when one year old (U.S. Forest Service 1948).

Mulberry is often propagated from softwood and hardwood cuttings because such cuttings root easily.

Bird uses. See Mulberries.

RED MULBERRY
Morus rubra L.
MORACEAE

Description. Red mulberry is native to eastern North America. While not as attractive as white mulberry, red mulberry is a prolific fruit producer, and its berries are preferred by birds.

Bark. Reddish-brown with smooth ridges.

Leaves. Alternate, simple, 3 to 10 inches long, irregularly shaped with two or more deeply cut lobes or with no lobes, rough above, hairy beneath. Autumn color: yellow.

Flowers. Green on pendant spikes, sexes occur on same or separate plants.

Fruits. Fleshy, dark red, or purple aggregate fruits, composed of many small, one-seeded drupes, resemble blackberries, and are sweet and delicious. Heavy fruiting may begin when trees are about ten years old.

Flowering period. April to June.

Fruiting period. June to August.

Habitat. Found scattered throughout moist places in eastern woodlands. Prefers fertile soils.

Range. Massachusetts south to southern Florida, west to Minnesota and Texas.

Hardiness zone. 6.

Landscape notes. Trees should be planted away from sidewalks or sitting areas so fallen fruits will not be a nuisance.

Propagation. The distribution of red mulberry is largely attributed to the dispersal of seeds by birds (Fordham 1967). Trees can be grown from seeds that are collected from mature fruits. Before planting, seeds must be separated from the pulp by mashing and soaking. They may be stratified in moist sand for 90 to 120 days at 41° F. to help break dormancy. Sow in fall or spring and cover with ¼-inch of soil followed by a layer of mulch to be removed upon germination. Seedlings should be kept in partial shade for two weeks and planted in the field when one year old or older (U.S. Forest Service 1948).

Birds That Use Mulberries

	Food	Cover	Nesting
Turkey*	F		
Bobwhite*	F		
Yellow-billed cuckoo	F		
Black-billed cuckoo	F		
Common flicker	F		
Red-bellied woodpecker	F		
Red-headed woodpecker*	F		
Hairy woodpecker*	F		
Downy woodpecker	F		
Eastern kingbird*	F		
Great crested flycatcher*	F		
Blue jay*	F		
Common crow*	F		
Fish crow*	F		
Tufted titmouse	F		
Mockingbird*	F		
Gray catbird*	F		
Brown thrasher*	F		
American robin*	F		
Wood thrush*	F		
Swainson's thrush	F		
Veery*	F		
Eastern bluebird*	F		
Cedar waxwing*	F		
Starling*	F		
White-eyed vireo*	F		
Red-eyed vireo*	F		
Bay-breasted warbler*	F		
Yellow warbler	F		
House sparrow	F		
Red-winged blackbird*	F		
Common grackle	F		
Orchard oriole*	F		
Northern oriole*	F		
Scarlet tanager*	F		
Summer tanager*	F		
Cardinal*	F		
Rose-breasted grosbeak*	F		
Indigo bunting*	F		
Purple finch*	F		
American goldfinch*	F		
Rufous-sided towhee	F		
White-throated sparrow	F		
Song sparrow*	F		

Note: *preferred food; F, fruit.
Sources: McKenny 1939; Davison 1967; Martin et al. 1951.

Red Mulberry

BLACK TUPELO

Nyssa sylvatica Marsh.
NYSSACEAE

Description. Black Tupelo is commonly found on wet sites. The branching pattern is distinctive, with branches growing at right angles to the trunk. It grows to 60 feet and produces fruits preferred by many birds, especially by thrushes and woodpeckers. Other common names are sour gum and blackgum.

Bark. Dark brown with deep furrows and tight, thick blocks.

Twigs. Slender, reddish-brown and smooth, with diaphragmed pith.

Leaves. Alternate, simple, often crowding into clusters at tips of twigs, 3 to 6 inches long, shiny, elliptic, leathery. Autumn colors: scarlet to orange.

Flowers. Inconspicuous, greenish-white, forming singly or in clusters, male and female flowers on separate plants.

Fruits. Small ovoid or oblong, blue-black drupes, about ½-inch long.

Flowering period. April to June.

Fruiting period. August to October.

Habitat. Grows best in moist, light, rich soils but does well on drier sites.

Range. Central Maine south to Florida, west to Michigan and eastern Texas.

Hardiness zone. 5.

Landscape notes. Very desirable as an ornamental, tupelo is attractive for its picturesque form and fiery red fall color, which lasts for weeks. The gnarled branches bear tiers of lustrous green foliage. It is most effective when planted in front of soft-textured evergreens such as pines or hemlocks. Black tupelo is an excellent choice for landscaping ponds, bottom lands, and hollows. Lowlands are the tree's natural habitat, but it will do equally well on drier sites. It is hardy, grows at a moderate rate—about 15 feet in ten years—and has a medium life span.

Propagation. Trees are difficult to transplant. Only small trees with an ample root ball are likely to succeed (Wyman 1951). They are usually propagated from seed, or by side or veneer grafting in the spring to the same variety of stock (Mahlstede and Haber 1957). Fruits should be collected when ripe, and macerated to separate seeds from pulp. Seeds should be stratified in moist sand for sixty to ninety days at 30°–50° F. and sown in spring. Those sown in the fall (not stratified) do not germinate as readily because of embryo dormancy (U.S. Forest Service 1948). Seeds should be sown ½- to 1 inch deep and kept moist (U.S. Forest Service 1948).

Black Tupelo

Birds That Use Tupelo

	Food	Cover	Nesting
Mallard	F		
Wood duck*	F		
Turkey*	F		
Ruffed grouse	F		
Bobwhite	F		
Ring-necked pheasant	F		
Common flicker*	F		
Pileated woodpecker	F		
Red-bellied woodpecker	F		
Red-headed woodpecker*	F		
Yellow-bellied sapsucker	F, sap		
Hairy woodpecker*	F		
Downy woodpecker	F		
Eastern kingbird*	F		
Blue jay	F		
Common crow	F		
Tufted titmouse	F		
Mockingbird*	F		
Gray catbird*	F		
Brown thrasher*	F		
American robin*	F		
Wood thrush*	F		
Hermit thrush	F		
Swainson's thrush	F		
Gray-cheeked thrush*	F		
Veery	F		
Eastern bluebird*	F		
Cedar waxwing*	F		
Starling*	F		
Red-eyed vireo	F		
Scarlet tanager	F		
Summer tanager*	F		
Rose-breasted grosbeak	F		
Purple finch	F		

Note: *preferred food; F, fruit.
Sources: McKenny 1939; Davison 1967; Martin et al. 1951; Collins 1965.

AMERICAN HOP-HORNBEAM
Ostrya virginiana (Mill.) K. Koch
BETULACEAE

Description. This usually small tree—20 to 30 feet, rarely to 60 feet tall—occurs as a scattered tree. Its fruits are most preferred by ruffed grouse. (Davison 1967:185). Other common names are Eastern hop-hornbeam and ironwood.

Bark. Lower bark gray to brownish, narrowly grooved and ridged, forming long, shreddy strips. The bark is probably the best field mark.

Twigs. Brown.

Leaves. Alternate, simple, 1 to 5 inches long, oblong to ovate, sharply pointed with fine hairs on both sides. Autumn color: yellow.

Flowers. Greenish catkins, often appearing in twos or threes scattered about the crown.

Fruits. Small nutlets enclosed in clustered papery sacs resembling hops.

Flowering period. April to June.

Fruiting period. August to October, persistent until winter.

Habitat. Grows in many different soils and sites from rich, fertile woods to open, gravelly ridges. Prefers partial shade.

Range. Nova Scotia south to Florida, west to southern Manitoba and Texas.

Hardiness zone. 5.

Landscape notes. American hop-hornbeam is a useful border tree for small yards. Its tolerance to shade makes it a good understory plant in woodlots. Trees are hardy, slow growing and moderately long-lived. Heavy fruiting occurs when trees are about twenty-five years old (U.S. Forest Service 1948).

Propagation. Hop-hornbeam can be propagated from ripe seeds that are collected while still on the tree. They should be dried and separated from their bladderlike sacs and sown immediately, or stratified in sand or peat at 41° F. for winter storage. Seed dormancy may be broken by stratifying seeds for 60 days at 68°–86° F., followed by 140 days at

41° F. Seeds sown ¼-inch deep in fall should be mulched to prevent winterkill (U.S. Forest Service 1948). Mulch should be removed upon germination.

Birds That Use American Hop-hornbeam

	Food	Cover	Nesting
Common merganser	F		
Turkey	F		
Ruffed grouse*	CK, F, BD		
Bobwhite	F, BD		
Ring-necked pheasant	F, BD		
Downy woodpecker	F		
Mockingbird	F		
Rose-breasted grosbeak	F		
Purple finch	F		

Note: *preferred food; F, fruit; CK, catkins; BD, buds.
Sources: Martin et al. 1951; Davison 1967; McKenny 1939.

WHITE SPRUCE
Picea glauca (Moench) Voss
PINACEAE

Description. White spruce, a northern tree, is a stately landscape specimen. It can grow to 100 feet. When grown in the open, its symmetrical, conical crown reaches to the ground. It is a favorite nest tree of the robin, mourning dove, mockingbird, and chipping sparrow (DeGraaf et al. 1975). The seed is a choice food of crossbills and other finches. Other common names are Canadian spruce and cat spruce.

Bark. Ash brown, thin.

Twigs. Brown, hairless.

Leaves. Linear, four-sided, bluish-green needles, ⅓- to ¾-inch long, appear crowded on the upper surfaces of branches.

Flowers. Inconspicuous sporophylls, both sexes occur on same plant.

Fruits. Borne in cylindrical brown cones, 1½ inches long, drop soon after maturing. Trees produce abundant cones when about twenty years old. Good crops occur every two to six years.

Flowering period. May.

Fruiting period. August to November.

Habitat. Typical of stream borders and lake shores. Prefers moist, sandy loams but grows in a variety of soils.

Range. Newfoundland south to northwestern Massachusetts, west to Minnesota.

Hardiness zone. 2.

Landscape notes. Widely used in landscaping, singly, in clumps, and in hedgerows. Long, single or double rows of trees make excellent windbreaks, and also form effective screens against unsightly views. The low crowns which extend to the ground are excellent backgrounds for colorful shrubbery. Plants are hardy, rapid growing—reaching 18 feet in ten years—and long-lived, surviving for 200 years. For large properties only.

Propagation. White spruce may be grown from seeds sown in fall or stratified over winter and sown in spring. Stratification is not nec-

White Spruce

essary for successful germination. Dried seeds have been stored for up to ten years at 36°–40° F. without loss of viability. Seeds should be broadcast or sown in drills and covered with ¼-inch of nursery soil or well-drained sandy loam. Fall-sown seeds should be mulched over winter; they generally germinate the following spring. Spring-sown seeds germinate in fifteen to thirty days (U.S. Forest Service 1948). Cuttings may be taken in late winter or early spring, but are difficult to grow (Hartmann and Kester 1968).
Bird uses. See Spruces.

COLORADO SPRUCE
Picea pungens Engelm.
PINACEAE

Description. The striking Colorado or blue spruce is readily used as a nest site, especially by the robin, mockingbird, chipping sparrow, and purple finch. Also known as prickly spruce, it grows to 100 feet, with a diameter of 18 to 30 inches.
Twigs. Smooth.
Leaves. Stiff, sharp, dense, green to bluish-green needles, ½- to 1 inch long.
Flowers. Inconspicuous sporophylls, sexes separate on same plant.
Fruits. Borne in cones, 2½ inches long, containing many small seeds. Good crops occur every year on mature trees.
Flowering period. April to May.
Fruiting period. September to winter.
Habitat. Abundant on the lower, middle, and upper slopes of the Rocky Mountains.
Range. Native to the mountains of Colorado to Utah, New Mexico, and Wyoming.
Hardiness zone. 2.
Landscape notes. Colorado spruce is widely used as an ornamental for its attractive shape and blue to silvery-green foliage which develops under satisfactory growing conditions. It is a popular lawn tree, either as a single specimen or in rows along property boundaries. Trees prefer full or partial sunlight. Growth is

[51] Trees

slow at first, more rapid after several years. Many cultivated varieties of superior form and color are available from local nurseries. It should be remembered that this spruce is most attractive during its first twenty years. As it ages, the lower branches die out, the tree loses its fullness, and it can eventually become unsightly (Wyman 1951). Use for large properties only.

Propagation. Colorado spruce may be readily raised from seed, a method of propagation which yields a variety of colors and shapes. It is often more practical to propagate by grafts and cuttings, which enables one to be selective of the most desirable qualities. Seeds may be stratified in moist sand for one to three months at 32°–41° F. (U.S. Forest Service 1948) before sowing.

Bird uses. See Spruces.

Colorado Spruce

RED SPRUCE
Picea rubens Sarg.
PINACEAE

Description. Red spruce, a commercial tree of the Northeast, is frequently used as a nest site. The seeds are preferred by crossbills and pine siskins. It grows 60 to 70 feet, with a diameter of 1 to 2 feet. Other common names are eastern spruce, yellow spruce, and he-balsam.

Bark. Grayish to reddish-brown.

Twigs. Orange-brown, hairy.

Leaves. Linear, ½- to ⅝-inch long, four-sided with blunt or sharp tips that often curve upward, yellow-green.

Flowers. Inconspicuous, both sexes occur on same plant.

Fruits. Cones, 1¼ to 2 inches long, ovoid to oblong, falling during the first winter or spring. Abundant cone production usually occurs on trees over forty years old (Harlow and Harrar 1968). Scattered cones may appear on trees as young as fifteen years old (U.S. Forest Service 1965).

Flowering period. April to May.

Fruiting period. September to October.

Habitat. Common in low, swampy areas but more vigorous on higher ground in well-drained, sandy loams.

Range. Nova Scotia, Prince Edward Island and Quebec west to Ohio, south generally in the mountains to North Carolina and Tennessee.

Hardiness zone. 2.

Landscape notes. Red spruce is a good landscape tree but grows more slowly than other spruces, so it is not a practical choice for sites requiring rapid results. Once established, it is hardy and usually long-lived. Best growth occurs in soils having a pH of 4.0 to 5.5 (U.S. Forest Service 1965).

Propagation. See White Spruce.

Bird uses. See Spruces.

	Food	Cover	Nesting
Mallard	S		
Spruce grouse*	NL	X	
Mourning dove	S	X	X
Pileated woodpecker	S		
Yellow-bellied sapsucker	sap	X	X (cavity)
Hairy woodpecker	S	X	X (cavity)
Downy woodpecker	S	X	X (cavity)
Blue jay		X	X
Black-capped chickadee	S	X	X (cavity)
Boreal chickadee	S	X	X (cavity)
Red-breasted nuthatch*	S	X	X (cavity)
Mockingbird		X	X
American robin		X	X
Wood thrush	S		
Swainson's thrush	S	X	X
Golden-crowned kinglet		X	X
Ruby-crowned kinglet		X	X
Cedar waxwing	S	X	
Magnolia warbler		X	X
Cape May warbler		X	X
Yellow-rumped warbler		X	X
Black-throated green warbler		X	X
Blackburnian warbler		X	X
Bay-breasted warbler		X	X
Blackpoll warbler		X	X
Evening grosbeak*	S	X	X
Purple finch*	S	X	X
Pine grosbeak	S	X	X
Pine siskin*	S	X	X
American goldfinch	S	X	
Red crossbill*	S	X	X
White-winged crossbill*	S	X	X
White-throated sparrow*	S	X	
Chipping sparrow		X	X

Note: *preferred food; S, seeds; NL, needles.
Sources: McKenny 1939; Martin et al. 1951; Davison 1967; Harrison 1975; Schutz 1974.

RED PINE
Pinus resinosa Ait.
PINACEAE

Description. Red pine is a stately tree with a straight trunk and dark green needles. The seed is a favorite food of the pine siskin. It can grow to 80 feet, with a diameter of 2 to 3 feet. Another common name is Norway pine.
Bark. Reddish, with large, flat, diamond-shaped plates.
Twigs. Orange-brown, lustrous.
Leaves. Long, lustrous needles, 3 to 8 inches long, forming in pairs.
Flowers. Inconspicuous, sexes occur separately on the same tree in clusters in spring.
Fruits. Thornless, woody cones, 1½ to 2½ inches long, containing many small seeds. Cones begin to appear when plants are about twelve years old. Heavy crops appear at three- to seven-year intervals.
Flowering period. April to June.
Fruiting period. August to October, persistent to summer.
Habitat. Thrives on light, acid, sandy soils, occasionally attains large size on heavier soils, often establishes itself in areas formerly occupied by white pine.
Range. Newfoundland south to northern New Jersey, west to Manitoba and Minnesota.
Hardiness zone. 2.
Landscape notes. Red pines are very attractive individually or in clumps and rows where they form effective screens and windbreaks. Very hardy, able to withstand temperatures from −60° to 105° F. They prefer open sunny situations, where they will grow in poor soil. Growth is usually rapid at first, with trees growing about 18 feet in ten years, but growth rate tapers off with age.
Propagation. Seeds of red pine have no dormancy conditions and need no stratification period. They may be collected from September to October and broadcast or sown in drills ¼-inch deep in well-drained sandy loam, and mulched until soon after the onset of germination (U.S. Forest Service 1948).
Bird uses. See White Pine.

PITCH PINE
Pinus rigida Mill.
PINACEAE

Description. In the Northeast, pitch pine is usually a small tree, 40 to 60 feet tall with a diameter of 1 to 2 feet. It grows on the poorest sand or on gravelly sites. It is frequently used as a nest tree and the seed is eaten by the red-breasted nuthatch, black-capped chickadee, and several types of finches.
Bark. Rough with deep fissures and irregular plates.
Leaves. Stiff needles, 3 to 3½ inches long, in groups of three.
Cones. Inconspicuous, sexes separate, forming on same plant.
Fruits. Heavy, stout cones, 1 to 3 inches long, spiny, often persisting for several years. Cones contain many small seeds which, upon ripening, are dispersed by wind and gravity.
Flowering period. April to May.
Fruiting period. November to April.
Habitat. Commonly found on dry, acidic, sterile soils in the northern part of its range where it develops a small scrubby habit. Farther south, in richer soils it reaches maximum height with a sturdy straight trunk, few low branches, and a small open crown. Prefers light, well-drained, sandy loams.
Range. Maine south to the mountains of Georgia and Tennessee.
Hardiness zone. 5.
Landscape notes. Pitch pine is an excellent tree for dry, sandy soils where other trees will not grow. It gives a fair amount of shade when planted in groups and requires little or no care. New England pitch pines are shorter than those to the south and may often appear grotesque, even picturesque. Cone production often begins on trees as young as three years old; heavy crops appear at intervals of three or more years. The cones often open in midwinter and release their seeds upon the snow, where they are readily spotted and consumed by wildlife (Harlow and Harrar 1969). Growth is usually slow for the first three to five years,

then becomes more rapid (U.S. Forest Service 1965). As trees approach the century mark, growth once again slows. Trees may live for 200 years. They produce new foliage after fire.
Propagation. Seeds should be collected from ripe cones that are sun- or kiln-dried and shaken. They may be sown in fall or spring by broadcasting or in drills 4 to 6 inches apart in well-drained, sandy loam. Recommended seed depth is ¼-inch (U.S. Forest Service 1948).

Birds That Use Pitch Pine

	Food	Cover	Nesting[1]
Horned grebe	S		
Wood duck	S		
Turkey*	S	X	
Bobwhite*	S	X	
Ring-necked pheasant	S		
Mourning dove	S	X	X
Pileated woodpecker	S		
Red-bellied woodpecker*	S		X (cavity)
Yellow-bellied sapsucker	S		
Hairy woodpecker	S	X	X (cavity)
Black-capped chickadee*	S	X	X (cavity)
Tufted titmouse	S	X	
White-breasted nuthatch*	S	X	X (cavity)
Red-breasted nuthatch*	S	X	X (cavity)
Brown creeper*	S		
Brown thrasher	S	X	X
Cedar waxwing	S		
Magnolia warbler		X	X
Yellow-rumped warbler	S	X	X
Yellow-throated warbler		X	X
Blackburnian warbler		X	X
Pine warbler	S	X	X
Eastern meadowlark	S		
Evening grosbeak	S	X	
Purple finch*	S	X	X
Pine grosbeak	S	X	

[54]

Pitch Pine

Pine siskin*	S	X	X
American goldfinch	S		
Red crossbill*	S	X	X
White-winged crossbill	S	X	X
Rufous-sided towhee*	S		
Northern junco	S		

Note: *preferred food; S, seeds; [1]often used by songbirds for nesting.
Sources: Martin et al. 1951; McKenny 1939; Davison 1967.

EASTERN WHITE PINE
Pinus strobus L.
PINACEAE

Description. Eastern white pine grows to the greatest size of any northeastern conifer, commonly to 100 feet. The plumelike, horizontal branches of older trees are distinctively graceful. White pine is a frequent nest site of robins, mourning doves, and blue jays, among others. The seeds are eaten by many species. The rapid growth of white pine makes it ideal for wildlife cover. Coniferous trees, in general, are important for protection from the elements and predators.
Bark. Old bark thick, gray, and deeply fissured, young bark thin, dark green, and smooth.
Twigs. Orange-brown.
Leaves. Needles, 3 to 5 inches long, occurring in bundles of five, deep bluish-green, slender and flexible.
Flowers. Inconspicuous sporophylls.
Fruits. Borne in cones, 4 to 8 inches long, tapering at tips, often curved, usually falling from the trees in winter or spring.
Flowering period. April to June.
Fruiting period. August to September.
Habitat. Grows on a variety of sites, from dry plateaus to wet swamps. Prefers moist, sandy loams.
Range. Newfoundland south to northern Georgia, west to Minnesota and Iowa.

Eastern White Pine

Hardiness zone. 4.

Landscape notes. This is a handsome tree singly or in groups on large properties. It is popular for its attractive shape during all stages of development. Shiny, deep-green needles provide excellent background for flowering trees and shrubs. The growth rate is moderate, with trees gaining about 10 feet in ten years (Wyman 1951), but they may reach 20 feet in that time under optimal conditions. Cone production may begin on ten-year-old plants, with heavy crops occurring in about twenty years. The trees are easily transplanted when young and tolerate pruning or even shearing. With good growing conditions, white pines may live for several hundred years. Tree growth may be affected by the white-pine weevil, a small insect that attacks and kills the terminal shoots.

Propagation. White pine is usually propagated from seed. Mature cones should be collected from September to October, sun-dried and shaken to release seeds. Seeds may be sown in the fall or stratified for thirty days at 50° F. and sown in spring. Seeds may be broadcast or sown in drills 4 to 6 inches apart and ¼-inch deep in sandy loam. Beds should be mulched lightly with either plant litter or cloth until germination begins (U.S. Forest Service 1948).

Birds That Use Eastern White Pine

	Food	Cover	Nesting
Horned grebe	S		
Wood duck	S		
Cooper's hawk		X	X
Spruce grouse*	S, ND	X	
Turkey*	S, ND	X	
Bobwhite*	S		
Ring-necked pheasant	S		
Rock dove	S		
Mourning dove*	S	X	X*
Pileated woodpecker	S		X (cavity)
Red-bellied woodpecker*	S		X (cavity)

	Food	Cover	Nesting
Yellow-bellied sapsucker	sap		X (cavity)
Hairy woodpecker	S		X (cavity)
Blue jay		X	X
Black-capped chickadee*	S	X	X (cavity)
Carolina chickadee*	S	X	X (cavity)
Boreal chickadee*	S	X	X (cavity)
Tufted titmouse*	S	X	X (cavity)
White-breasted nuthatch*	S	X	X (cavity)
Red-breasted nuthatch*	S	X	X (cavity)
Brown-headed nuthatch*	S	X	X (cavity)
Brown creeper*	S	X	
Carolina wren	S		
Brown thrasher	S	X	X
Wood thrush		X	X
American robin		X	X
Cedar waxwing	S		
Magnolia warbler		X	X
Yellow-rumped warbler		X	X
Yellow-throated warbler		X	X
Blackburnian warbler		X	X
Pine warbler*	S	X	X
Eastern meadowlark	S		
Common grackle*	S	X	X
Cardinal*	S	X	X
Evening grosbeak*	S	X	X
Purple finch	S	X	X
House finch	S	X	
Pine grosbeak*	S	X	X
Pine siskin*	S	X	X
American goldfinch	S		
Red crossbill*	S	X	X
White-winged crossbill*	S	X	X
Rufous-sided towhee*	S	X	
Northern junco*	S	X	
Chipping sparrow*	S	X	X
White-throated sparrow*	S	X	

Note: *preferred food; S, seeds; ND, needles.
Sources: Martin et al. 1951; McKenny 1939; Davison 1967; Harrison 1975; Terres 1968; DeGraaf et al. 1975.

Scotch Pine

SCOTCH PINE

Pinus sylvestris L.

PINACEAE

Description. Scotch pines are used for wind-breaks and ornamentals. Occasionally used by birds as a nest site, its seeds are preferred by red crossbills. (Davison 1967:201).

Bark. Orange and shreddy on upper part of young trunks, dark and fissured on full-grown trees.

Twigs. Yellow to brown.

Leaves. Long, sharp, bluish-green needles in pairs, 1½ to 3 inches long.

Flowers. Inconspicuous sporophylls, male and female are separate on same plant.

Fruits. Borne in cones, 1½ to 3 inches long, stoutly pyramidal, spineless. Good seed crops occur every two to five years.

Flowering period. May to June.

Fruiting period. September to October, persistent to April.

Habitat. Native to Europe and Siberia. Grows well in a variety of soils, but prefers sandy loams and sunny, protected locations.

Range. Naturalized throughout New England south to New Jersey, west to Ohio and Iowa. (Fernald 1950:56).

Hardiness zone. 2.

Landscape notes. Scotch pine is attractive for its upright crown, blue-green foliage, and orange upper bark. It is a common choice in landscaping because it is easily cultivated and requires little or no care. Occasionally it grows crooked but is no less picturesque. Trees are grown commercially for lumber and for use at Christmas. Scotch pine is hardy, grows rapidly, and is long-lived.

Propagation. Trees are usually propagated from seed. Cones may be gathered from October to March, air-dried, and shaken to remove seeds. Seeds usually do not require stratification. They may be broadcast or sown in drills and covered with ¼-inch of sandy loam (U.S. Forest Service 1948).

Birds That Use Scotch Pine[1]

	Food	Cover	Nesting
Red crossbill*	S	X	X

Note: [1]probably used by the same birds that are attracted to Eastern white pine; *preferred food; S, seeds.

Source: Davison 1967.

EASTERN COTTONWOOD

Populus deltoides Marsh.

SALICACEAE

Description. Eastern cottonwood, while able to grow on dry sites, is naturally found in wet areas, especially stream banks. It grows 80 to 100 feet, with a diameter of 3 to 4 feet. It is of moderate value to wildlife—the open branching habit of mature trees is not conducive to open nesting, but woodpeckers frequently excavate nests in the soft wood, and the buds are taken by some birds. Another common name is eastern poplar.

Bark. Greenish-yellow and thin on young stems, becoming gray, thick, and deeply fissured with age.

Leaves. Alternate, simple, 3 to 6 inches long, 4 to 5 inches wide, triangular shaped with coarse teeth along margins, tips sharply pointed, dark green above, lighter beneath, leaf stalks flattened. Autumn colors: orange-yellow to gold.

Flowers. Inconspicuous, male and female catkins form on separate trees.

Fruits. Three- or four-parted oval capsules, ¼- to ⅓-inch long, forming on long, caterpillarlike catkins. Capsules release large quantities of silky-haired seeds which often accumulate on the ground and resemble snow. Seed production begins when trees are about ten years old (U.S. Forest Service 1965). Good seed crops occur every year.

Flowering period. February to May.

Fruiting period. April to June.

Habitat. Best growth occurs on moist, alluvial soils where a young tree may grow up to 5 feet per year. Commonly grows in pure stands in old fields or in association with sycamore and black willow.

Range. New Hampshire south to Florida, west to Kansas.

Hardiness zone. 2.

Landscape notes. Eastern cottonwood is useful in areas where abundant fruits and "cotton" will not be regarded as a nuisance. Trees can be planted in wet or dry soils. Once established, they grow very rapidly. Plants are hardy in the Northeast, where they may live a century or more. Trees should not be planted within 100 feet of dwellings because their brittle limbs are readily broken by storms.

Propagation. Trees are propagated by seeds or hardwood cuttings. Seeds should be collected when capsules begin to open and planted immediately. They should be sown on bare, moist, shaded ground and left uncovered. Germination should occur in a few days because ripe seeds are not dormant (U.S. Forest Service 1948). Cuttings taken from one-year-old sprouts and treated with indolebutyric acid root well. Trees reproduce naturally by seeds, root suckers, and stump sprouts (U.S. Forest Service 1965).

Birds That Use Eastern Cottonwood

	Food	Cover	Nesting[1]
Ruffed grouse*	BD, CK		
Yellow-bellied sapsucker	sap	X	X (cavity)
Evening grosbeak	BD		
Purple finch	BD		

Note: *preferred food; BD, buds; CK, catkins;
[1]young trees are frequent nest sites of songbirds.
Sources: Martin et al. 1951; Davison 1967.

BIGTOOTH ASPEN

Populus grandidentata Michx.
SALICACEAE

Description. Bigtooth aspen is a fairly common northeastern tree. It grows 60 to 70 feet, occasionally with a diameter of 2 feet. Its main wildlife value lies in the fact that ruffed grouse prefer its buds and catkins. The yellow-bellied sapsucker also commonly excavates its nest in bigtooth aspen. Other common names are poplar, popple, and largetooth aspen.

Bark. Upper trunk smooth, yellowish-green in youth becoming furrowed and brown with age.

Leaves. Alternate, simple, 2 to 6 inches long, rounded and coarsely toothed with flattened stalks, undersides of young leaves are white and woolly when young. Autumn color: orange-yellow.

Flowers. Inconspicuous, forming on male and female catkins.

Fruits. Capsules on pendulous catkins containing many seeds covered with silky hairs.

Flowering period. April to May.

Fruiting period. May to June.

Habitat. Often found mixed with quaking aspen or growing in pure stands in forest clearings and along roadways. Trees grow in a variety of soils with sunny exposures.

Range. Nova Scotia south to North Carolina, west to Manitoba and Iowa.

Hardiness zone. 4.

Landscape notes. Bigtooth aspen is well known for its attractive autumn color. The leaves are especially striking when trees are planted in front of a dark background of evergreens. The trees are hardy, rapid growing, and short-lived, generally deteriorating in forty-five to fifty years. They require little or no care.

Propagation. See Eastern Cottonwood.

Birds That Use Bigtooth Aspen

	Food	Cover	Nesting
Ruffed grouse*	BD, CK		
Yellow-bellied sapsucker	sap	X	X (cavity)
Downy woodpecker		X	X (cavity)
Hairy woodpecker		X	X (cavity)
Black-capped chickadee		X	X (cavity)
Evening grosbeak	BD		
Purple finch	BD		

Note: *preferred food; BD, buds; CK, catkins.
Sources: Martin et al. 1951; Harrison 1975.

QUAKING ASPEN
Populus tremuloides Michx.
SALICACEAE

Description. The quaking aspen is probably the most widely distributed tree in North America (Harlow and Harrar 1969). The buds are preferred by ruffed grouse, and the northern oriole frequently nests in its upper branches. Quaking aspen is a fairly small tree, 50 to 60 feet tall. It is also known as trembling aspen or popple.

Bark. Rough with dark gray patches at base, becoming smooth and yellow-green in the crown area.

Leaves. Alternate, simple, 1½ to 3 inches in diameter, broadly ovate with rounded bases and pointed tips, margins with close fine teeth, dark green above, light green beneath, leaf stalks laterally flattened causing them to tremble in the slightest breeze. Autumn colors: bright yellow or gold.

Flowers. Inconspicuous, male and female catkins form on separate plants.

Fruits. Capsules on pendulous catkins containing many seeds covered with silky hairs.

Flowering period. April to May.

Fruiting period. May to June.

Habitat. Quaking aspen is the most common aspen in the Northeast. Occurs in dry forests and damp soils along ponds, streams, and rivers and in upland meadows. Commonly grows in areas cleared by fire and logging, where it often is later dominated by other trees.

Range. Newfoundland west to Alaska, south to West Virginia, Iowa, and locally through the Rockies and Coast Ranges.

Hardiness zone. 1.

Landscape notes. A delicate, airy tree that will grow in almost any good soil having adequate moisture and a sunny exposure. Autumn colors are highly ornamental and most effective when trees are planted in clumps in front of taller evergreens. Trees are hardy and grow rapidly but are short-lived, particularly when dominated by taller trees.

Propagation. See Eastern Cottonwood.

Birds That Use Quaking Aspen

	Food	Cover	Nesting
Ruffed grouse*	BD, CK		
Ring-necked pheasant	CK		
Yellow-bellied sapsucker	sap	X	X (cavity)
Downy woodpecker		X	X (cavity)
Hairy woodpecker		X	X (cavity)
Black-capped chickadee		X	X (cavity)
Northern shrike	BD		
Northern oriole	BD	X	X
Rose-breasted grosbeak	BD		
Purple finch	BD		
Pine grosbeak	BD		

Note: *preferred food; BD, buds; CK, catkins.
Sources: Davison 1967; Martin et al. 1951; McKenny 1939; Harrison 1975; Rushmore 1969.

PIN CHERRY
Prunus pensylvanica L.
ROSACEAE

Description. Pin cherry is a small tree—10 to 30 feet tall—that grows in a great variety of places, especially in dry, disturbed or waste places. The fruits are valuable as bird food, especially for the eastern bluebird. Other common names are fire cherry, bird cherry, and wild red cherry.

Bark. Reddish-brown, shiny and smooth, marked with short horizontal bars.

Leaves. Alternate, simple, 2 to 5 inches long, lanceolate, yellow-green on upper surfaces.

Flowers. Small, white blossoms forming in umbels on the sides of branchlets.

Fruits. Small, red, rounded drupes, ¼-inch in diameter, edible.

Flowering period. March to July.

Fruiting period. July to September, sometimes persistent to winter.

Habitat. Often occurs in association with aspens in areas that have been burned.

Range. Newfoundland south to the mountains of Georgia, west to Colorado and Iowa.

Hardiness zone. 2.

Landscape notes. More attractive in clumps than as a specimen, pin cherry should be planted in areas away from walks and patios where juicy cherries will not get underfoot. This tree is useful for creating a low tree layer between mature woodlands and shrubbery. It is a frequent host of the fall webworm and eastern tent caterpillar. Trees are hardy, rapid growing, and short-lived.

Propagation. Pin cherry can be propagated from seeds gathered when fruits ripen, and dried with or without the pulp. They may be stored for one year in airtight containers at 41° F. Seeds should be sown in July or August of the year they are collected, or stratified and sown in spring. Stratification gives only fair results. Approximately two-thirds of the seeds will grow after exposure for two months at 68° F. (night) and 86° F. (days), followed by three months at 41° F. They should be sown in beds in drills 8 to 12 inches apart and ½-inch deep, and mulched lightly until they germinate (U.S. Forest Service 1948).

Birds That Use Pin Cherry

	Food	Cover	Nesting
Mallard	F		
Ruffed grouse*	F		
Bobwhite	F		
Ring-necked pheasant*	F		
Common flicker*	F		
Pileated woodpecker	F		
Red-bellied woodpecker	F		
Red-headed woodpecker*	F		
Yellow-bellied sapsucker	F, sap		
Hairy woodpecker	F		
Downy woodpecker	F		
Eastern kingbird*	F		
Great crested flycatcher	F		
Blue jay	F		
Common crow*	F		
Mockingbird	F		
Gray catbird*	F		
Brown thrasher*	F		
American robin*	F		
Wood thrush*	F		
Hermit thrush	F		
Swainson's thrush*	F		
Gray-cheeked thrush*	F		
Veery*	F		
Eastern bluebird*	F		
Cedar waxwing*	F		
Starling*	F		
Red-eyed vireo*	F		
Warbling vireo	F		
Common grackle	F		
Northern oriole	F		
Scarlet tanager	F		
Summer tanager	F		
Cardinal	F		
Rose-breasted grosbeak*	F		
Evening grosbeak*	F		
Pine grosbeak	F		

	Food	Cover	Nesting
American goldfinch	F		
Rufous-sided towhee	F		
White-crowned sparrow	F		
White-throated sparrow	F		
Song sparrow	F		

Note: *preferred food; F, fruit.
Sources: McKenny 1939; Davison 1967; Martin et al. 1951.

BLACK CHERRY
Prunus serotina Ehrh.
ROSACEAE

Description. Black cherry is found throughout the eastern United States, and grows 50 to 60 feet tall. It invades abandoned fields and has only moderate tolerance. The northern oriole is one species that nests in it, and its early-ripening fruits are readily taken by many birds. Black cherry is also known as rum cherry.

Bark. Dark and rough with squarish plates on old trunks, smooth and reddish on branches, both marked with short horizontal lines, inner bark aromatic.

Twigs. Slender, reddish-brown with bitter almond taste.

Leaves. Alternate, simple, 2 to 6 inches long, narrowly oval to oblong or lanceolate with fine teeth and thinly pointed leaf tips, upper surfaces bright green, lower surfaces paler with reddish-brown hairs along base of midrib. Autumn colors: yellow to orange-red.

Flowers. Small, creamy-white blossoms forming on long racemes appearing with the leaves.

Fruits. Small, round, dark-purple drupes, 1/3- to 1/2-inch in diameter, fleshy, juicy, sweet, and edible. Heavy fruit crops occur every three to four years.

Flowering period. March to June.

Fruiting period. June to October.

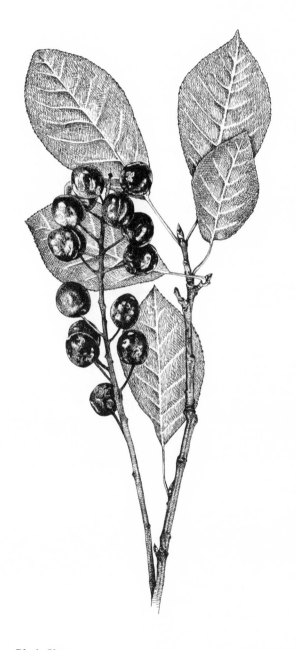

Black Cherry

Habitat. Occurs on rich, moist, deep soils in pure stands or, more commonly, mixed with hardwoods and evergreens. Also grows on light, sandy soils.

Range. Quebec south to Florida, west to North Dakota and Arizona.

Hardiness zone. 4.

Landscape notes. This is an excellent fruit producer that is sure to attract many birds. The narrow open crown and overall shape of this tree make it more suitable for border plantings and woodlands than for open lawns. It should be placed where falling fruits and twigs will not cause problems. The shiny leaves, dense drooping branches, and profuse white blooms are highly ornamental, yet the tree is often overlooked by landscape professionals. Trees are hardy, rapid growing, and may live for 150 to 200 years.

Propagation. Black cherry may be grown from ripe seeds that are separated from the pulp, then cleaned and dried. Seeds may be stored for two years in airtight containers at 41° F. without losing viability, or sown in fall for spring germination. The seeds may also be stratified in moist sand or peat for three to four months at 41° F. to hasten breaking of dormancy. They should be sown in drills 8 to 12 inches apart and covered with ½-inch of nursery soil. Seedlings grow well in partial shade or sunny locations (U.S. Forest Service 1948).

Birds That Use Black Cherry

	Food	Cover	Nesting[1]
Mallard	F		
Turkey	F		
Ruffed grouse*	F		
Bobwhite*	F		
Ring-necked pheasant	F		
Common flicker*	F		
Pileated woodpecker	F		
Red-bellied woodpecker*	F		
Red-headed woodpecker*	F		
Yellow-bellied sapsucker*	F, sap		
Hairy woodpecker	F		
Downy woodpecker	F		
Eastern kingbird*	F		X
Great crested flycatcher	F		
Blue jay*	F		
Common crow*	F		
Mockingbird*	F		
Gray catbird*	F		
Brown thrasher*	F		
American robin*	F		X
Wood thrush*	F		
Hermit thrush*	F		
Swainson's thrush*	F		
Gray-cheeked thrush*	F		
Veery*	F		
Eastern bluebird*	F		
Cedar waxwing*	F		
Starling*	F		
Red-eyed vireo*	F		
Warbling vireo*	F		
Red-winged blackbird	F		
Common grackle	F		
Orchard oriole*	F	X	X
Northern oriole*	F	X	X
Scarlet tanager	F		
Summer tanager*	F		
Cardinal*	F		
Rose-breasted grosbeak*	F		
Evening grosbeak*	F		
Pine grosbeak	F		
American goldfinch	F		
Rufous-sided towhee	F		
White-crowned sparrow	F		
White-throated sparrow*	F		
Song sparrow	S		

Note: *preferred food; F, fruit; [1]occasionally used for nest sites by songbirds.
Sources: McKenny 1939; Davison 1967; Martin et al. 1951.

COMMON CHOKECHERRY
Prunus virginiana L.
ROSACEAE

Description. Common chokecherry is a small tree or shrub, 6 to 20 feet tall, usually found growing along fence rows or hedges from seed dropped by birds. Many birds, especially the eastern bluebird, eat the fruit. Another common name is cabinet cherry.
Bark. Gray-brown and smooth on old trunks, reddish-brown and glossy on young trunks and branches, nonaromatic.
Leaves. Alternate, simple, 2 to 5 inches long, ovate or obovate with fine sharp teeth. Autumn colors: deep bronze to yellow.
Flowers. White, fragrant, forming in clusters on 3- to 5-inch racemes.
Fruits. Small, round, purplish-black (frequently red) drupes, 5/16-inch diameter, tart, often used in pies and jellies.
Flowering period. April to July.
Fruiting period. July to October.
Habitat. Grows in thickets along streams, pastures, and roadsides and scattered about in old fields, waste areas, and young woodlands. Tolerates many kinds of soil including sand. Best growth occurs in rich, well-drained, moist soils having a sunny exposure (Van Dersal 1938).
Range. Newfoundland south to northwest Georgia, west to California.
Hardiness zone. 2.
Landscape notes. This tree is useful for small properties, and is attractive for its flowers and fruits. It is good for naturalistic plantings along boundaries and in sparse woodlands where dropped fruits will not be a nuisance. Trees are easy to transplant when young and will do well in sun or shade. Although frequently used by webworms, they are hardy, rapid growing, and moderately long-lived. As with other cherries, the wilted leaves are poisonous to livestock, so common chokecherry should not be planted or maintained near pastures.
Propagation. Trees may be propagated from

Common Chokecherry

[65] Trees

seeds collected in August to September. They should be left in the pulp and sown in fall, or stratified and sown in spring, or cleaned, dried, and stored. Seeds stored in airtight containers at 26° F. will remain viable for one year. Seeds to be sown in spring should be stratified for three to five months at 41° F. They should be sown in drills, covered with ½-inch of nursery soil, followed by a layer of mulch to be removed upon germination (U.S. Forest Service 1948).

Birds That Use Common Chokecherry

	Food	Cover	Nesting[1]
Mallard	F		
Turkey	F		
Ruffed grouse*	F		
Bobwhite	F		
Ring-necked pheasant*	F		
Common flicker*	F		
Pileated woodpecker*	F		
Red-bellied woodpecker*	F		
Red-headed woodpecker*	F		
Yellow-bellied sapsucker*	F,sap		
Hairy woodpecker	F		
Downy woodpecker	F		
Eastern kingbird*	F		
Great crested flycatcher	F		
Blue jay	F		
Common crow*	F		
Mockingbird	F		
Gray catbird*	F		
Brown thrasher*	F		
American robin*	F		
Wood thrush*	F		
Hermit thrush	F		
Swainson's thrush*	F		
Gray-cheeked thrush*	F		
Veery	F		
Eastern bluebird*	F		
Cedar waxwing*	F		
Starling*	F		
Red-eyed vireo	F		
Warbling vireo	F		
Common grackle	F		
Northern oriole	F		
Scarlet tanager	F		
Summer tanager	F		

	Food	Cover	Nesting[1]
Cardinal	F		
Rose-breasted grosbeak*	F		
Evening grosbeak*	F		
Pine grosbeak	F		
American goldfinch	F		
Rufous-sided towhee	F		
White-crowned sparrow	F		
White-throated sparrow	F		
Song sparrow	F		

Note: *preferred food; F, fruit; [1] occasionally used for nest sites by songbirds.
Sources: McKenny 1939; Davison 1967; Martin et al. 1951.

WHITE OAK
Quercus alba L.
FAGACEAE

Description. White oak is a valuable timber tree, and is used for tight cooperage. It is also valuable to wildlife. White oak reaches great heights—up to 90 feet—and is a magnificent shade tree, whose acorns are a choice food of the blue jay, ruffed grouse, and brown thrasher. Other common names are ridge white oak and stave oak.
Bark. Light gray on young trees with thin plates which may later develop fissures and ridges.
Twigs. Stout, purplish-gray to greenish-red, hairless.
Leaves. Alternate, simple, 5 to 9 inches long, 2 to 4 inches wide, with 7 to 9 lobes along margins, upper surface bright green, lower surface paler. Autumn colors: rusty red to dark purple.
Flowers. Inconspicuous, male flowers on pendulous catkins, female flowers solitary or clustered on spikes from axils of new leaves.
Fruits. Acorn, ½- to ¾-inch long, partially enclosed in scaly cup, paired or solitary, each containing a single seed.
Flowering period. March to May.
Fruiting period. September to November, first autumn after flowering.

Habitat. Grows in many types of soil. Develops best in deep, moist, well-drained loam in sun or shade.

Range. Central Maine south to northwestern Florida, west to Minnesota and Texas.

Hardiness zone. 5.

Landscape notes. This majestic tree is valued in landscaping for the massive crown it develops when planted in the open. The long, large, nearly horizontal branches of old trees are characteristic. Open-grown trees may fruit in as early as twenty years but more commonly bear heavy crops after their fortieth year.

Acorns develop the first fall after flowering, but trees bear heavy crops irregularly, usually every four to ten years. Trees may reach 14 feet by the tenth year of growth (Wyman 1951). They are hardy, grow moderately fast in full sunlight, and may live for 500 years.

Propagation. White oaks may be propagated by seeds and grafting. The seeds may be planted the same season they ripen because of low embryo dormancy, or they may be dried and stored in sealed containers at 32°–36° F. until ready to plant.

Bird uses. See Oaks.

[67] Trees

SCARLET OAK
Quercus coccinea Muenchh.
FAGACEAE

Description. Scarlet oak is a medium-sized
tree, 70 to 80 feet tall, that is often used as an
ornamental because of its fall color. Occasionally used as a nest site, scarlet oak acorns are
preferred by the common grackle, blue jay,
and turkey.
Bark. Dark brown to nearly black on mature
trees, with irregular ridges and fine grooves.
Twigs. Slender, smooth, reddish-brown.
Leaves. Alternate, simple, 4 to 7 inches long, 3
to 5 inches wide, 5 to 9 lobes along margins
separated by deep, rounded sinuses, surfaces
bright, shiny green above, paler beneath. Autumn colors: bronze to scarlet.
Flowers. Inconspicuous, on pale yellow spikes.
Fruits. Acorn, ½- to 1 inch long, oval to
round. As much as half the nut may be covered by the deep, bowllike cup.
Flowering period. April to May.
Fruiting period. September to November of
second fall after flowering.
Habitat. Usually found on dry, sandy soil.
Particularly common east of the Appalachians
where it occasionally forms pure stands or is
mixed with other oaks and hickories.
Range. Southwest Maine south to northeast-
ern Arkansas and northern Georgia, west to
Michigan.
Hardiness zone. 5.
Landscape notes. An attractive tree valued for
its shade and ornamental qualities, the scarlet
oak is hardy, rapid growing, and long-lived.
It is an excellent choice wherever a medium-
sized specimen is desired. Trees larger than
seedlings are difficult to transplant.
Propagation. See Northern Red Oak.
Bird uses. See Oaks.

Scarlet Oak

Pin Oak

PIN OAK

Quercus palustris Muenchh.
FAGACEAE

Description. The pin oak is usually found on moist soils. It retains its lower, drooping, dead branches for a long time. When these are removed, the pin oak makes a fine ornamental.

Bark. Dark brown to gray, smooth when young, becoming rougher with age as ridges and shallow fissures develop.

Twigs. Slender, reddish-brown, and shiny.

Leaves. Alternate, simple, 3 to 5 inches long, 2 to 5 inches wide, 5 to 9 lobes along margin with either wide or narrow sinuses, surfaces bright green and shiny above, paler beneath. Autumn colors: bronze to scarlet.

Flowers. Inconspicuous, on pale yellow spikes.

Fruits. Acorn, single or clustered, 1/2-inch long, nearly round, base covered by thin, saucerlike cup.

Flowering period. April to May.

Fruiting period. September to November of the second fall after flowering.

Habitat. Tolerates many soils. Thrives on rich bottomlands, swamp borders, as well as on poorly drained clay flats. Prefers sun or partial shade.

Range. Central Massachusetts south to North Carolina and Tennessee, west to southern Michigan and Oklahoma.

Hardiness zone. 5.

Landscape notes. Pin oak is attractive for its unusual broadly pyramidal crown with deeply cut leaves. It is commonly used along streets, in yards and in parks. Pin oak is hardy, generally grows more rapidly than other oaks, is moderately long-lived, and needs little care. Trees are easy to transplant because of a fibrous root system (no taproots).

Propagation. See Northern Red Oak.

Bird uses. See Oaks.

NORTHERN RED OAK

Quercus rubra L.
FAGACEAE

Description. Northern red oak is a valuable timber tree. Its acorns are eaten by many bird species, but preferred by grackles, ruffed grouse, and turkey. It grows 60 to 80 feet tall, with a diameter of 2 to 3 feet.

Bark. Greenish-brown and smooth on young trunks, darkening to brownish-black and becoming rough with age. Middle-aged trees have flat-topped ridges separated by narrow fissures which become narrower and deeper through the years.

Twigs. Greenish to reddish-brown, stout and smooth.

Leaves. Alternate, simple, 5 to 8 inches long, 4 to 5 inches wide, oblong to ovate with 7 to 11 lobes, lobe tips usually toothed, dull or shiny green above, paler beneath. Autumn colors: red to reddish-bronze.

Flowers. Inconspicuous, on long green spikes.

Fruits. Acorn, 1/2- to 1 inch long, partially covered at the base by the flat, saucerlike cup which encloses less than one-third of the nut. Trees begin to fruit heavily when about twenty-five years old. Some acorns are produced every year, with heavy crops at irregular intervals.

Flowering period. April to May.

Fruiting period. September to October (second autumn after flowering), persistent to December.

Habitat. Grows on sandy loams but prefers richer soils. Tolerates almost any well-drained soil in full sunlight or partial shade.

Range. Quebec south to northwestern Pennsylvania and the mountains of North Carolina, west to Minnesota.

Hardiness zone. 4.

Landscape notes. This excellent shade tree develops a sturdy trunk and attractive symmetrical crown when grown in the open. Seedlings grow rapidly in good soil and may grow 3 feet the first year (Harlow and Harrar 1969). Decomposing leaves improve soil structure and maintain soil acidity. Mature trees usually bear fruits the second autumn after flowering, and heavy crops usually occur at two- to five-year intervals. Red oaks are hardy and may live for 200 to 300 years (Harlow and Harrar 1969).

Propagation. Trees may be propagated from seed or by grafting (Mahlstede and Haber 1957). Seeds of most species of the black oak group to which northern red oak belongs generally have dormant embryos which require either stratification or fall sowing. Stratification may be achieved by chilling seeds at 32°–35° F. for one to three months (Hartmann and Kester 1968).

Bird uses. See Oaks.

BLACK OAK

Quercus velutina Lam.

FAGACEAE

Description. Black oak is generally larger than red oak—100 to 150 feet tall—and has a more irregular shape. Acorn crops are intermittent —often several years pass between crops.
Bark. Young bark is smooth and dark brown, older bark is thick, dark gray, and rough with ridges and fissures.
Twigs. Stout, smooth, reddish-brown.
Leaves. Alternate, simple, 5 to 7 inches long, 3 to 5 inches wide, 5 to 7 lobes along margins often with several teeth on each, surfaces dark, shiny green above, paler and somewhat hairy beneath. Autumn colors: dull red to orange-brown.
Flowers. Inconspicuous, on pale yellow spikes.
Fruits. Acorns, paired or solitary, ½- to ¾-inch long, base surrounded by a saucer-shaped cup, mature in two years.
Flowering period. April to May.
Fruiting period. September to November of the second fall after flowering, persistent to December.
Habitat. Grows best on rich soils that are moist but well drained. Often found on drier

sites having poor soil. Thrives in sun or partial shade.
Range. Southern Maine south to northwestern Florida, west to eastern Texas and Minnesota.
Hardiness zone. 5.
Landscape notes. Black oak is a popular shade tree for lawns, parks, roadsides, and woodlots, and is a good choice for poor, dry, sandy soils where other trees have difficulty growing. The species is hardy, slow growing, and moderately long-lived, occasionally surviving for 200 years. A large taproot makes plants larger than seedlings difficult to transplant.
Propagation. See Northern Red Oak.
Bird uses. See Oaks.

Birds That Use Oaks

	Food	Cover	Nesting
Mallard	F		
Northern shoveler	F		
Wood duck	F		
Green-winged teal	F		
Turkey*	F, BD		
Ruffed grouse*	F, BD		
Bobwhite*	F, BD		
Ring-necked pheasant	F		
Mourning dove	F		
Common flicker	F		
Red-bellied woodpecker	F		
Red-headed woodpecker	F		
Yellow-bellied sapsucker	F		
Hairy woodpecker	F		
Downy woodpecker	F		
Blue jay*	F		
Common crow	F	X	X
Tufted titmouse	F		
White-breasted nuthatch	F		
Carolina wren	F		
Brown thrasher*	F		
American robin			X
Hermit thrush	F		
Starling	F		
Northern oriole		X	X

	Food	Cover	Nesting
Eastern meadowlark	F		
Rusty blackbird	F		
Common grackle*	F		
Scarlet tanager		X	X
Cardinal	F		
Rose-breasted grosbeak	FL	X	X
Rufous-sided towhee*	F		

Note: *preferred food; F, fruit; BD, buds; FL, flowers.

Sources: McKenny 1939; Martin et al. 1951; Davison 1967.

BLACK WILLOW

Salix nigra Marsh.

SALICACEAE

Description. Black willow is a wetland tree, common to swamp borders or stream banks. It is a frequent nest site.

Bark. Thick, dark brown, deeply fissured.

Twigs. Reddish-brown, brittle.

Leaves. Alternate, simple, 1 to 6 inches long, narrow with rounded bases, fine teeth along margins.

Flowers. Inconspicuous, sexes form on separate plants.

Fruits. Capsules, ¼-inch long, oval to conical with short stalks. Seed production begins when plants are about ten years old (U.S. Forest Service 1965).

Flowering period. February to June.

Fruiting period. April to July.

Habitat. Commonly found growing on wet soils along ponds and watercourses throughout the northeastern United States, except northern Maine.

Range. New Brunswick south to Florida, west to Minnesota and Texas.

Hardiness zone. 5.

Landscape notes. Black willow's natural growth form is more attractive in the Southeast than in the Northeast, but the tree is equally valuable in both regions. It is a useful plant for naturalizing low, wet ground where few other trees can survive. It grows rapidly, 50 feet in ten years (Harlow and Harrar 1969), and seldom lives beyond seventy years (U.S. Forest Service 1965). The tree is hardy and requires little care, but should not be planted near dwellings—the brittle limbs are frequently broken by storms.

Propagation. Trees may be propagated from seeds, root cuttings, and stem cuttings. Seeds must be collected when ripe, and sown within a day or two due to rapid loss of viability. Germination occurs in a day or two if seeds are kept moist (Hartmann and Kester 1968).

Birds That Use Black Willow

	Food	Cover	Nesting[1]
Ruffed grouse*	BD, T		
Red-bellied woodpecker		X	X
Evening grosbeak	BD		
Pine grosbeak*	BD		
Common redpoll		X	X

Note: *preferred food; BD, buds; T, twigs; [1]often used for nest sites by songbirds.

Sources: Collins 1965; Martin et al. 1951.

COMMON SASSAFRAS
Sassafras albidum (Nutt.) Nees
LAURACEAE

Description. Sassafras is generally considered a weed tree—it is intolerant and invades abandoned lands. It is seldom used by birds for nesting because of its open branching pattern, but its blue or blue-black fruits are a choice food of many birds. Usually 10 to 50 feet tall with a diameter of 2 to 12 inches, sassafras is a large shrub or low tree in the northern parts of its range.

Bark. Reddish-brown, rough, with fissures and ridges.

Twigs. Green, smooth, aromatic.

Leaves. Alternate, simple, 2 to 9 inches, with three shapes occurring on the same tree: a three-fingered hand, a mitten, and an egg. All are without teeth and are aromatic. Autumn color: orange-red.

Flowers. Greenish-yellow, male and female flowers occur on the same or separate plants in loose, drooping cymes.

Fruits. Oval, dry, shiny blue or blue-black drupes, ½-inch long on red stems. Heavy fruit production begins when trees are eight to ten years old.

Flowering period. April to June.

Fruiting period. August to October.

Habitat. Trees attain greatest size on moist, rich, sandy loams in open woodlands. They grow on many sites including dry and sandy soils.

Range. Maine south to Florida, west to Oklahoma and Iowa.

Hardiness zone. 5.

Landscape notes. An attractive ornamental for small areas, sassafras is especially colorful in autumn with its orange leaves, green stems, and blue fruits. It may be planted singly in good soil where it will develop maximum size, or in borders with other plants where its growth will be restricted. The lower branches die as the tree grows, but they are not retained.

Propagation. Plants may be produced by seeds and cuttings. Seeds should be picked from the trees when they ripen, and cleaned of pulp and debris. They may be dried and stored in sealed containers at 35°–41° F. or stratified over winter in sand at 35°–41° F. (U.S. Forest Service 1948). Seeds should be sown ¼- to ½-inch deep in moist loam and mulched with leaves or straw until germination takes place. Seed beds may be located in full sunlight (U.S. Forest Service 1948).

Trees are easily transplanted when young. Two faster ways to propagate are to take root cuttings that bear sprouts, or to root-prune suckers which can be transplanted the following year (Pogge 1975).

Birds That Use Common Sassafras

	Food	Cover	Nesting[1]
Turkey*	F		
Bobwhite*	F		
Common flicker	F		
Pileated woodpecker*	F		
Yellow-bellied sapsucker	sap		
Eastern kingbird*	F		
Great crested flycatcher*	F		
Eastern phoebe	F		
Mockingbird	F		
Gray catbird*	F		
Brown thrasher	F		
American robin*	F		
Hermit thrush	F		
Swainson's thrush	F		
Gray-cheeked thrush	F		
Veery	F		
Eastern bluebird*	F		
White-eyed vireo	F		
Red-eyed vireo*	F		
Warbling vireo	F		
Yellow-throated warbler	F		
Common yellowthroat	F		
Rufous-sided towhee	F		

Note: *preferred food; F, fruit; [1]seldom used by songbirds for nest sites.
Sources: McKenny 1939; Davison 1967; Martin et al. 1951; Gude 1973; Pogge 1975.

AMERICAN MOUNTAIN-ASH

Sorbus americana (Marsh.) DC.
ROSACEAE

Description. American mountain-ash is a
hardy, small tree or large shrub usually found
on rocky hillsides. It grows to 40 feet, with a
diameter of 12 inches. It is an ideal specimen
for the small lawn. The clusters of red berries
are a choice, early-fall food of many birds including the eastern bluebird.
Bark. Grayish to yellowish-brown, smooth.
Leaves. Alternate, compound, with 13 to 17
long, sharply toothed, blue-green, smooth
leaflets, 6 to 9 inches long. Autumn color: orange-red.
Flowers. Small, white or pink blossoms, ¼-
inch in diameter, forming in clusters.
Fruits. Orange-red berries, ¼-inch in diameter, forming in clusters, persistent.
Flowering period. May to July.
Fruiting period. August to October, sometimes
persistent to March, but usually consumed by
birds when ripe.
Habitat. Dry, rocky slopes to rich, moist
woods and clearings.
Range. Quebec south to the mountains of
Georgia, west to Manitoba and Illinois.
Hardiness zone. 2.
Landscape notes. This native species is not
widely used as an ornamental, but perhaps
deserves more attention. It has finely cut
leaves, brilliant autumn colors, and produces
abundant fruits. It is a good choice for small
suburban lawns. The European mountain ash,
S. aucuparia, a common introduced ornamental, differs from the native specimen by having bluntly pointed, pubescent leaflets. Japanese beetles seem to prefer its foliage, but
seldom damage the tree. It grows best in full
sun.
Propagation. Plants may be produced from
seeds sown in fall or spring. Seeds may be
separated from ripe fruits by maceration, or
left intact and sown immediately, or stratified
in moist sand for ninety days at 68° F.
(nights) and 86° F. (days). Seeds may be

broadcast or sown in drills and covered with
1/16-inch of soil. Seedlings grow rapidly particularly in cool, moist, sunny locations. Trees
are hardy and short-lived (U.S. Forest Service
1948).

Birds That Use American Mountain-ash

	Food	Cover	Nesting
Ruffed grouse*	F		
Red-headed woodpecker*	F		
White-breasted nuthatch	F		
Gray catbird*	F		
Brown thrasher*	F		
American robin*	F		
Wood thrush	F		
Swainson's thrush	F		
Veery	F		
Eastern bluebird*	F		
Cedar waxwing*	F		
Common grackle*	F		
Northern oriole*	F		
Evening grosbeak*	F		
Pine grosbeak*	F		

Note: *preferred food; F, fruit.
Sources: Martin et al. 1951; Davison 1967; Petrides
1972; McKenny 1939; Collins 1965.

NORTHERN WHITE CEDAR
Thuja occidentalis L.
PINACEAE

Description. Northern white cedar actually prefers alkaline soils, although it also grows in wet, acid soils. Its thick branching pattern and dense foliage afford fine protective cover for birds and it is frequently used for nesting. The seed is preferred by pine siskins. Other common names are swamp cedar and eastern arbor-vitae.

Bark. Grayish surface, reddish-brown fibers underneath.

Leaves. Small, scalelike, 1/8- to 1/4-inch long, flattened and overlapping, often glandular, soft and flexible, yellowish to bright green.

Flowers. Inconspicuous, male and female flowers borne separately on same tree.

Fruits. Borne in cones, 1/3- to 1/2-inch long, which form annually and persist into winter after releasing seeds in autumn. Seeds may occur on trees as young as six years old, with heaviest production occurring after 20 years in three- to five-year intervals (U.S. Forest Service 1965).

Flowering period. April to May.

Fruiting period. August to October.

Habitat. Occurs on a variety of soils, but grows best on those containing limestone. Trees do well in swampy locations, but grow more rapidly on drier ground. Extensive stands often develop in more favorable areas.

Range. Quebec south to North Carolina, west to Minnesota.

Hardiness zone. 2.

Landscape notes. Northern white cedar is used extensively as an ornamental in shrub and tree form because it is very tolerant of pruning and will form dense hedges. For best results, locate plants in areas with high atmospheric and soil moisture, or keep surrounding soil watered and fertilized. Plants are hardy, slow growing, and long-lived.

Propagation. Plants may be propagated from seeds and cuttings. Seeds may be fall-sown when ripe, or stratified for sixty days at 40° F. Recommended planting depth is 1/8- to 1/4-inch (U.S. Forest Service 1948). Cuttings may be taken in midsummer and rooted out-of-doors in a shaded, closed frame, or they may be taken in midwinter and rooted under light mist in a greenhouse. They should be removed in 6-inch lengths from the tips of new or mature branches (Hartmann and Kester 1968; U.S. Forest Service 1948).

Birds That Use Northern White Cedar

	Food	Cover[1]	Nesting[2]
American robin	S	X	X
House finch		X	X
Common redpoll	S		
Pine siskin*	S		

Note: *preferred food; S, seeds; [1]provides excellent winter cover for many songbirds; [2]common nest site.

Sources: McKenny 1939; Petrides 1972; Martin et al. 1951.

Northern White Cedars

EASTERN HEMLOCK
Tsuga canadensis (L.) Carr.
PINACEAE

Description. Eastern hemlock is probably our most tolerant tree—it grows in very dense shade. When young, it is a handsome tree with graceful, feathery branches. It is a preferred nest site of the robin, blue jay, and wood thrush, among others (DeGraaf et al. 1975). The seed is eaten by red crossbills, white-winged crossbills, chickadees, pine siskins, and goldfinches.

Bark. Reddish-brown to gray.

Leaves. Linear needles, ⅓- to ⅔-inch long, flat with two white lines beneath, distinct short petioles, tips blunt.

Flowers. Inconspicuous, sexes occur separately on the same plant.

Fruits. Borne in small, flexible cones, ½- to ¾-inch long, persistent. Open-grown trees bear heavily when twenty to forty years old and produce heavy crops in two- to three-year intervals (U.S. Forest Service 1965).

Flowering period. May to June.

Fruiting period. September to October, persistent to winter.

Habitat. Commonly grows on rocky ridges, in ravines, and on moist, cool mountain slopes.

Range. Nova Scotia south to the mountains of Georgia, west to Minnesota.

Hardiness zone. 5.

Landscape notes. Eastern hemlock is very attractive as an ornamental when grown under proper conditions. It responds well to shearing, and may be planted singly, in clumps, or in hedges. Plants are hardy, rapid growing, and long-lived, occasionally surviving for 450 years (U.S. Forest Service 1965). Hemlock is easy to transplant when given good soil. It does best in deep, moist, well-drained loam in full sun, as well as in dense shade. It does poorly in cities (Wyman 1951) and in places where hot, dry conditions prevail.

Propagation. Hemlock can easily be propagated from seed. For best results, stratify seeds for

two to four months at 40°F., and sow in spring in ⅛-inch of soil. Seedlings should be partly shaded during the first season of growth. Trees may also be propagated by cuttings and layering (U.S. Forest Service 1948).

Birds That Use Eastern Hemlock

	Food	Cover	Nesting
Red-shouldered hawk			X[1]
Ruffed grouse	NL	X	
Mourning dove		X	X
Common flicker	S		
Blue jay		X	X
Black-capped chickadee	S		
Boreal chickadee*	S	X	X
Gray catbird		X	
Brown thrasher		X	
American robin		X	X
Wood thrush		X	X
Hermit thrush		X	
Magnolia warbler		X	X
Black-throated green warbler		X	X
Black-throated blue warbler		X	X
Blackburnian warbler		X	X
Bay-breasted warbler		X	X
Common grackle		X	X
Pine siskin*	S	X	X
American goldfinch*	S		
Red crossbill*	S	X	X
White-winged crossbill*	S	X	X
Northern junco	S	X	
White-throated sparrow		X	
Fox sparrow		X	
Song sparrow		X	

Note: *preferred food; NL, needles; S, seeds; [1]uses leafy twigs to line nests.
Sources: McKenny 1939; Davison 1967; Martin et al. 1951.

AMERICAN ELM
Ulmus americana L.
ULMACEAE

Description. Dutch elm disease is rapidly eliminating this magnificent tree. It is the most preferred nest site of the northern oriole (DeGraaf et al. 1975). The warbling vireo is frequently associated with the open-grown elms, especially in New England. American elm grows to 100 feet, with a diameter of 4 to 5 feet.
Bark. Grayish, rough, with flat-topped ridges and often diamond-shaped fissures.
Twigs. Brown, thin, hairless, often zig-zag.
Leaves. Alternate, simple, 4 to 6 inches long, 1 to 3 inches wide, oblong to elliptic, margins coarsely toothed, uneven at base, surfaces usually equally rough above and beneath. Autumn colors: yellow to russet.
Flowers. Brownish-red, small, appear before the leaves in clusters.
Fruits. Flattened, nearly rounded samaras. Heavy seed production may begin on trees fifteen years old and continue until they are about 150 years old (U.S. Forest Service 1965). Good crops occur every year.
Flowering period. February to May.
Fruiting period. April to June.
Habitat. Rich, moist soils of bottomlands and stream margins to drier uplands.
Range. Newfoundland south to Florida, west to Saskatchewan and Texas.
Hardiness zone. 2.
Landscape notes. American elm is a majestic shade tree with a wide-spreading, vase-shaped crown. It is less frequently found in forests, yards, and parks today than in years past due to the rapid spread of Dutch elm disease. This fatal disease is caused by a fungus spread by bark beetles. Phloem necrosis, a deadly virus spread by leaf hoppers, is also taking its toll in the Mississippi Valley. The tree is exceedingly picturesque in all seasons. When healthy, this elm is hardy, rapid-growing— occasionally reaching 30 feet in ten years

(Wyman 1951)—and long-lived, surviving for 200 years.

Propagation. Trees may be propagated by softwood cuttings taken in summer, hardwood cuttings taken in fall and winter, grafts (whip and tongue and splice) made in winter, and budding in summer (Mahlstede and Haber 1957). Trees may be grown from ripe seeds collected from the ground and sown immediately. They should germinate the following spring. Dormant seeds stratified in sand at 41° F. for sixty days should germinate the same season they are sown. Seeds may be sown in drills and covered with ¼-inch soil (U.S. Forest Service 1948).

Birds That Use American Elm

	Food	Cover	Nesting
Wood duck	S		
Turkey*	S		
Ruffed grouse*	S		
Bobwhite	S		
Ring-necked pheasant	S		
Common flicker		X	X (cavity)
Red-bellied woodpecker		X	X (cavity)
Yellow-bellied sapsucker	sap		
Hairy woodpecker		X	X (cavity)
Downy woodpecker		X	X (cavity)
Black-capped chickadee	S	X	X (cavity)
Carolina chickadee	S	X	X (cavity)
White-breasted nuthatch		X	X (cavity)
American robin			X
Red-eyed vireo		X	X (small trees)
Yellow warbler		X	X (small trees)
Yellow-rumped warbler	S		
American redstart		X	
House sparrow	S		
Northern oriole	S	X	X
Cardinal	S		
Rose-breasted grosbeak	S, BD		
Evening grosbeak*	S, BD		
Purple finch*	S, BD		
Common redpoll	S		
Pine siskin	S		
American goldfinch*	S, BD		

Note: *preferred food; S, seeds; BD, buds.
Sources: Martin et al. 1951; Davison 1967; McKenny 1939; Petrides 1972; Collins 1965; Schutz 1974.

SHRUBS

SPECKLED ALDER
Alnus rugosa (Du Roi) Spreng.
BETULACEAE

Description. Speckled alder is common along stream banks and in wet meadows in the northeastern United States. Alders are closely related to the birches, a relationship revealed by the similarity of their catkins. The seeds of alders are most important to goldfinches, pine siskins, and redpolls. Speckled alder grows to 25 feet, with a spread of about 20 feet. Another common name is hoary alder.

Bark. Brown to blackish gray, speckled with many light, linear lenticels.

Leaves. Alternate, simple, 2 to 5 inches long, oval, margins often double-toothed and wavy, bases of leaves broadly rounded to heart-shaped, dark green above, paler and hairless or velvety beneath, veins prominent. Autumn colors: green to brown or black.

Flowers. Male and female flowers appear on separate catkins which form the previous fall. Males are slender and cylindrical and hang in clusters of 3 to 5 from short leafless branches. Females are conelike, ¼- to ⅜-inch long, and pendant.

Fruits. Cones—composed of woody scales and wingless seeds which are released in autumn and early winter—usually form in clusters of threes. The dry, empty cones remain until the following summer.

Flowering period. March to May.

Fruiting period. August to October, persistent to December.

Habitat. Usually found near stream borders, pond edges, and swamps, in sun or shade.

Range. Nova Scotia south to Pennsylvania, west to Michigan.

Hardiness zone. 5.

Landscape notes. Excellent shrub for naturalizing pond shores and stream banks. Leaves appear earlier in the spring than those of most shrubs. Plants spread rapidly by seeds and form thickets; they are hardy and have a moderate growth rate. The empty, woody cones are attractive in dried-flower arrangements.

Propagation. Speckled alder will germinate from seeds collected in September or October and sown in November. They can be sown in drills or broadcast and covered with a thin layer of sand mixed with humus. The beds should be protected from winter cold with a layer of mulch to be removed upon germination. Beds must be kept moist, cool, and shaded until fall (U.S. Forest Service 1948). Young seedlings should be transplanted after the second or third year (Liscinsky 1972).

If later sowing is desired, seeds may be cleaned, air-dried, and stored at 34°–38° F. for up to ten years without losing viability (Heit 1967d). Plants may also be propagated from hardwood cuttings taken in winter.

Bird uses. See Alders.

SMOOTH ALDER

Alnus serrulata (Ait.) Willd.
BETULACEAE

Description. Like speckled alder, smooth alder is also found along watercourses (Petrides 1972:309). It usually occurs as a shrub thicket, 6 to 12 feet tall, but may become a small, 25-foot tree. Other common names are common alder and hazel alder.

Bark. Smooth, brownish-green in youth becoming grayish-green with age, lacks speckles, or has fewer and smaller ones than speckled alder.

Leaves. Alternate, simple, 2½ to 4½ inches long, oval or obovate, very finely toothed, veins conspicuous. Young leaves have fine, resinous dots on upper surfaces and may have fine hairs beneath. Autumn colors: green to brown or black.

Flowers. Occur briefly in spring, before leaves develop, on greenish-brown catkins which form the previous fall. Male and female flowers form on same plant. Female catkins often appear above the male catkins and are usually erect instead of pendant.

Fruits. Small, woody cones filled with many wingless seeds.

Flowering period. April to May.

Fruiting period. August to October, persistent to December.

Habitat. Commonly grows in damp soils along stream banks and swamp borders, in wet meadows and flood plains.

Range. Nova Scotia south to northwestern Florida, west to Illinois and Oklahoma.

Hardiness zone. 5.

Landscape notes. This shrub is useful for naturalizing pond and stream margins or for massed plantings. It is hardy and has a moderate growth rate.

Propagation. Reproduces naturally by seeds, layers, suckers, and underground stems. Growth is more vigorous in full sunlight than in shade. Plants can be propagated from seed or transplanted from the wild. Seeds should be collected in September and October and sown in November in drills, or broadcast and covered with sand mixed with humus. Mulch should be applied to the beds to protect seeds from cold and removed upon germination. Beds should be kept moist and shaded until fall (U.S. Forest Service 1948). Seeds may be stored for later planting if cleaned, air-dried, and refrigerated at 31°–38° F. They should remain viable for at least ten years (Heit 1967d). Seedlings should be removed to permanent locations after second or third year (Liscinsky 1972). Stem and root cuttings are not recommended.

Bird uses. See Alders.

Birds That Use Alders

	Food	Cover	Nesting
Mallard	S	X	
American wigeon	S	X	
Green-winged teal	S	X	
Bufflehead	S	X	
Turkey	S	X	
Ruffed grouse	BD, S		
Bobwhite	S		
Ring-necked pheasant	S	X	
American woodcock		X	X[1]
Mourning dove	S		
Willow flycatcher		X	X
Alder flycatcher		X	X
Yellow warbler		X	X
Wilsons warbler		X	X
Red-winged blackbird		X	X
Rusty blackbird		X	X
Rose-breasted grosbeak	S	X	X
Purple finch	S		
Common redpoll*	S		
Pine siskin*	S		
American goldfinch*	S		
Tree sparrow	S		
Fox sparrow		X	X
Song sparrow		X	X

Note: *preferred food; S, seeds; BD, buds; [1]nests on ground in alder swales.

Sources: McKenny 1939; Davison 1967; Martin et al. 1951.

BARTRAM SERVICEBERRY
Amelanchier bartramiana (Tausch) Roemer
ROSACEAE

Description. Bartram serviceberry is the only serviceberry that has flowers occurring in groups of 1 to 4 in the leaf axils. All others have long clusters of flowers (Petrides 1972:322). This species grows 2 to 4 feet tall, and it flowers and fruits somewhat later than other serviceberries. Other common names are shadbush, serviceberry, and mountain juneberry.

Leaves. Alternate, simple, 2 to 3 inches, elliptic, pointed at both ends, membranous, closely toothed. Autumn colors: orange to rusty red.

Flowers. White or pink, forming singly at tips of branches and in inflorescences of 1 to 4 blossoms scattered in the angles of leaves.

Fruits. Small, purple-black, oblong pome, ½-inch long, containing numerous seeds.

Flowering period. May to August.

Fruiting period. June to September.

Habitat. A northern shad. Grows on rich, peaty, moist soils as well as on dry upland slopes of mountains.

Range. Labrador south through New England to southeastern Pennsylvania, west to Minnesota.

Hardiness zone. 3.

Landscape notes. This is a graceful shrub with delicate blossoms and fruits. It is good for naturalistic plantings under taller trees.

Propagation. Seed and stock are available commercially but are expensive. Suckers, root cuttings, and softwood cuttings may be taken in the spring and fall and the cuttings rooted with the aid of root-inducing hormone (Harris 1961). This may be a practical method of propagation if only a small number of plants is desired.

Seeds may be collected, dried, and stored in sealed containers at 41° F. Seeds may be stratified at low temperatures and scarified by placing them in concentrated sulfuric acid for thirty minutes to help overcome dormancy.

(For a complete discussion of acid treatment of seeds, see U.S. Forest Service 1948, p. 2.) Seeds may be planted in the fall or, if stratified, they may be sown in the spring. Seeds should be covered with ¼-inch of rich soil followed by a layer of mulch where temperatures are extremely cold. Seedlings should be given partial shade the first year and transplanted when one year old. They can be planted in the field after the second or third year (U.S. Forest Service 1948).

Bird uses. See Serviceberries.

Birds That Use Serviceberries

	Food	Cover	Nesting
Ruffed grouse	F		
Bobwhite	F		
Ring-necked pheasant	F		
Mourning dove	F		
Common flicker*	F		
Red-headed woodpecker*	F		
Hairy woodpecker	F		
Downy woodpecker	F		
Eastern kingbird	F		
Eastern phoebe	F		
Blue jay	F		
Gray jay	F		
Common crow*	F		
Black-capped chickadee	F		
Tufted titmouse	F		
Mockingbird	F		
Gray catbird*	F		
Brown thrasher*	F		
American robin*	F		
Wood thrush	F	X	X
Hermit thrush*	F	X	
Swainson's thrush*	F		
Veery*	F		
Eastern bluebird	F		
Bohemian waxwing*	F		
Cedar waxwing*	F		
Red-eyed vireo	F		
American redstart*	F		
Red-winged blackbird	F		
Common grackle	F		
Northern oriole*	F		

	Food	Cover	Nesting
Scarlet tanager	F		
Cardinal	F		
Rose-breasted grosbeak	F		
Evening grosbeak*	F		
Pine grosbeak	F		
American goldfinch	F		
Rufous-sided towhee	F	X	
Northern junco	F		
Song sparrow	F		

Note: *preferred food; F, fruit.

Sources: Martin et al. 1951; Davison 1967; McKenny 1939.

DEVIL'S WALKINGSTICK
Aralia spinosa L.
ARALIACEAE

Description. The very spiny devil's walking-stick is most frequently encountered in moist, fertile woodlands, especially in the southern Appalachians, although its range extends to the Great Plains. Among the birds, thrushes most prefer the fleshy fruit, but other than this preference, its wildlife value is considered to be quite low (Martin et al. 1951:348). It grows 5 to 15 feet tall, with a spread of 10 to 12 feet. Devil's walkingstick is uncommon north of Pennsylvania. Other common names are Hercules-club and angelica-tree.

Bark. Covered with coarse spines.

Leaves. Alternate, compound (singly, doubly, or triply), up to 4 feet long, leaflets ovate, margins toothed, leafstalks thorny. Autumn color: purple.

Flowers. Small, white, occur in broad, flat-topped clusters which give a delicate, lacy appearance to the top of the shrub.

Fruits. Black, fleshy, two- to five-seeded berries, ¼-inch in diameter, small, nutlike seed.

Flowering period. July to August.

Fruiting period. September to October.

Habitat. Grows in rich soils of woodlands and riverbanks.

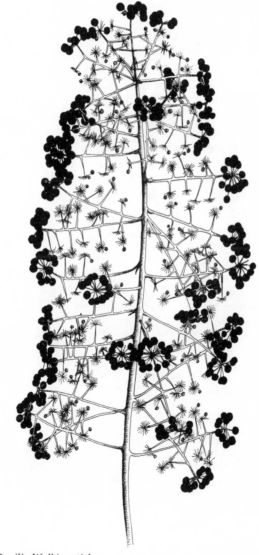

Devil's Walkingstick

[83] Shrubs

Range. Southern New England south to Florida, west to Iowa and Texas.

Hardiness zone. 6.

Landscape notes. Devil's walkingstick is attractive in summer as a background shrub when mixed with other hedge-forming vegetation. The leaves are bronze when they unfold in spring and take on a blue-green cast when fully expanded. The creamy white plumes of flower clusters grow to three feet tall and contribute to the exotic effect of this plant. It is fairly hardy and has a moderate growth rate.

Propagation. Devil's-walkingstick spreads by seeds and root suckering. Plants may be propagated from seeds and root cuttings. Seeds should be collected from fruits that are beginning to fall from the plant and separated from the pulp by maceration. Seeds are mildly dormant and should be stratified at low temperatures for spring sowing (U.S. Forest Service 1948). Suckers and small plants can be transplanted to moist, rich soil in full or partial sunlight.

Birds That Use Devil's Walkingstick

	Food	Cover	Nesting
Ruffed grouse	F	X	
Bobwhite	F	X	
Blue jay	F	X	
Gray catbird	F	X	
Wood thrush*	F	X	
Swainson's thrush*	F	X	
Eastern bluebird	F	X	
Cardinal	F	X	X (occasional)
Pine grosbeak	F		
White-throated sparrow	F		

Note: *preferred food; F, fruit.

Sources: McKenny 1939; Davison 1967; Martin et al. 1951.

COMMON BEARBERRY

Arctostaphylos uva-ursi (L.) Spreng.

ERICACEAE

Description. This prostrate evergreen shrub occurs north of the Canadian border and on mountains and seacoasts farther south. It grows in low mats up to 5 feet across. Other common names are red bearberry, kinnikinic, bilberry, bear's grape, and barren myrtle.

Bark. Red on stems, fine hairs on twigs.

Leaves. Alternate, simple, ¾- to 1¼ inches long, elliptic, surfaces dark shiny green, evergreen. Autumn color: reddish-brown.

Flowers. Small, pink or white drooping bells.

Fruits. Red or pink fleshy drupes the size of peas, persistent through winter.

Flowering period. April to July.

Fruiting period. July to October, persistent to March.

Habitat. Prefers sand or well-drained, gravelly, light loam, in sun or partial shade. Generally found along the coast, at high elevations, and in northern latitudes.

Range. The Arctic south to Virginia, west to California.

Hardiness zone. 2.

Landscape notes. Common bearberry forms low, evergreen mats that are useful as ground cover. Plants are ornamental in fruit and are useful for stabilizing low north-, east-, or west-facing slopes by preventing erosion (Zak et al. 1972). It is a slow-growing, hardy species that withstands extreme cold, relentless winds, barren soils, and scorching sun.

Propagation. Common bearberry can be propagated from seeds and stem cuttings. Seeds should be planted under controlled nursery conditions rather than by direct seeding. Seed germination may be induced by soaking seeds in concentrated sulfuric acid for three to six hours and then stratifying them in moist sand at 68° F. (night) to 86° F. (day) for sixty days, followed by a cooler exposure of 40° F. for sixty days (U.S. Forest Service 1948). Sod transplants usually do not grow well (Zak et al. 1972).

Birds That Use Common Bearberry[1]

	Food	Cover	Nesting
Ruffed grouse	F		
Ruby-throated hummingbird	N		
Gray jay	F		
Fox sparrow	F		

Note: [1]over 34 species of songbirds consume fruits, including those listed; F, fruit; N, nectar.
Sources: Martin et al. 1951; McKenny 1939.

RED CHOKEBERRY
Aronia arbutifolia Ell.
ROSACEAE

Description. Red chokeberry is a small, deciduous shrub that grows 2 to 8 feet tall. Like black chokeberry (*A. melanocarpa*), it is confined to the eastern United States. Chokeberries occur in wet areas—swamps, wet woodlands, and especially in wet fence-rows.
Bark. Grayish-brown on stems, grayish-white and woolly on twigs.
Leaves. Alternate, simple, 2 to 5 inches long, elliptic, finely toothed, smooth above, densely hairy beneath. Autumn colors: rich red and orange.
Flowers. White or purple, rose-shaped blossoms, ½- to ⅝-inch in diameter, form in terminal clusters.
Fruits. Dry, fleshy, sweet, red berries about ¼-inch diameter, persistent into winter.
Flowering period. April to July.
Fruiting period. August to November, or longer.
Habitat. Grows on wet and dry soils in sun and partial shade.
Range. Nova Scotia to Florida, west to Minnesota and Louisiana.
Hardiness zone. 5.
Landscape notes. Red chokeberry is of ornamental value for its foliage, flowers, and fruits. Attractive in borders and clumps, it also grows in coastal areas. It is very hardy and has a moderate growth rate.
Propagation. This shrub spreads by seeds and suckers. It transplants well, especially to good garden soil (Robinson 1960). Fruits may be collected by hand as soon as they ripen, and dried without removing seeds. Seeds may be stratified in moist peat for ninety days at 33°–41° F., and sown in spring in moist garden soil (U.S. Forest Service 1948).

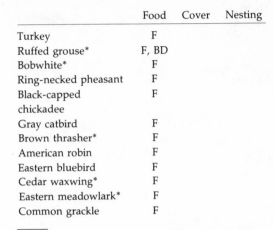

	Food	Cover	Nesting
Turkey	F		
Ruffed grouse*	F, BD		
Bobwhite*	F		
Ring-necked pheasant	F		
Black-capped chickadee	F		
Gray catbird	F		
Brown thrasher*	F		
American robin	F		
Eastern bluebird	F		
Cedar waxwing*	F		
Eastern meadowlark*	F		
Common grackle	F		

Note: *preferred food; F, fruit, BD, buds.
Sources: Davison 1967; McKenny 1939; Petrides 1972; Martin et al. 1951; McAtee 1942.

BLACK CHOKEBERRY
Aronia melanocarpa Ell.
ROSACEAE

Description. Although black chokeberry is taller—to 10 feet—than red chokeberry (*A. arbutifolia*), it is found in similar habitats—moist roadsides, wet woods, and fence-rows.
Bark. Brown, smooth.
Leaves. Alternate, simple, 1 to 3 inches long, oval or elliptic, no hairs beneath. Autumn color: bright red.
Flowers. Similar to red chokeberry.
Fruits. Similar to red chokeberry but black and shiny, persistent into winter.
Flowering period. April to July.
Fruiting period. August to November, or longer.
Habitat. Grows on moist or dry sites. Commonly found along roadsides and field borders.
Range. Newfoundland to South Carolina and Tennessee.
Hardiness zone. 5.
Landscape notes. Valuable for its brilliant sum-

Red Chokeberry

mer and autumn foliage, black chokeberry is attractive in borders. It is hardy and has a moderate growth rate.

Propagation. This plant spreads naturally by seeds and suckers. It is easily transplanted to dry or wet soil in full sun or partial shade. Fruits should be collected when ripe, and then dried. They may be stratified in moist sand for a minimum of ninety days at 41° F. to hasten germination, and sown in spring in garden soil (U.S. Forest Service 1948).

Birds That Use Black Chokeberry

	Food	Cover	Nesting
Black-capped chickadee	F		
Ruffed grouse	F, BD		
Bobwhite	F		
Gray catbird	F		
Brown thrasher	F		
Cedar waxwing*	F		
Eastern meadowlark	F		

Note: *preferred food; F, fruit; BD, buds.
Sources: Petrides 1972; McKenny 1939; Martin et al. 1951.

JAPANESE BARBERRY
Berberis Thunbergii DC.
BERBERIDACEAE

Description. Widely used as an ornamental shrub, Japanese barberry has escaped from cultivation and is widely distributed in woodlands and fence-rows from seeds dropped by birds. It grows to 5 feet. It fruits prolifically, but fruits of individual plants evidently vary in palatability—birds will readily strip one plant of fruits in early fall, while an adjacent plant's fruits will go untouched. A good winter food of the mockingbird and cedar waxwing, Japanese barberry is a preferred nest site of the chipping sparrow (DeGraaf et al. 1975).

Bark. Brown outer bark, yellow inner bark and wood, unbranched or doubly branched thorns.
Leaves. Alternate, simple, ½- to 1½-inches long, wedge-shaped, without teeth. Autumn colors: orange to scarlet.
Flowers. Small, yellow blossoms forming singly or in umbellike clusters.
Fruits. Long or globular red berries, often persisting through winter.
Flowering period. April to June.
Fruiting period. July to winter, or longer.
Habitat. Escaped from cultivation and naturalized in pastures and other open areas. Tolerates a variety of soils.
Range. Nova Scotia south to North Carolina, west to Michigan and Missouri.
Hardiness zone. 5.
Landscape notes. Very ornamental in all seasons, these shrubs are useful as hedge plants and on slopes to prevent erosion. The variety *atropurpurea* has leaves that turn deep purple in full sun. Plants are very hardy and grow slowly. Japanese barberry, unlike other barberries, is not an alternate host of the black stem rust of wheat, and may therefore be planted in wheat-producing areas.
Propagation. See European Barberry.

Birds That Use Japanese Barberry

	Food	Cover	Nesting
Ruffed grouse	F	X	
Bobwhite	F	X	
Ring-necked pheasant	F	X	
Mockingbird*	F	X	
Gray catbird	F	X	X[1]
American robin	F		
Cedar waxwing*	F		
Cardinal	F		
Northern junco	F	X	
Chipping sparrow		X	X[1]
Song sparrow		X	X[1]

Note: *preferred food; F, fruit; [1]preferred nest site.
Sources: Petrides 1972; Martin et al. 1951; Schutz 1974; Holweg 1964; DeGraaf et al. 1975.

EUROPEAN BARBERRY

Berberis vulgaris L.

BERBERIDACEAE

Description. European barberry is a vase-shaped, ornamental shrub that is taller—to 10 feet—and less common than Japanese barberry (*B. Thunbergii*). The fruits of European barberry are not as readily taken by birds, but serve as emergency food for several species. Another common name is common barberry.

Bark. Outer bark gray, inner bark yellow, branches thorny.

Leaves. Alternate, simple, 1½ to 3 inches long, obovate, crowded with short, bristlelike teeth, bright green above, lighter beneath. Autumn colors: green or purplish-green.

Flowers. Small, yellow blossoms forming in drooping clusters along branches.

Fruits. Small, scarlet, edible, ornamental berries ½-inch long, forming in clusters along branches.

Flowering period. April to June.

Fruiting period. July, persistent to spring.

Habitat. Found in thickets and hedgerows and scattered throughout pasturelands, in sun or shade. Plants grow on many soils.

Range. Nova Scotia south to Pennsylvania, west to Minnesota and Missouri.

Hardiness zone. 4.

Landscape notes. This is a useful shrub for landscaping purposes. Its graceful habit is attractive when the shrub is planted singly or in clumps. Flowers and fruits are highly ornamental. The bright-red berries remain on the plants well into winter. European barberry is hardy throughout the northeastern United States. It grows rapidly at first but slows as plants mature.

Propagation. European barberry can be propagated from softwood cuttings taken in June and July. Cuttings should be inserted into a moist rooting medium in a closed frame where surrounding air remains humid. The sash should be raised daily for a half hour of ventilation, and the cuttings should be sprinkled with water occasionally (Free 1957).

Plants are alternate hosts of the black stem rust of wheat and should be located away from wheat fields. To plant from seed, hand pick the fruits when ripe and sow the whole berry immediately, or remove the seeds by maceration. Seeds should be dried and stratified in moist sand for fifteen to forty days at 32°–41° F., or stored in sealed containers and kept just above 32° F. (U.S. Forest Service 1948). Barberries may also be propagated by layering and grafting. Best growth occurs on moist, light loam.

Birds That Use European Barberry

	Food[1]	Cover	Nesting
Ruffed grouse	F		
Bobwhite	F		
Ring-necked pheasant	F		
Mockingbird	F		
American robin	F		
Cedar waxwing	F		
Song sparrow	F	X	X

Note: [1]persistent fruits serve as emergency food in winter for many birds; F, fruit.

Sources: Davison 1967; Petrides 1972; Martin et al. 1951.

EASTERN CHINKAPIN
Castanea pumila (L.) Mill.
FAGACEAE

Description. The eastern chinkapin resembles sprouts of American chestnut (*Castanea dentata*). It usually grows 10 to 15 feet tall, with a spread of 10 to 15 feet. Another common name is Allegany chinkapin.

Bark. Dark brown on stems; twigs and buds somewhat hairy.

Leaves. Alternate, simple, 3 to 5 inches long, oblong with prominent, pinnate veins and coarse teeth, dark green and smooth above, pale green or white with dense hairs below. Autumn colors: bright yellow and russet.

Flowers. Male and female flowers form separately on same plant. Male flowers form on spreading catkins, 3 to 5 inches long. Fragrant female flowers form at bases of catkins on prickly, burrlike balls, less than 1 inch in diameter.

Fruits. Small, brown, pea-sized nut surrounded by a leathery, spine-covered husk. Kernel is sweet. Whole fruit is about 1 inch in diameter.

Flowering period. June to July.

Fruiting period. August to September.

Habitat. Thrives in dry, rocky woodlands.

Range. Massachusetts south to northern Florida, west to eastern Texas.

Hardiness zone. 6.

Landscape notes. This is a good cover plant on dry, rocky embankments. It is also useful in thickets and unpruned hedgerows having a sunny exposure. Plants are moderately hardy and rapid growing.

Propagation. Plants reproduce naturally from seeds—many of which are spread by squirrels—and vegetatively by sporadic suckering. They may be propagated by seeding, layering, grafting, or budding.

The following techniques are used for American chestnut and may be applied to chinkapin: if planting from seed, separate ripe nuts from their husks and sow immediately, or stratify them in moist sand, sawdust, or peat at 32°–40° F. until sprouting occurs; if germination begins in midwinter, seeds may be chilled slightly below 32° F. to inhibit growth, and sown outside in spring in 1 inch of soil. Seedlings may be transplanted to the field after the first or second year (U.S. Forest Service 1948).

Eastern Chinkapin

Birds That Use Eastern Chinkapin

	Food	Cover	Nesting[1]
Turkey	F		
Blue jay	F		
Red-headed woodpecker	F		

Note: F, fruit; [1]occasional nest site of songbirds.
Sources: Martin et al. 1951; Davison 1967.

COMMON BUTTONBUSH
Cephalanthus occidentalis L.
RUBIACEAE

Description. Buttonbush is a shrub of fresh-
water wetlands. It often grows in water 1 to 2
feet deep and may form dense, islandlike
stands. It is a frequent nest site of birds found
in wetlands. It grows 3 to 12 feet tall. Other
common names are buttonwillow, globeflower, and honey balls.

Bark. Dark gray on stems, red-brown on
branchlets with large lenticels.

Leaves. Opposite or whorled in threes or fours
around stems, simple, 3 to 6 inches long,
without teeth, dark shiny green above, paler
below. Autumn color: dull yellow or green.

Flowers. Small, white, tubular, densely clustered on round heads, hold abundant nectar,
very fragrant.

Fruits. Small, dry schizocarps containing one
or two seeds.

Flowering period. June to September.

Fruiting period. September to December, often
persistent to spring.

Habitat. Shallow water and wet shores of
ponds, swamps, and stream banks in full sun
or partial shade.

Range. Nova Scotia south to Florida, west to
Minnesota and California.

Hardiness zone. 5.

Landscape notes. Buttonbush is worthy of cultivation on low, swampy soils, pond edges, or
on drier ground in any good garden soil.
Plants are hardy and grow at a moderate rate.

Propagation. Plants may be propagated from
seeds or cuttings. Ripe seeds may be extracted from the fruit balls and sown immediately, or dried and stored in wax-sealed jars
at 41° F. for several years, but not without
substantial loss of viability. They may be
sown in sandy, moist nursery beds and later
transplanted to similar soil or any good garden loam (U.S. Forest Service 1948).

Birds That Use Common Buttonbush

	Food	Cover	Nesting
Mallard	S	X	
Gadwall	S	X	
American wigeon	S	X	
Northern shoveler	S	X	
Green-winged teal	S	X	
Blue-winged teal	S	X	
Wood duck	S	X	
Virginia rail		X	X
Ruby-throated hummingbird*	N		
Red-winged blackbird		X	X
Common grackle		X	X

Note: *preferred food; S, seeds; N, nectar.
Sources: Martin et al. 1951; Davison 1967.

Common Buttonbush

SWEETFERN
Comptonia peregrina (L.) Coult.
MYRICACEAE

Description. This low-growing shrub occurs on dry, gravelly sites, commonly with scrub oak and gray birch. The broken twigs are aromatic. It grows 2 to 4 feet tall, with a spread of 2 to 4 feet.

Bark. Yellowish to copper-brown, aromatic, young branches covered with dense, soft hairs.

Leaves. Alternate, simple, 3 to 6 inches long, fernlike with many pointed lobes along margins, sprinkled with small, resinous dots.

Flowers. Male and female flowers occur on same or separate plants. Male flowers are ½-inch long and form at the end of the twig. Female flowers are round and resemble burs.

Fruits. Small, nonwaxy, olive-brown nuts, ¼- to ⅜-inch in diameter, surrounded by bristly scales.

Flowering period. April to June.

Fruiting period. August to October.

Habitat. Common in dry, open areas across the Northeast. Grows in full or partial sunlight.

Range. New Brunswick south to the mountains of Georgia, west to Indiana.

Hardiness zone. 2.

Landscape notes. This is an attractive low shrub or ground cover for barren, sandy soils. Nodules on plant roots fix nitrogen from the air. Large clumps scent the air with spice after a rain. Plants are very hardy, grow at a moderate rate, and are excellent for stabilizing steep embankments.

Propagation. Sweetfern can be propagated from root cuttings or purchased from nurseries. Young plants should be mulched. Root cuttings ¼-inch in diameter can be taken from healthy plants in early spring and planted in 8-by-10-inch plastic containers. Plants can be set out in late summer, fall, or the following spring (Zak et al. 1972). Wild shrubs should be transplanted to sandy soil when dormant and stems cut back to ground level (Robinson 1960).

Birds That Use Sweetfern

	Food	Cover	Nesting
Ruffed grouse	BD, CK		
Mourning dove	F		
Common flicker	F		

Note: BD, buds; CK, catkins; F, fruit.
Sources: Martin et al. 1951; McKenny 1939; Petrides 1972.

ALTERNATE-LEAF DOGWOOD
Cornus alternifolia L.f.
CORNACEAE

Description. Alternate-leaf dogwood usually occurs as a shrub, especially in woodlands. In relatively open spaces it occasionally grows as a small, stately tree to 30 feet with wide-spreading branches. It is much too rarely planted as an ornamental. It makes a fine specimen in somewhat shady, moist areas, and is very valuable to wildlife. Other common names are pagoda dogwood, blue dogwood, and green osier.

Bark. Brown to gray with low ridges and shallow fissures on trunk, green and smooth on branches.

Leaves. Alternate on sterile branches, simple and grouped as if in whorls on fertile branches, 2 to 4 inches long, elliptic, ovate or acuminate, surfaces dark green, hairy beneath, veins prominent, petioles slender. Autumn color: deep red.

Flowers. Cream colored, appear on broad, flat-topped, terminal cymes.

Fruits. Bluish-black round drupes, ⅓-inch in diameter on red stems.

Flowering period. May to early June.

Fruiting period. Late July to September.

Habitat. Grows most commonly in moist, rich soils of woodlands, woodland borders, and occasionally along stream banks. Tolerates sun or shade.

Range. Newfoundland south to northwestern Florida, west to Minnesota and Arkansas.

[91] Shrubs

Hardiness zone. 4.

Landscape notes. Alternate-leaf dogwood is very attractive as both shrub and tree. It is an excellent border and understory plant. To achieve the best shape, allow it to spread freely without pruning. Plants are hardy and grow slowly until well established.

Propagation. Stock is available from commercial sources. Plants may be propagated from seed or vegetatively by the following methods: softwood cuttings, hardwood cuttings, grafting, layering, and budding (Mahlstede and Haber 1957). Gather seeds when fruits are ripe and separate them from the pulp by soaking in water for a few days. Sow seeds immediately, or stratify them in moist sand or peat moss for two months at 68° F. (night) and 86° F. (day), followed by three to four months at 41° F., and then plant in April or May. Sow seeds in drills, or broadcast and cover with ¼- to ½-inch of soil depending on seed size. If sown in fall, cover with thick layer of mulch, to be removed upon germination (U.S. Forest Service 1948).

For details of vegetative propagation, see Flowering Dogwood. Plants become thick and bushy when pruned. When allowed to grow with single trunks, they form delicate trees.

Birds That Use Alternate-leaf Dogwood
(See Dogwoods)

	Food	Cover	Nesting
Turkey*	F, BD	X	
Ruffed grouse*	F, BD	X	
Bobwhite*	F, BD		
Ring-necked pheasant	F, BD		
Common flicker*	F		
Pileated woodpecker	F		
Red-headed woodpecker	F		
Yellow-bellied sapsucker*	F (sap)		
Downy woodpecker*	F		
Eastern kingbird*	F	X	X
Great crested flycatcher	F		
Tree swallow	F		
Common crow	F		
Mockingbird	F		
Gray catbird*	F		
Brown thrasher*	F		
American robin*	F	X	X
Wood thrush*	F	X	X
Hermit thrush*	F	X	
Swainson's thrush*	F		
Gray-cheeked thrush*	F	X	
Veery	F	X	
Eastern bluebird*	F		
Cedar waxwing*	F	X	X
Starling	F		
Red-eyed vireo*	F	X	X
Warbling vireo*	F		
Scarlet tanager	F	X	X
Cardinal*	F		
Evening grosbeak*	F		
Purple finch*	F	X	X
Pine grosbeak*	F		
White-throated sparrow	F		
Song sparrow	F		

Note: *preferred food; F, fruit, BD, buds.
Sources: Martin et al. 1951; Davison 1967; Van Dersal 1938; Vines 1960.

SILKY DOGWOOD

Cornus amomum Mill.

CORNACEAE

Description. Silky dogwood is often mistaken for red-osier dogwood, although the twigs of silky dogwood are not as red as those of the latter. Silky dogwood is very common, especially on wet sites such as stream banks, wet meadows, and fence-rows. The fruits are readily taken by many kinds of birds. It grows as a many-stemmed shrub, 4 to 10 feet tall. Other common names are red willow, silky cornel, and squawbush.

Bark. Reddish-brown and smooth on stems, new shoots silky with brown hairs.

Leaves. Opposite, simple, 3 to 5 inches long, narrow, commonly has soft, reddish hairs on surfaces. Autumn colors: purple to red.

Flowers. Creamy white on flat cymes 1½ to 2½ inches in diameter.

Fruits. Blue or bluish-white round drupes, ¼-inch to ⅜-inch in diameter, usually abundant.

Flowering period. June to July.

Fruiting period. August to October.

Habitat. Grows in low, moist locations, especially along streams, ponds, and swamps, usually in thickets. Very common within its range in the Northeast.

Range. Southern Maine to southern Illinois and Indiana, south to South Carolina and Alabama.

Hardiness zone. 6.

Landscape notes. This is an excellent shrub for borders and clumps. Plants can be shaped by pruning or left to spread freely by layering. They are also useful in preventing stream-bank erosion. They are hardy and grow rapidly.

Propagation. Plants may be propagated from seed or vegetatively by cuttings, grafting, division, and layering. Seeds may be planted in September or October, or stratified and planted in the spring (Heit 1968; Miller 1959). Seeds may be stratified in sand, peat, or a mixture of the two for three to four months at 41° F. (U.S. Forest Service 1948).

For details of vegetative propagation see Flowering Dogwood.

Birds That Use Silky Dogwood
(See Dogwoods)

	Food	Cover	Nesting
Wood duck	F	X	
Turkey*	F		
Ruffed grouse*	F		
Bobwhite*	F		
Ring-necked pheasant	F		
American woodcock		X	
Common flicker*	F		
Red-headed woodpecker	F		
Downy woodpecker*	F		
Eastern kingbird*	F		
Gray catbird*	F	X	X
Brown thrasher*	F		
American robin*	F		
Wood thrush*	F		
Swainson's thrush*	F		
Eastern bluebird*	F		
Cedar waxwing*	F		
Purple finch*	F		
American goldfinch		X	X
Song sparrow	F	X	

Note: *preferred food; F, fruit.

Sources: Martin et al. 1951; Davison 1967; Van Dersal 1938; Vines 1960.

BUNCHBERRY
Cornus canadensis L.
CORNACEAE

Description. Bunchberry is a tiny shrub native to cool, northeastern woodlands and open, sunny mountainsides. It grows 5 to 12 inches tall. Other common names are bunchberry dogwood and dwarf cornel.

Leaves. Evergreen, ovate, toothless, 5 to 7 parallel veins, form in whorls of 6, borne horizontally.

Flowers. Small, greenish, forming in dense heads on a single stalk, surrounded by 4 to 6 large, greenish-white bracts.

Fruits. Brilliant scarlet berries.

Flowering period. May to July.

Fruiting period. August.

Habitat. Cool, damp, mossy woods, damp openings.

Range. Labrador south to West Virginia, west to Alaska and California.

Hardiness zone. 2.

Landscape notes. Bunchberry has highly ornamental flowers and fruit. It is used extensively as a ground cover in natural compositions and in wildflower gardens.

Propagation. Seeds may be stratified in sand or peat for 30 to 60 days at 70° F., followed by 120 to 150 days at 33° F. They should be sown in drills, or broadcast and covered with ¼- to ½-inch of nursery soil and mulched until the onset of germination. Seeds that are sown without treatment usually take two years to germinate (U.S. Forest Service 1948).

Birds That Use Bunchberry

	Food	Cover	Nesting
Ruffed grouse	F, BD		
Bobwhite	F		
Ring-necked pheasant	F		
Veery*	F		
Philadelphia vireo*	F		
Warbling vireo*	F		
Pine grosbeak	F		
Savannah sparrow	F		
Lapland longspur	F		

Note: *preferred food; F, fruit; BD, buds.
Sources: Martin et al. 1951; McKenny 1939.

Bunchberry

GRAY DOGWOOD
Cornus racemosa Lam.
CORNACEAE

Description. Gray dogwood is a common, thicket-forming shrub of dry forest edges and fence-rows. Its fruits are readily eaten by many birds. Other common names are gray-stemmed dogwood and panicled dogwood.
Bark. Gray on stems, purplish on branches.
Leaves. Opposite, simple, 1 to 5 inches long with 3 to 5 pairs of veins, narrow to oval in shape, slightly hairy beneath. Autumn color: dull red.
Flowers. Small, white, in loose cymes 1½ to 2 inches in diameter.
Fruits. Round, white drupes, ¼-inch in diameter, on red stalks in conical clusters.
Flowering period. May to July.
Fruiting period. July to October, persistent to early winter.
Habitat. Grows on a variety of sites from moist lowlands to dry uplands. Adapts well to a wide range of climatic conditions and soil types. Found in thickets and hedgerows along fields and forest borders. Prefers partial shade.
Range. Central Maine south to West Virginia, west to Missouri and Oklahoma.
Hardiness zone. 5.
Landscape notes. This is an excellent thicket-forming shrub for pond shores or drier woodland borders. Plants are hardy and slow growing, seldom exceeding 6 feet in height in ten years (Liscinsky 1974). Mature height to 9 feet. They can withstand city smoke (Terres 1968).
Propagation. Seed and stock can be purchased from nurseries or collected in the wild. To propagate plants from seed, collect mature fruits and clean seeds by maceration. Plant in early August of the same year, or air-dry and store at 41° F., or stratify seeds in sand or peat for 60 days at 68° F. (night) and 86° F. (day), followed by 120 days at 41° F., and plant in April or early May (U.S. Forest Service 1948; Heit 1967d). Sow seeds ¼- to ½- inch deep in soil and transplant when one or two years old. Plants can also be propagated from root cuttings, layers, and division (Liscinsky 1960; U.S. Forest Service 1948).

Birds That Use Gray Dogwood
(See Dogwoods)

	Food	Cover[1]	Nesting
Turkey*	F		
Ruffed grouse*	F, BD		
Bobwhite*	F		
Ring-necked pheasant	F		
American woodcock		X	
Common flicker*	F		
Red-headed woodpecker	F		
Downy woodpecker*	F		
Eastern kingbird*	F		
Gray catbird*	F	X	X[2]
American robin*	F		
Swainson's thrush*	F		
Eastern bluebird*	F		
Cedar waxwing*	F		
Cardinal*	F		
Pine grosbeak*	F		

Note: *preferred food; F, fruit; BD, buds; [1]excellent cover and nest site for many songbirds; [2]preferred nest site.
Sources: McKenny 1939; Davison 1967; Liscinsky 1974.

Gray Dogwood

RED-OSIER DOGWOOD
Cornus stolonifera Michx.
CORNACEAE

Description. Red-osier dogwood is most commonly found in wet areas—swamps, low meadows, and stream banks—but it occasionally grows in much drier sites. The fruits are eaten by a great variety of birds and the upright twigs are a preferred nest site of the goldfinch. Plants are generally 4 to 8 feet tall with a spread of 10 feet. Other common names are red-stemmed cornel and squaw-bush.
Bark. Thin, greenish-red in summer turning brilliant red in autumn. There is also a yellow-stemmed variety.
Leaves. Opposite, simple, 4 to 6 inches long, ovate to oblong, pointed at the tips. Autumn color: dark red.
Flowers. Creamy white, forming on small flat cymes 1 to 2 inches across.
Fruits. Small white drupes, ¼-inch in diameter.
Flowering period. May to August.
Fruiting period. July to October.
Habitat. Grows singly or in thickets on dry soils (Grimm 1952), but is more often found on wet sites along ponds and streams in association with alders and willows, and in lowlands with poplars and black spruce (Conway 1949).
Range. Newfoundland south to West Virginia, west to California and Alaska.
Hardiness zone. 2.
Landscape notes. Red-osier dogwood is valued for its flowers and foliage in summer and its brilliant red stems in winter which contrast sharply with a background of snow or evergreens. It is excellent as a border shrub, and useful for holding soil on banks. It is hardy and grows rapidly in cultivated soil and adequate light. Plants may grow to 3 feet tall the first season in good, rich topsoil (Smithberg 1974).

Propagation. This dogwood reproduces naturally by stolons in moist locations (Smithberg 1974), by layering, seed or root shoots. It can be propagated from cuttings or seed, or acquired more easily by digging up small plants or suckers. Plants grow well in soils having a pH of 5.0 to 6.0 (Wilder 1946), but can tolerate a range of 3.2 to 8.0 (Jewell and Brown 1929).

To propagate from seed, gather seeds when fully ripe. Clean, air-dry, and store seeds in sealed glass containers at 34°–38° F. if later planting is desired. For planting in fall (September to October or earlier), they should be soft; if hard, soak in water. If seed coats are too hard and are not mechanically scarified before planting, germination may be delayed until the second spring (Laurie and Chadwick 1931). Sow in ¼-inch of garden soil and cover with a mulch of leaves or straw. Remove mulch at the first signs of germination (U.S. Forest Service 1948).

To use hardwood cuttings, cut 6- to 8-inch lengths and set in sand (Smithberg 1964). Transplant after one growing season.
Branches may be layered. Roots form after several weeks, at which time the shoot can be cut away from the parent plant and transplanted (Hartmann and Kester 1968).

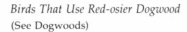

Birds That Use Red-osier Dogwood
(See Dogwoods)

	Food	Cover[1]	Nesting[2]
Turkey*	F		
Ruffed grouse*	F	X	
Bobwhite*	F		
Ring-necked pheasant	F	X	
Common flicker*	F		
Red-headed woodpecker	F		
Downy woodpecker*	F		
Eastern kingbird*	F		
Common crow*	F		
Gray catbird*	F		
Brown thrasher*	F		
American robin*	F		
Swainson's thrush*	F		
Eastern bluebird*	F		
Cedar waxwing*	F		
Purple finch*	F		
American goldfinch		X	X[3]
White-throated sparrow	F		
Song sparrow	F		

Note: *preferred food; F, fruit; [1]important cover plant for birds; [2]often a nest site for songbirds; [3]preferred nest site.
Sources: Davison 1967; Smithberg 1974; McKenny 1939.

Birds That Use Dogwoods

	Food	Cover	Nesting
Wood duck	F		
Turkey*	F	X	
Spruce grouse	F	X	
Ruffed grouse*	F	X	
Bobwhite*	F	X	
Ring-necked pheasant	F	X	
American woodcock		X	
Common flicker*	F		
Pileated woodpecker	F		
Red-bellied woodpecker	F		
Yellow-bellied sapsucker*	F		
Hairy woodpecker	F		
Downy woodpecker*	F		
Eastern kingbird*	F	X	
Great crested flycatcher	F		
Willow flycatcher		X	X
Tree swallow	F		
Common crow*	F		
Mockingbird	F	X	
Gray catbird*	F	X	
Brown thrasher*	F	X	
American robin*	F	X	
Wood thrush*	F	X	
Hermit thrush*	F	X	
Swainson's thrush*	F	X	
Gray-cheeked thrush*	F	X	
Eastern bluebird*	F	X	
Cedar waxwing*	F		
Starling	F		
Red-eyed vireo*	F		
Warbling vireo*	F		
Pine warbler*	F		
Scarlet tanager	F		
Cardinal*	F	X	
Evening grosbeak*	F		
Purple finch*	F		
Pine grosbeak*	F		

Note: *preferred food; F, fruit.
Sources: Martin et al. 1951; Davison 1967; Holweg 1964; Van Dersal 1938; McKenny 1939; DeGraaf et al. 1975; Harrison 1975; McAtee 1942.

AMERICAN HAZEL
Corylus americana Walt.
CORYLACEAE

Description. American hazel grows in clumps to 10 feet tall in clearings (Stearns 1974). The nuts are readily eaten by jays, ruffed grouse, hairy woodpeckers, and pheasants, and by deer, squirrels, and chipmunks. Other common names are American filbert and hazelnut.
Bark. Color varies from russet brown to yellow-gray.
Leaves. Alternate, simple, 3 to 6 inches long, ovate to heart-shaped, toothed, dark yellowish-green above and pale green beneath. Autumn color: pale yellow.
Flowers. Flowers of both sexes appear on same plant—usually on same stem—before leaves unfold. Males form on 3- to 4-inch catkins. Females form in starlike tufts projecting above buds.
Fruits. Oval or oblong, brown nuts, ½-inch long, kernel sweet.
Flowering period. March to April.
Fruiting period. July to October, persistent into winter.
Habitat. Grows in dense clumps and thickets along roadsides, stonewalls, and edges of woods. Grows on a variety of soils, but requires full sun for part of each day.
Range. Maine south to Georgia, west to Missouri and Oklahoma.
Hardiness zone. 5.
Landscape notes. Good for naturalistic plantings in large areas, these plants have little ornamental value but provide good cover for wildlife. They are hardy in the Northeast and grow rapidly.
Propagation. Plants can be raised from seed or vegetatively from cuttings, layers, sprouts, and grafting. Seeds should be gathered when husks begin to turn brown; otherwise, the squirrels and chipmunks may get them first. Spread them out to dry for two to three days, then knock the husks off by flailing. Store them without further drying in a sealed con-

tainer at 41° F., where they should remain viable for two years. If you plan to sow seeds during the following spring, stratify them in moist sand at 41° F. for 90 to 120 days (Swingle 1939), or at 41° F. for 60 days, plus 65° F. for 67 days, then reduce the temperature to 41° F. for another 30 days (U.S. Forest Service 1948).

Take cuttings in the fall after the leaves have dropped and place them in sand beds until spring. Plant them just before the buds break (Deam 1932).

Birds That Use American Hazel

	Food	Cover	Nesting
Turkey	F		
Ruffed grouse*	F, BD, CK		
Bobwhite	F		
Ring-necked pheasant*	F		
American woodcock		X	
Red-bellied woodpecker	F		
Hairy woodpecker*	F		
Blue jay*	F		

Note: *preferred food; F, fruit; BD, buds; CK,catkins.
Sources: Martin et al. 1951; Davison 1967; Petrides 1958.

American Hazel

BEAKED FILBERT
Corylus cornuta Marsh.
CORYLACEAE

Description. Beaked filbert is very similar to American hazel (*C. americana*) in form, but is found in somewhat wetter, shadier sites (Stearns 1974). Ruffed grouse and blue jays prefer the nuts. Also known as beaked hazel, it can grow to 9 feet.
Bark. Yellowish gray or reddish gray on stems, slightly hairy on twigs.
Leaves. Alternate, simple, 2 to 4 inches long, ovate to obovate, prominently veined, upper surfaces bright green with or without hairs, lower surfaces paler and slightly hairy. Autumn color: bright yellow.
Flowers. Male and female flowers occur on same plants, usually on the same stem. Staminate flowers develop on long, pendulous catkins. Pistillate flowers form in tufts projecting above short buds.
Fruits. Pale brown oval nuts are enclosed in husks twice their length which form long hairy beaks.
Flowering period. April to May.
Fruiting period. July to September, persistent into winter.
Habitat. Commonly found in open woods, pastures, and thickets in well-drained, light soils of slightly acid pH, but tolerates many soil types. Prefers sunshine to shade.
Range. Nova Scotia to Georgia, west to Kansas and Colorado.
Hardiness zone. 5.
Landscape notes. Beaked filbert is good for dense hedgerows and clumps, but has little ornamental value. Plants are hardy and grow moderately fast.
Propagation. Plants can be propagated by seed or vegetatively by layers, sprouts, and cuttings. To produce plants from seed, gather fruits when husks begin to turn brown and spread them out to dry. Remove husks in a few days and, if later sowing is desired, place seeds in a closed container and store at 41° F. for up to one year. Do not dry seeds. If spring sowing is desired, stratify seeds in moist sand at 41° F. for 90 to 120 days (Swingle 1939).

Cuttings should be made in the fall after the leaves have dropped, placed in sand beds until spring, and transplanted just before the buds break (Deam 1932).

Birds That Use Beaked Filbert

	Food	Cover	Nesting
Turkey	F		
Ruffed grouse*	F, BD, CK		
American woodcock		X	
Red-bellied woodpecker	F		
Hairy woodpecker	F		
Blue jay*	F		

Note: *preferred food; F, fruit; BD, buds; CK, catkins.
Sources: Martin et al. 1951; Davison 1967.

HAWTHORNS
Crataegus spp.
ROSACEAE

Description. The hawthorns comprise a widespread group of deciduous, thorny shrubs and small trees which show so little variation among species that accurate identification is difficult even for expert botanists. Individual plants commonly hybridize and add to the confusion. As a group, they are distinctive from other thorny shrubs in several ways: the thorns are hard and smooth, straight or slightly bent and form in leaf axils; all thorns are without buds and leaves and persist year-round. Hawthorns are 5 to 30 feet tall, depending on the species.
Leaves. Variable size and shape. Some are finely toothed and elliptical, others are deeply lobed and triangular, often with several

Hawthorn

shapes appearing on a single plant.

Flowers. Blossoms form singly or in clusters and vary in size. Colors vary with species from shades of white, to rose and scarlet.

Fruits. Rounded pomes, early fruits usually soft and perishable, late-summer fruits hard and persistent, colors vary from yellow to orange and red.

Habitat. Hawthorns are common throughout the Northeast along fence-rows and in abandoned fields and pastures, often in association with sumacs and brambles. They are found in well-drained, moist, and waterlogged soils, usually in full sunlight. They cannot tolerate full shade.

Landscape notes. These are excellent shrubs or trees for yard or border. They have attractive foliage, flowers, and fruits. Plants that fruit heavily in late summer display their ornamental red and orange colors well into winter. Hawthorns can be planted close together and pruned to create a living fence of thorns, impenetrable by animals and humans.

Hawthorns are susceptible to rusts, blights, and insect damage. The eastern red cedar is the alternate host of two destructive rusts and should not be planted nearby. Thin-leaved varieties are less resistant to damage than those with thick leaves. Washington hawthorn is probably most resistant to rusts, and provides excellent food and nest sites for birds.

Propagation. Plants may be propagated from seed collected from wild or cultivated species. It is best to collect seeds of species having characteristics best suited to one's needs. Seeds usually have double dormancy and may require sulfuric acid scarification and a warm-cold stratification for germination (Flemion 1938). For spring sowing, seeds should be cleaned, dried, mixed with sand, and stored outside in a rodent-proof box until spring and then planted in rows in good garden soil.

Direct-seeding and grafting are other means of propagation, but good results are often difficult to achieve (Sharp 1974).

Some Recommended Hawthorns

Species	Height	Leaves	Flower		Fruit		Range
			Period	Color	Period	Color	
NATIVE							
Cockspur Hawthorn *Crataegus crusgalli*	20′–30′	length and shape variable, orange in autumn	May	white	August to February	red	Thickets and open ground, often in dry, rocky places. SE Canada to South Carolina, W to Minnesota and Texas. Hardiness zone: 5.
Washington Hawthorn *Crataegus phaenopyrum*	20′–30′	length and shape variable, orange to scarlet autumn foliage	June	white	*annually,* September persistent to winter	orange-red	Thickets and open woods. Pennsylvania to Florida, W to Missouri and Arkansas. Hardiness zone: 5.
INTRODUCED							
Pauls Scarlet Hawthorn *Crataegus oxycantha pauli*	20′–30′	length and shape variable, poor color in autumn	May	double scarlet or pink, fragrant	September to October	scarlet	Escaped from cultivation to roadsides and borders of woods. Intro. from Europe and Asia. Hardiness zone: 5.

Birds That Use Hawthorns

	Food	Cover	Nesting		Food	Cover	Nesting
Wood duck	F			American robin	F	X	X
Turkey	F			Hermit thrush	F		
Ruffed grouse*	F			Cedar waxwing*	F		
Bobwhite	F			Cardinal	F	X	X
Ring-necked pheasant	F			Evening grosbeak	F		
Common flicker	F			Purple finch	F		
Yellow-bellied sapsucker	sap			Pine grosbeak	F		
Willow flycatcher		X	X	Fox sparrow*	F	X	
Blue jay	F		X				
Gray catbird	F	X	X	Note: *preferred food; F, fruit.			
Mockingbird	F	X	X	Sources: Martin et al. 1951; Petrides 1972; Davison 1967; Schutz 1974; McKenny 1939.			
Brown thrasher	F	X	X				

RUSSIAN OLIVE

Elaeagnus angustifolia L.

ELAEAGNACEAE

Description. This exotic has been widely planted for windbreaks. It is extremely hardy, grows in virtually any soil, and produces abundant fruit that is eaten by many birds. It grows to 20 feet and is also known as oleaster, wild olive, and Jerusalem willow.

Bark. Twigs silvery, fuzzy, sometimes thorny.

Leaves. Alternate, simple, 1½ to 3 inches long, without teeth, oblong, linear, or lanceolate, green above, silvery beneath. Autumn color: silver-green.

Flowers. Inconspicuous, fragrant blossoms, silver outside, yellow inside, borne in leaf axils in groups of two or three.

Fruits. Silvery yellow, ovoid drupes, dry and mealy, sweet, persistent into winter.

Flowering period. May to July.

Fruiting period. August to October, persistent to spring.

Habitat. Thrives in dry, sandy loam or clay soil. Will do well in any good garden soil in full sunlight or shade. Salt tolerant and drought resistant.

Range. Native of southern Europe and Asia. Escaped from cultivation in the northeastern United States.

Hardiness zone. 2.

Landscape notes. This shrub is useful for windbreaks, snowtraps, hedgerows, and banks, and is good for beautifying unsightly areas. Plants normally develop into shrubs with five or six main stems. If all but one stem is removed and optimal growth conditions are present, the plant may develop into a shade tree up to 40 feet tall (Borell 1962). Growth is rapid under favorable conditions with heights reaching 12 feet in two years (Borell 1962).

Propagation. See Autumn Olive.

Birds That Use Russian Olive

	Food	Cover[1]	Nesting
Mallard	F		
Turkey	F		
Ruffed grouse	F		
Bobwhite	F		
Ring-necked pheasant	F		
Mourning dove	F	X	X
Common flicker	F		
Common crow	F		
Mockingbird	F	X	X
Gray catbird	F		
Brown thrasher	F		
American robin*	F		
Eastern bluebird	F		
Cedar waxwing*	F		
Starling	F		
House sparrow	F		
Common grackle	F		
Cardinal	F		
Evening grosbeak*	F		
House finch	F		
Pine siskin	F		
Rufous-sided towhee	F		
Northern junco	F		
White-crowned sparrow	F		
Song sparrow	F		

Note: *preferred food; F, fruit; [1]used for food and cover by many birds and small mammals (National Wildlife Federation 1974.)

AUTUMN OLIVE
Elaeagnus umbellata Thunb.
ELAEAGNACEAE

Description. Autumn olive is a shrub or small tree introduced from Asia. It can be planted in a variety of sites, and grows to about 12 feet, with a widely spreading crown. It is a very valuable food plant for birds. Other common names are autumn elaeagnus and Japanese silverberry.

Bark. Brown or yellowish-brown and smooth on young stems, branches often thorny.

Leaves. Alternate, simple, 1 to 3 inches long, elliptic to ovate or oblong, edges often wavy, dark green above, silvery-white beneath. Autumn color: silver-green.

Flowers. Yellowish, fragrant, slender tubes resembling small trumpets forming in clusters along the twigs.

Fruits. Reddish-brown to pink drupes, juicier than those of Russian olive, each containing one soft pit. Production is usually heavy.

Flowering period. May to June.

Fruiting period. Fall, persistent to midwinter.

Habitat. Tolerant of a variety of soils from acid to alkaline sands and clay loams that are dry or moist. Grows well in the sun in areas having adequate drainage. Plants are drought resistant. They may be injured by extremely cold temperatures (−30° F.), but they usually recover.

Range. Native to China, Korea, and Japan. Escaping from cultivation and spreading to waste areas and roadside thickets from Maine to New Jersey and Pennsylvania.

Hardiness zone. 4.

Landscape notes. Silvery foliage and reddish berries contrast well with darker green background plants. It is attractive as a single shrub or in clumps. For best clumping effects, space groups of plants at least 8 feet apart. Autumn olive is recommended for dry, sandy slopes along roadsides and bridge abutments and is useful in sandy areas along the coast. It is also excellent for erosion control and screening. Autumn olive is hardy and grows moderately fast throughout its range. It may be pruned to desired shape (Zak et al. 1972; U.S. Soil Conservation Service 1969; Robinson 1960).

The cardinal autumn olive, developed by the U.S. Soil Conservation Service, is an exceptionally attractive variety and a prolific producer of fruit. It grows rapidly under favorable conditions, reaching 8 feet in height and bearing fruit in three to five years (Allan and Steiner 1965).

Propagation. Plants may be grown from seeds and stem cuttings, root cuttings, layers, and grafts. Seeds can be obtained by macerating the ripe fruits in water and floating off the pulp. Seeds may be sown in drills ¾-inch deep or broadcast and covered with no more than 2 inches of mulch. If planting during the spring following collection, prechill them for sixty to ninety days at 41° F. to break embryo dormancy. One- to two-year-old seedlings may be transplanted in spring or fall when dormant. Seedlings should be planted deep enough to extend the root vertically without bending it. Mulched trees do well on dry sites. (Zak et al. 1972; U.S. Forest Service 1948; U.S. Soil Conservation Service 1969).

Birds That Use Autumn Olive

	Food	Cover[1]	Nesting[2]
Mallard	F		
Turkey	F	X	
Ruffed grouse	F	X	
Bobwhite	F	X	
Ring-necked pheasant	F	X	
Mourning dove	F	X	
Tree swallow*	F		
Black-capped chickadee	F		
Mockingbird*	F	X	
Gray catbird*	F	X	
American robin*	F	X	
Hermit thrush*	F		
Veery	F		
Eastern bluebird*	F		
Cedar waxwing*	F		
Starling	F		
Yellow-rumped warbler	F		
House sparrow	F		
Common grackle	F		
Cardinal*	F	X	
Evening grosbeak	F		
Purple finch	F		
Rufous-sided towhee	F	X	
Northern junco	F	X	
Fox sparrow	F	X	
Song sparrow	F	X	

Note: *preferred food; F, fruit; [1]thickets provide good protective cover for many birds and mammals; [2]good nesting site for many songbirds.
Source: Allan and Steiner 1965.

Huckleberries *Gaylussacia* spp.
Four species of huckleberry occur in the Northeast. Each is discussed separately.

BLACK HUCKLEBERRY
Gaylussacia baccata (Wang.) K. Koch
ERICACEAE

Description. This deciduous shrub grows to 3 feet, with a crown spread of 2 to 4 feet. Another common name is high-bush huckleberry.
Leaves. Alternate, simple, 1 to 3 inches long, elliptic, without teeth, green above, yellowish beneath with yellow resin dots on both surfaces. Autumn color: red.
Flowers. Greenish-white or greenish-red in clusters on one-sided racemes, buds covered with resinous dots.
Fruits. Black, shiny berries occasionally blue or white, ¼-inch in diameter, sweet, edible.
Flowering period. May to June.
Fruiting period. July to September.
Habitat. Found in dry, rocky, and sandy acidic soil in open meadows and on forest floors. Commonly grows among blueberries.
Range. Newfoundland west to Saskatchewan, south to Georgia and Louisiana.
Hardiness zone. 2.
Landscape notes. Black huckleberry becomes an attractive ornamental shrub under cultivation. The sweet, firm, shiny fruits are as appealing to the palate as they are to the eye. It is useful in the yard wherever low shrubbery is desired or for naturalizing under trees and among rocks.
Propagation. Black huckleberry can be propagated by seed, hardwood cuttings, softwood cuttings, division, and layering. To plant from seed, collect fruits when ripe and remove pulp by mashing and washing. Viable seeds should sink when placed in a container of water. They can be sown immediately in a mixture of sand and peat or stratified for spring planting. To stratify, alternate day and night temperatures of seeds placed in peat between 68° F. (night) and 86° F. (day) for thirty days, followed by constant cooling at 50° F. Seeds should germinate during the cooling period (U.S. Forest Service 1948).

Birds That Use Black Huckleberry

	Food	Cover	Nesting[1]
Turkey	F	X	
Ruffed grouse	F	X	
Bobwhite	F	X	
Mourning dove	F	X	
Common flicker	F		
Blue jay	F		
Gray catbird*	F		
American robin	F		
Hermit thrush	F	X	
Eastern bluebird	F		
Pine grosbeak	F		
Rufous-sided towhee	F	X	

Note: *preferred food; F, fruit; [1]frequent nest site.
Sources: McKenny 1939; Petrides 1972; Davison 1967; Van Dersal 1938.

BOX HUCKLEBERRY
Gaylussacia brachycera (Michx.) Gray
ERICACEAE

Description. This is a low evergreen shrub, 6 to 18 inches tall.
Leaves. Alternate, simple, ¼- to 1 inch long, oval, with finely rounded teeth, dark green, thick and leathery.
Flowers. Small pink or white bells on small racemes.
Fruits. Small, rounded, black drupes.
Flowering period. May to June.
Fruiting period. July to August.
Habitat. Prefers dry, acidic, woodland soils.

Range. Maryland south to West Virginia, Tennessee, and Kentucky.

Hardiness zone. 6.

Landscape notes. This shrub may be used as a ground cover in woodlands where it spreads by creeping stems and forms thick masses. The dense foliage that forms on this low species gives protection to ground-feeding birds.

Propagation. Box huckleberry spreads naturally by rhizomes which send up new shoots. For general propagation information, see Lowbush Blueberry.

Bird uses. See Huckleberries.

Box Huckleberry

DWARF HUCKLEBERRY
Gaylussacia dumosa (Andr.) T. & G.
ERICACEAE

Description. This deciduous shrub is 1 to 2 feet tall.

Bark. Gray on stems, brownish and hairy on twigs.

Leaves. Alternate, simple, 1 to 1½ inches long, obovate to oblong or oblanceolate, without teeth, shiny green above, slightly hairy and covered with resin dots beneath.

Flowers. White, pink, or red bells, drooping on loose racemes.

Fruits. Round, black, shiny berries, ¼-inch in diameter, bland.

Flowering period. May to June.

Fruiting period. June to October.

Habitat. Low, sandy, acidic soils of wet meadows and bogs.

Range. Newfoundland south to Florida, west to Mississippi and Tennessee.

Hardiness zone. 5.

Landscape notes. Dwarf huckleberry is useful as a low ground cover in wet meadows and boggy areas.

Propagation. Plants can be grown from seed, cuttings, division, and layering, and are easily transplanted. See Lowbush Blueberry.

Birds That Use Dwarf Huckleberry
(See Huckleberries)

	Food	Cover	Nesting
Turkey	F		
Bobwhite	F	X	
Blue jay	F		
Mockingbird	F		
Gray catbird	F		
Cardinal	F		
Rufous-sided towhee	F	X	

Note: F, fruit.
Sources: McKenny 1939; Davison 1967.

DANGLEBERRY

Gaylussacia frondosa (L.) T. & G.

ERICACEAE

Description. This deciduous shrub is 3 to 6 feet tall. Other common names are bluetangle, tangleberry, and tall huckleberry.

Bark. Dark brown.

Leaves. Alternate, simple, 1 to 2 inches long, oblong or oval, margins without teeth, pale green above, pale and covered with small, resinous dots beneath. Autumn color: red.

Flowers. Greenish-pink, clustered along the stem in loose racemes.

Fruits. Dark-blue berries with whitish powder, ⅓-inch in diameter, sweet.

Flowering period. May to June.

Fruiting period. June to September.

Habitat. Prefers acidic soils with a pH of 4.5 to 6.0 (Spurway 1941) that are well-drained and exposed to full sunlight. Plants commonly grow in old fields and along borders of upland woods.

Range. Southern New Hampshire south to Florida, west to Ohio and Louisiana.

Hardiness zone. 5.

Landscape notes. In the Northeast, dangleberry is not as compact in branching habit or as prolific in fruit production as highbush huckleberry. Plants are attractive in borders and clumps on moist, well-drained soils.

Propagation. Dangleberry can be grown from seed, hardwood cuttings, softwood cuttings, division, and layering. Since little information is available on seed propagation, the use of vegetative techniques will probably result in greater success. Small plants can be successfully transplanted from the wild. See Highbush Blueberry.

Birds That Use Dangleberry
(See Huckleberries)

	Food	Cover	Nesting
Turkey	F	X	
Ruffed grouse	F	X	
Bobwhite	F	X	
Mourning dove	F	X	
Common flicker	F		
Blue jay	F		
Mockingbird	F		
Gray catbird	F		
Cedar waxwing	F		
Orchard oriole	F		
Scarlet tanager	F		
Pine grosbeak	F		
Rufous-sided towhee	F	X	

Note: F, fruit.
Sources: McKenny 1939; Van Dersal 1938.

Dangleberry

Birds That Use Huckleberries

	Food	Cover	Nesting
Turkey	F	X	
Ruffed grouse*	F	X	
Bobwhite	F	X	
Ring-necked pheasant	F		
Mourning dove	F	X	
Common flicker	F		
Red-headed woodpecker	F		
Eastern kingbird	F		
Great crested flycatcher	F		
Blue jay*	F		
Fish crow	F		
Mockingbird	F	X	X
Gray catbird*	F	X	X
Brown thrasher	F		
American robin	F	X	X
Wood thrush	F		
Hermit thrush	F	X	
Eastern bluebird	F		
Cedar waxwing	F		
Orchard oriole	F		
Scarlet tanager	F		
Pine grosbeak	F		
White-winged crossbill	F		
Rufous-sided towhee	F	X	

Note: *preferred food; F, fruit.
Sources: McKenny 1939; Davison 1967; Martin et al. 1951; Van Dersal 1938.

WITCH-HAZEL
Hamamelis virginiana L.
HAMAMELIDACEAE

Description. Witch-hazel is a fall flowering understory shrub of wide distribution. It grows 20 to 30 feet tall, with a spread of 20 to 25 feet. Just before flowering, the old seed capsules split, scattering the seed. Other common names are winter-bloom and snapping-alder.
Bark. Yellowish-gray, hairy.
Leaves. Alternate, simple, 2 to 6 inches long, obovate or oval to suborbicular, wavy toothed, straight veined. Autumn colors: bright yellow to brown.
Flowers. Yellow, ⅝- to ⅞-inch long, petals thin and curled.
Fruits. Obovoid capsule, ½- to ¾-inch long, densely covered with fine hairs.
Flowering period. September to November, after leaves have fallen.
Fruiting period. Spring to fall of second year.
Habitat. Commonly grows along edges of woods and fields and on banks of gullies in dry and rocky, or moist and fertile soils. Prefers sun or partial shade. Tolerates city conditions. Grows in a wide range of climatic conditions.
Range. Quebec south to Georgia west to Minnesota and Missouri.
Hardiness zone. 5.
Landscape notes. Witch-hazel is the last native shrub in the Northeast to flower in fall. Its dense foliage is effective in screening out unsightly views when planted in masses or hedgerows, and is useful for creating windbreaks for wildlife. Plants provide good background for lower ornamentals. They are very hardy and slow growing.
Propagation. Witch-hazel is difficult to transplant from the wild without prior root pruning (Robinson 1960). It can be propagated from cuttings or seeds. To obtain seeds from the wild, gather ripe fruits and store them in a dry place until seeds are ejected. They can be stored at 41° F. for at least one year (U.S.

Witch-hazel

Forest Service 1948). Ripe seeds, under natural conditions, ordinarily require two years in the ground to germinate (Van Dersal 1938), but those collected and stratified over the first winter should germinate in one year. Stratify the seeds in a mixture of sand and peat for sixty days at 68° F. (night) and 86° F. (days), followed by ninety days at 41° F. Seeds sown in late summer should be covered with mulch to prevent freezing, and uncovered upon germination. Stratified seeds may be sown in the spring as soon as the ground thaws. The soil should be kept moist (U.S. Forest Service 1948).

Cuttings should be placed in a sand medium early enough to allow for good root development before winter. Seed production is greater on plants receiving full or partial sunlight.

Birds That Use Witch-hazel

	Food	Cover	Nesting[1]
Turkey	S		
Ruffed grouse*	S, BD		
Bobwhite	S		
Ring-necked pheasant	S		
Cardinal	S		

Note: *preferred food; S, seeds; BD, buds; [1]only occasionally used as a nest site.
Sources: Martin et al. 1951; Davison 1967; Petrides 1972; Wood 1974b.

SHRUBBY ST. JOHNSWORT
Hypericum spathulatum (Spach) Steud.
GUTTIFERAE

Description. This coarse, stiff shrub has a rather widespread crown, and is all too uncommon as an ornamental. It grows 1 to 4 feet tall, occasionally to 7 feet, with a spread of 1 to 4 feet.
Bark. Reddish-brown and peeling.

Leaves. Opposite, simple, 1 to 3 inches long, narrowly oblong, surfaces a rich, shiny green covered with translucent dots. Autumn color: greenish-yellow.

Flowers. Yellow, 1 to 1½ inches in diameter, forming in upper leaf axils and on branch tips.

Fruits. Three-parted, reddish-brown capsules containing many seeds, persistent.

Flowering period. July to September.

Fruiting period. August, persistent into winter.

Habitat. Grows in open areas in rocky or sandy soil. Prefers partial shade.

Range. Massachusetts south to Georgia, west to Minnesota and Arkansas.

Hardiness zone. 5.

Landscape notes. These highly ornamental plants respond well to cultivation, growing to unusual heights (c. 7 feet) and producing abundant showy flowers from July to September. They are especially attractive in borders among other green shrubbery which enhances the blooms.

Propagation. Ripe seeds may be collected from the wild when capsules have turned brown, and broadcast over garden loam. Plants may also be propagated from late-summer cuttings of branch tips showing new growth. Cuttings should be rooted under high humidity (Hartmann and Kester 1968). Root cuttings and division are other techniques (Mahlstede and Haber 1957). If not too large, plants may be transplanted.

Birds That Use Shrubby St. Johnswort

	Food	Cover	Nesting
Ruffed grouse	S	X	
Bobwhite	S	X	
Ring-necked pheasant	S	X	
Northern junco	S	X	
Tree sparrow	S	X	

Note: S, seeds.
Sources: Davison 1967; Mason 1965.

INKBERRY
Ilex glabra (L.) Gray
AQUIFOLIACEAE

Description. The hollies are often difficult to identify because the group contains both deciduous and evergreen plants, with no obvious characteristic recurring throughout the family. This evergreen variety produces fruits especially valuable to birds because they persist through winter and spring. Inkberry grows 6 to 10 feet tall. Other common names are low gallberry holly, bitter gallberry, and evergreen winterberry.

Bark. Gray, twigs hairy.

Leaves. Alternate, simple, 1 to 3 inches long, oblanceolate to obovate, base tapering, usually a few teeth present near apex, leathery, remain bright green and shiny throughout the winter.

Flowers. Inconspicuous, male and female flowers occur on separate plants. Female flowers solitary. Male flowers clustered on long stalks.

Fruits. Glossy black drupes, ¼-inch in diameter, globular, solitary, very persistent.

Flowering period. March to June.

Fruiting period. Fall, persistent to spring.

Habitat. Commonly found in either sandy or peaty soil. Abundant in the acid soils of pine and oak barrens. Tolerates shade but prefers sunny situations.

Range. Isle au Haut, Maine, south along the coast to southern Florida and Louisiana.

Hardiness zone. 4.

Landscape notes. This is an attractive, small-to-medium-sized shrub with upright stems and a loose, branching habit which becomes more compact when cultivated. It has long been cultivated in England where it is valued for its striking year-round beauty. Inkberry is extremely hardy and grows slowly. It transplants well in almost any stage of growth—when dormant and stripped of its leaves—and can be pruned to improve shape and density. It adapts well to garden conditions

and tolerates shady, dry, and windy locations (Keeler 1969; U.S. Forest Service 1948).
Propagation. Fruits may be collected when ripe, and dried with the pulp on, or the pulp may be separated from the seeds by maceration. Seeds to be stored over winter may be dried thoroughly and placed in airtight containers at low temperatures or stratified in moist sand. Germination usually takes as long with scarification (one to three years) as with natural conditions because of dormancy. Scarification has not been very successful.

Plants may also be propagated by layering, cuttings, and grafting (U.S. Forest Service 1948).

Birds That Use Inkberry

	Food	Cover	Nesting
Turkey*	F		
Bobwhite	F		
Common flicker	F		
Mockingbird	F	X	X
American robin*	F	X	X
Hermit thrush	F		
Eastern bluebird	F		
Cedar waxwing*	F		
Rufous-sided towhee	F		

Note: *preferred food; F, fruit.
Sources: Davison 1967; McKenny 1939.

Inkberry

SMOOTH WINTERBERRY
Ilex laevigata (Pursh) Gray
AQUIFOLIACEAE

Description. Smooth winterberry resembles common winterberry, but its leaves are not as variable nor as wide as those of the latter. It grows 10 to 20 feet tall.
Bark. Stems gray, twigs and branches brownish-green.
Leaves. Alternate, simple, 2 to 3 inches long, oval to oblong with fine teeth on margins, shiny above, smooth beneath. Autumn color: bright yellow.
Flowers. Inconspicuous, male and female flowers form on separate plants. Male flowers occur singly or in pairs on slender stalks. Female flowers are solitary, sessile, or on short stalks in leaf axils.
Fruits. Bright red, berrylike drupes, ¼-inch in diameter. Larger than those of *I. verticillata* but not as persistent.
Flowering period. May to June.
Fruiting period. September to January.
Habitat. Wooded swamps and lowland thickets. Has greater tolerance to drier soils than does *I. verticillata*.
Range. Southern Maine to Georgia.
Hardiness zone. 5.
Landscape notes. The bright-red fruits give this hardy, slow-growing shrub an attractive appearance into late autumn after the leaves have fallen. For best results, plant several together to form a clump or hedge.
Propagation. See Common Winterberry.

Birds That Use Smooth Winterberry
(See Hollies)

	Food	Cover	Nesting
Bobwhite	F		
Common flicker	F		
Gray catbird*	F		
Brown thrasher*	F		
American robin*	F		
Hermit thrush*	F		

Note: *preferred food; F, fruit.
Source: McKenny 1939.

COMMON WINTERBERRY
Ilex verticillata (L.) Gray
AQUIFOLIACEAE

Description. In New England this widespread
deciduous holly is often called black alder. It
can become quite large—5 to 15 feet tall—
with many stems. This shrub is striking when
its leaves fall and the red fruits become fully
visible. Other common names are northern
holly and swamp holly.

Bark. Dark gray to black, smooth.

Leaves. Opposite, simple, pinnately veined, 2
to 3 inches long, oval, oblong to lanceolate
and serrate. Autumn colors: green until late
autumn, then brown to black.

Flowers. Small, greenish-white, male and female blossoms borne on separate plants. Male
flowers borne in clusters. Female flowers
borne singly or in small clusters.

Fruits. Bright scarlet drupes, 1/4- to 5/16-inch
in diameter, solitary or in clusters of twos or
threes. Persistent into winter.

Flowering period. April to July.

Fruiting period. August to October, persisting
into winter.

Habitat. Commonly found throughout the
Northeast on wet soils near swamps and
ponds or in wet woods. Will tolerate cool,
moist, upland soils. Prefers soils with fairly
high organic content and pH of 5.5 (Curtis
1959). Best growth occurs in full sun or partial
shade away from aggressive competitors.
However, moist, shady locations are sug-
gested for landscaping (Kammerer 1934; Holweg 1974).

Range. Newfoundland west to Minnesota,
south to Missouri and Georgia.

Hardiness zone. 4.

Landscape notes. This erect-growing, handsome
shrub is useful for enhancing pond shores
and other low, moist ground. Deep-scarlet,
persistent berries contrasting with dark-gray
bark give plants ornamental value long after
the leaves have dropped. They are excellent
for Christmas decorations. Hardy and slow
growing, common winterberry is becoming

Common Winterberry

[113] Shrubs

available at nurseries and garden centers because of its striking landscape values.

Propagation. Common winterberry reproduces naturally by means of seed, suckers, and layering. Seedlings and rooted cuttings can be purchased from nurseries or can be propagated. Small shoots may be separated from parent plants when at least two years old and transplanted. Male and female plants should flower simultaneously and should be located within 40 feet of each other for best cross-pollination and fruit production (Link 1945).

Plants should bear fruits in three to five years (Spinner and Ostrum 1945). To start plants from seed, gather seeds when fresh, and sow or stratify immediately. Or if later planting is desired, dry and refrigerate at low temperatures in airtight containers. Seeds will remain viable for up to one year. Seeds sown immediately after they are collected will normally germinate the second spring (Kains 1938). If stratified in moist sand for two months at 68° F. (night) and 86° F. (day), followed by a cooler period of two months at 41° F. (day and night) and left in the moist sand for an additional sixty days, seeds should germinate the first spring (U.S. Forest Service 1948).

Foliated summer and hardwood cuttings that are 3 to 6 inches long will develop roots in approximately eighteen days if they are treated with growth hormone on the lower third of the stem, put into moist peat moss, and covered with glass or plastic to maintain high humidity. They should be kept at 80° F. (Holweg 1974).

Birds That Use Common Winterberry
(See Hollies)

	Food	Cover	Nesting
Black duck	F		
Bobwhite	F		
Common flicker	F		
Common crow	F		
Mockingbird*	F		
Gray catbird*	F		
Brown thrasher*	F		

	Food	Cover	Nesting
American robin	F		
Hermit thrush*	F		
Veery	F	X	X
Cedar waxwing	F		
Red-winged blackbird	F	X	X

Note: *preferred food; F, fruit.
Sources: McKenny 1938; Davison 1967.

Birds That Use Hollies

	Food	Cover	Nesting
Black duck	F		
Wood duck	F		
Turkey*	F		
Ruffed grouse	F		
Bobwhite	F		
Ring-necked pheasant	F		
Mourning dove	F		
Common flicker	F		
Pileated woodpecker*	F		
Red-bellied woodpecker	F		
Yellow-bellied sapsucker*	F, sap		
Eastern phoebe	F		
Common crow	F		
Mockingbird*	F	X	X
Gray catbird*	F		
Brown thrasher*	F		
American robin*	F	X	X
Wood thrush	F		
Hermit thrush*	F		
Swainson's thrush*	F		
Gray-cheeked thrush	F		
Veery	F	X	X
Eastern bluebird*	F		
Cedar waxwing*	F		
White-eyed vireo	F		
Red-winged blackbird		X	X
Cardinal	F		
Purple finch	F		
Rufous-sided towhee	F		
White-throated sparrow	F		

Note: *preferred food; F, fruit.
Sources: Davison 1967; McKenny 1939; Martin et al. 1951; Petit 1949; National Wildlife Federation 1974.

[114]

COMMON JUNIPER
Juniperus communis L.
PINACEAE

Description. In the Northeast, common or pasture juniper grows as a dense, prickly shrub. It invades pastures and old fields where it may grow 1 to 4 feet tall, with a spread of 8 to 12 feet or more. Other common names are pasture juniper, dwarf juniper, and old field juniper.

Bark. Reddish-brown, shreddy.

Leaves. Sharp, grooved, three-sided needles, ¼- to ⅞-inch long, in whorls of 3, whitish above, aromatic.

Flowers. Small, inconspicuous sporophylls, male and female form on same or separate plants.

Fruits. Hard, round, blue-black berries, ¼-inch in diameter, covered with white powder, each containing 2 to 4 seeds. Take two years to mature, may persist for three years.

Flowering period. May.

Fruiting period. September to November.

Habitat. Common on hillsides and sandy plains on a variety of soils. Tolerates sterile conditions and strong winds. In New England, it often grows in abandoned pastures undergoing early stages of secondary succession.

Range. Canada south through New England to the mountains of Georgia, west to California.

Hardiness zone. 2.

Landscape notes. This is an excellent cover shrub for sandy waste places and low-nutrient soils. It grows well on embankments. Plants are hardy, slow growing, and easily transplanted. In the wild, this juniper becomes established adjacent to exposed pasture stumps or stones on which robins alight, and, having fed on the berries, deposit seed (Livingston 1972).

Propagation. Plants can be propagated by stem cuttings of softwood taken early in the growing season, or by hardwood cuttings made in October, November, and December. Both

should be treated with root-inducing hormone, inserted in sand, and soaked thoroughly. They should be placed in a cold frame for the winter. In cold areas, the frame should be covered with a sash and further protected with an old blanket or layer of hay over the entire frame (Free 1957). Both should be field-planted when sturdy roots develop. They can be successfully transplanted when a large root ball is taken to prevent root disturbance and drying.

Seeds of *Juniperus communis* have impermeable coats and under natural conditions germinate the second or third spring following dispersal (U.S. Forest Service 1948). To propagate from seed, store fruits for one year. Then clean and scarify them in sulfuric acid and sow ¼-inch deep in rich soil in the fall. Germination should take place the following spring (U.S. Forest Service 1948).

Birds That Use Common Juniper

	Food	Cover	Nesting
Ruffed grouse	F	X	
Bobwhite	F	X	
Ring-necked pheasant	F	X	
Common flicker	F		
Downy woodpecker	F		
Mockingbird	F		
Gray catbird	F		
American robin*	F		
Eastern bluebird*	F		
Cedar waxwing*	F		
Yellow-rumped warbler	F		
Evening grosbeak*	F		
Purple finch*	F		
Pine grosbeak*	F		
Chipping sparrow		X	X

Note: *preferred food; F, fruit.
Sources: McKenny 1939; Petrides 1972; Martin et al. 1951; Mason 1965.

COMMON SPICEBUSH
Lindera benzoin (L.) Blume
LAURACEAE

Description. This common but scattered forest understory shrub occurs throughout the eastern United States. The fruits are preferred by many songbirds. It grows to 15 feet with a spread of 2 to 8 feet. Other common names are allspice bush and feverbush.
Bark. Olive green, with a spicy fragrance when bruised.
Leaves. Alternate, simple, 3 to 6 inches long, ½- to 3 inches wide, narrow and wedge-shaped at the base. Autumn color: yellow.
Flowers. Small, greenish-yellow blossoms forming in clusters in the axils of the previous year's leaves, each cluster composed of secondary clusters of 4 to 6 flowers. Flowers develop before the leaves.
Fruits. Thin-skinned, aromatic scarlet drupes about ½-inch long, forming singly or in groups of up to five.
Flowering period. March to May, before the leaves.
Fruiting period. July to October.
Habitat. Grows in moist, fertile soil of northern slopes, river bottomlands, and along woodland streams. In the Northeast it can often be found growing in the shade of hardwoods such as sugar and red maples, beech, and birch (Wood 1974a).
Range. Southwestern Maine, south to Florida, west to Iowa and Kansas.
Hardiness zone. 5.
Landscape notes. This shrub is lovely when blossoming in the spring and when fruiting in the fall. It is useful as an understory or border shrub, singly or in clumps.
Propagation. Spicebush reproduces naturally from seeds, sprouts, and suckers. Propagation may be difficult because seeds ordinarily lose their viability quickly (U.S. Forest Service 1948) and cuttings usually do not root easily (Hottes 1931). September cuttings of shoots

Common Spicebush

have been successfully propagated (Doran 1957; Osborn 1933).

Fruits should be picked when ripe in September or October, separated from the pulp, and air-dried. Seed growth may be induced by stratification by exposing seeds to 77° F. temperatures for 15 to 30 days, followed by exposure at 41° F. for 90 to 120 days. If seeds are sown in the fall, cover them with mulch and remove it in the spring (U.S. Forest Service 1948). Where winters are severe, stratify the seeds below the frost line in the fall and remove and plant them in rich, moist soil the following spring. They will probably do best in full sunlight or partial shade where there is adequate moisture (Wood 1974a). Plants are very hardy and slow growing.

Birds That Use Common Spicebush

	Food	Cover	Nesting[1]
Ruffed grouse	F		
Bobwhite	F		
Ring-necked pheasant	F		
Common flicker	F		
Eastern kingbird	F		
Great crested flycatcher	F		
Gray catbird	F		
American robin	F		
Wood thrush*	F		
Hermit thrush	F		
Gray-cheeked thrush	F		
Veery*	F		
Red-eyed vireo	F		
Cardinal	F		
White-throated sparrow	F		

Note: *preferred food; F, fruit; [1]not usually used as a nest site.
Sources: Martin et al. 1951; Davison 1967; Petrides 1972.

HONEYSUCKLES
Lonicera spp.
CAPRIFOLIACEAE

Description. Six honeysuckles are included: two native species and four introduced and naturalized species. Honeysuckles grow up to 10 feet, occasionally taller, with a spread of 6 to 10 feet.

Bark. Gray or brown, often papery on branches and twigs.

Leaves. Opposite, simple, oval or oblong, margins without teeth, upper leaves not united on shrub forms. Autumn colors: yellow, green, or blue-green.

Flowers. Blossoms are generally white, pink, or red, occasionally yellow or even purple.

Fruits. Berries with several seeds, usually red or yellow.

Habitat. Found in a variety of habitats but most commonly grow on soils that are rich and moist. Thrive in sun or shade in waste areas along roadsides, hedgerows, and neglected fields.

Landscape notes. Species introduced from Europe and Asia have greater ornamental value than do native plants. All plants take well to any good garden soil and are valued for their flowers, foliage, and fruits. They are handsome standing alone, in clumps, or in long hedges where they serve as windbreaks, snow fences, and provide shelter for wildlife. They are hardy, usually grow rapidly, and require little care.

Propagation. Seeds and seedlings of exotic honeysuckle species are available from some nurseries. Seeds and seedlings of native species may be collected in the wild. Fruits should be collected when ripe, and the seeds separated from the pulp by maceration. They may be dried for a short period and stored in sealed containers at 34°–38° F. (U.S. Forest Service 1948; Heit 1967d).

Lonicera oblongifolia may be sown immediately or stratified in peat for sixty days at 68° F. (night) and 86° F. (day), followed by ninety days at 41° F. (U.S. Forest Service 1948).

Lonicera tatarica may be stratified in sand or peat for thirty to sixty days at 41° F. (U.S. Forest Service 1948).

Hardwood and softwood cuttings may be treated with root-inducing hormone and inserted in sand or a sand-peat mixture (Doran 1957). They should be watered thoroughly.

Birds That Use Honeysuckles [1]

	Food	Cover	Nesting
Turkey	F	X	
Ruffed grouse	F	X	
Bobwhite	F	X	
Ring-necked pheasant	F	X	
Ruby-throated hummingbird	N		
Common flicker	F		
Eastern kingbird	F		
Mockingbird	F	X	X
Gray catbird*	F	X	X
Brown thrasher	F	X	X
American robin*	F		
Hermit thrush	F		
Eastern bluebird	F		
Cedar waxwing	F		
Starling	F		
Evening grosbeak	F		
Purple finch	F		
Pine grosbeak	F		
American goldfinch*	F		
Northern junco	F	X	
White-throated sparrow	F	X	

Note: [1]Most species of honeysuckles are used by wildlife. Native species are generally less prolific bearers of fruit and foliage than are introduced species, but are more widespread; therefore, their overall wildlife values are not diminished. *L. maackii* is especially valuable for birds because it holds its profuse fruit crops through late fall; *preferred food; F, fruit; N, nectar.
Source: U.S. Soil Conservation Service 1966.

Amur Honeysuckle

Tatarian Honeysuckle

Six Common Northeastern Honeysuckles, Lonicera *spp.*

Species	Height	Leaves	Flowering		Fruiting		Range
			Period	Color	Period	Color	
NATIVE							
American Fly Honeysuckle L. canadensis	3'–5'	1"–3"	April to June	yellowish-green	June to August	red	Rich, cool woodlands of Quebec S to mountains of North Carolina. Hardiness zone: 4.
Swamp Fly Honeysuckle L. oblongifolia	2'–5'	1"–3½"	May to July	greenish-yellow, fragrant	July to September	deep red	Wet woodlands of Quebec S to Pennsylvania, W to Minnesota. Hardiness zone: 4.
INTRODUCED AND NATURALIZED							
Tatarian Honeysuckle L. tatarica	to 10'	1½"–2½"	May to June	pink or white, very fragrant	June to November	red or yellow	Intro. from Eurasia. Escaped from cultivation. Quebec S to Kentucky, W to Iowa. Hardiness zone: 4.
Standish Honeysuckle L. standishi	5'–6'	2"–4"	April	white	June to August	red	Intro. from Asia. Escaped from cultivation on Long Island and in New York State. Hardiness zone: 5.
Amur Honeysuckle L. maackii	to 15'	1½"–2½"	May to July	white, becoming yellowish	July to November	red	Intro. from Korea, Manchuria. Escaped from cultivation. New England S to Pennsylvania, W to Michigan. Hardiness zone: 2.
Morrow Honeysuckle L. Morrowi	6'–8'	1"–2"	May to June	white or yellow	June to August	red or yellow	Intro. from Eurasia. Escaped from cultivation. Maine to Pennsylvania, W to Michigan. Hardiness zone: 5.

NORTHERN BAYBERRY
Myrica pensylvanica Loisel.
MYRICACEAE

Description. Northern bayberry is a common deciduous shrub of northeastern seacoasts and dune areas, where red-winged blackbirds commonly use it for nesting. Many birds eat the waxy berries. It grows 3 to 8 feet tall. Another common name is candleberry.

Bark. Brownish-gray, aromatic, twigs covered with droplets of resin.

Leaves. Alternate, simple, 2 to 5 inches long with a few rounded teeth at tips, bright green and leathery when mature, lightly covered with resin dots. Autumn colors: bronze or dark green.

Flowers. Small, inconspicuous, male and female flowers form on separate plants.

Fruits. Small, waxy berries, pale gray when ripe, 1/8-inch in diameter, aromatic, borne in clusters along main stems, persistent for two to three years.

Flowering period. May to July.

Fruiting period. June to April, very persistent.

Habitat. Grows on dry, sandy sites inland and along the coast.

Range. Newfoundland south to North Carolina, west to the Great Lakes.

Hardiness zone. 2.

Landscape notes. This highly adaptable hardy plant will grow in swampy soil and on sand dunes. It is a good border shrub for dry, exposed areas and is excellent for controlling erosion of poor soils. In wind-free locations, the bronze-green leaves may persist throughout winter but usually they are blown off, revealing the shrub's angular twigginess and clusters of berries.

Propagation. Plants can be propagated from seeds and stem cuttings. Seeding can be done in the fall by broadcasting or by spacing at 4-foot intervals and covering with mulch. Waxy seed coats must be removed before planting. For spring sowing, remove seed coats and chill seeds for sixty to ninety days at 41° F. in order to break dormancy (Zak et al. 1972).

Northern Bayberry

[121] Shrubs

Two-year-old seedlings obtained from nurseries can be planted in sandy soil. Avoid sod. Mulch plants for the first two years with straw, sawdust, or wood chips (U.S. Soil Conservation Service 1960).

Birds That Use Northern Bayberry

	Food	Cover[1]	Nesting[2]
Turkey	F		
Ruffed grouse	F		
Bobwhite	F		
Ring-necked pheasant	F		
Common flicker	F		
Red-bellied woodpecker*	F		
Downy woodpecker	F		
Eastern phoebe	F		
Tree swallow*	F		
Common crow	F		
Fish crow	F		
Black-capped chickadee	F		
Carolina chickadee	F		
Carolina wren	F		
Mockingbird	F		
Gray catbird*	F		
Brown thrasher*	F		
Hermit thrush	F		
Eastern bluebird*	F		
Red-winged blackbird		X	X
Starling*	F		
Eastern meadowlark*	F		
White-eyed vireo*	F		
Yellow-rumped warbler*	F		
Scarlet tanager	F		
Rufous-sided towhee	F		

Note: *preferred food; F, fruit; [1]provides excellent protection for songbirds when grown in larger thickets; [2]furnishes good nest sites for songbirds. Sources: Martin et al. 1951; Petrides 1972; Davison 1967; McKenny 1939.

SCARLET FIRETHORN
Pyracantha coccinea Roem.
ROSACEAE

Description. This shrub, which may grow to 8 feet (occasionally taller), is especially popular in southern areas of the Northeast and southward where it has escaped from cultivation. It is valued for its flat-topped clusters of small but conspicuous white flowers in summer and for its masses of small, brilliant reddish-orange berries in fall and winter. Other common names are pyracantha and evergreen thorn.
Bark. Gray on young branches, thorny.
Leaves. Evergreen in the South, deciduous in the Northeast, alternate, simple, ½- to 2 inches long, narrowly oval or oblanceolate with wedge-shaped bases and rounded or pointed tips, wavy margins, upper surfaces dark shiny green when leaves are mature.
Flowers. White, ¼-inch in diameter, forming in clusters about 1½ inches across.
Fruits. Bright reddish-orange berries, ¼-inch in diameter, forming in dense clusters, bitter.
Flowering period. May to June.
Fruiting period. September to April.
Habitat. Introduced from Europe and naturalized in thickets, in fence-rows, and along roadsides.
Range. Pennsylvania, south to Florida, west to Louisiana.
Hardiness zone. 6.
Landscape notes. This plant is very handsome, especially when in fruit. It is useful along walls where it can be pruned and trained artistically. It is also good for formal hedges and shrub borders as well as rocky slopes. It does well in many soil types that are well drained and exposed to sunlight.
Propagation. Plants are usually propagated by taking cuttings of stems that developed during the most recent growing season. Cuttings develop good root systems in a greenhouse or in mist-propagating beds, and should be ready to transplant in six months (Hartmann and Kester 1968).

Firethorn may be grown from seeds that have been stratified as soon as ripe, or stored for no longer than one year in airtight containers and then stratified. The stratification process calls for three months at 40° F. (Wyman 1977).

Birds That Use Scarlet Firethorn

	Food	Cover	Nesting
Bobwhite	F		
Pileated woodpecker*	F		
Blue jay	F		
Gray catbird*	F		
Brown thrasher*	F		
Mockingbird*	F		
American robin*	F		
Eastern bluebird*	F		
Hermit thrush	F		
Wood thrush	F		
Cedar waxwing*	F		
Purple finch*	F		
Cardinal	F		
Fox sparrow	F		
House sparrow	F		
Song sparrow	F		
White-crowned sparrow	F		

Note: *preferred food; F, fruit.
Sources: Davison 1967; Martin et al. 1951.

Scarlet Firethorn

ALDERLEAF BUCKTHORN
Rhamnus alnifolia L'Her.
RHAMNACEAE

Description. Alderleaf buckthorn is a low-growing shrub, commonly 2 to 3 feet tall.
Bark. Mature stems have gray outer bark, yellowish inner bark.
Leaves. Alternate, simple, 2 to 4 inches long, elliptic with prominent veins which tend to curve along leaf edges, dark green when mature. Autumn color: green.
Flowers. Small, yellow, inconspicuous, male and female flowers usually borne on separate plants.
Fruits. Small, fleshy, black drupes, 1/5-inch in diameter, containing two to four flat seeds.
Flowering period. May to July.
Fruiting period. August to October.
Habitat. Occurs in damp to wet soils of low woodlands and swamps.
Range. Newfoundland west to British Columbia, south to northern California and West Virginia.
Hardiness zone. 5.
Landscape notes. The black fruits and dark green leaves of alderleaf buckthorn are very ornamental. The dense foliage makes it an ideal choice for borders and clumps. It grows

easily under cultivation, is hardy, and has a moderate growth rate.

Propagation. Plants can be propagated from seeds which have been collected from ripe fruits in late summer or fall. The easiest means of separating seeds from pulp is by maceration. After seeds are thoroughly dry, they may be sown immediately or stored at 41° F. in sealed containers, where they should retain viability for two years (U.S. Forest Service 1948).

Natural germination normally occurs the first spring after seed dispersal. Germination can be induced earlier if seeds are stratified in moist sand for sixty to ninety days at 41° F. (U.S. Forest Service 1948). Seeds should be sown in drills 8 inches apart, covered with ½-inch of soil, and kept moist. Occasionally buckthorns are propagated by layering, cuttings, and grafting (U.S. Forest Service 1948).

Bird uses. See Buckthorns.

COMMON BUCKTHORN
Rhamnus cathartica L.
RHAMNACEAE

Description. This buckthorn is European in origin, and is the only buckthorn with spines. It can grow to 25 feet but is more commonly 12 feet tall or less.

Bark. Dark brown, branch tips bear leafy thorns.

Leaves. Alternate, often opposite, simple, 1 to 2½ inches long, elliptic or broadly ovate, teeth rounded, surfaces smooth, dark green above, paler below. Autumn color: green well into autumn.

Flowers. Small, green, inconspicuous flowers form in the leaf axils in early summer, male and female flowers on separate plants.

Fruits. Small, shiny, black drupes, 1/5-inch in diameter, persisting into winter. Production usually begins when plants are five to seven years old.

Flowering period. April to July.

Fruiting period. June to October, persisting into winter.

Habitat. Tolerates a variety of soils. Grows well in sun or shade in open woods, pastures, and fence-rows.

Range. Introduced from Europe and Asia but now naturalized in much of the northeastern United States.

Hardiness zone. 2.

Landscape notes. A useful hedge plant, common buckthorn adapts well to most soils and withstands city smoke. It is an excellent background shrub for lower-growing, colorful plants. The juice of its berries is used for producing dyes. Roots do not send up suckers. Plants are easily transplanted, tolerate heavy pruning, and need little care. They are hardy and have a moderate growth rate. The foliage reaches to the ground (Keeler 1969; Robinson 1960).

Propagation. Methods are similar to those of alder buckthorn. Common buckthorn seedlings prefer drier soils so require less water for good development.

Bird uses. See Buckthorns.

GLOSSY BUCKTHORN
Rhamnus frangula L.
RHAMNACEAE

Description. This European species has been grown in the United States since colonial times. It has escaped from cultivation and is a common understory shrub in moist northeastern forests. Glossy buckthorn grows 8 to 12 feet tall, with a spread of 6 to 10 feet. Its foliage is low to the ground. Another common name is European buckthorn.

Bark. Reddish-brown with prominent white lenticels, young twigs covered with fine, soft hairs.

Leaves. Alternate, simple, 1½ to 3 inches long, oval, with prominent veins, dark, glossy green above, hairy beneath, without teeth.

Flowers. Small, whitish, inconspicuous in small, sessile umbels.

Fruits. Small, round drupes, ¼-inch in diameter, red changing to dark purple or black, not persistent.

Flowering period. May to July.

Fruiting period. July to October.

Habitat. Commonly seen in fence-rows, thickets, and open woods on many types of soil. Prefers full or partial shade.

Range. Introduced from Europe and naturalized throughout the Northeast. Nova Scotia south to New Jersey, west to Minnesota and Illinois.

Hardiness zone. 2.

Landscape notes. The large rounded crown with compact spreading branches and dense foliage and fruits give the shrub a pleasing appearance. The dark green leaves are particularly striking. An ornamental variety, *R.f. Columnaris*, is commercially available. Glossy buckthorn is attractive alone or in masses. It does especially well in peaty soils.

Propagation. See Alderleaf Buckthorn.

Bird uses. See Buckthorns.

Birds That Use Buckthorns

	Food	Cover	Nesting
Ruffed grouse	F		
Ring-necked pheasant	F		
Pileated woodpecker*	F		
Hairy woodpecker	F		
Downy woodpecker	F		
Eastern kingbird	F		
Great crested flycatcher	F		
Mockingbird*	F		
Gray catbird*	F		
Brown thrasher*	F		
American robin	F		
Wood thrush	F		
Hermit thrush	F		
Cedar waxwing	F		
Northern oriole	F		

Note: *preferred food; F, fruit.

Sources: Schutz 1974; Martin et al. 1951; Mason 1965.

FLAMELEAF SUMAC
Rhus copallina L.
ANACARDIACEAE

Description. Flameleaf or winged sumac is usually a small shrub—4 to 10 feet tall—that forms a thicket. Its main wildlife value is as an emergency food. Other common names are dwarf sumac, shining sumac, wing-rib sumac, and mountain sumac.

Bark. Old stems dark, smooth, grayish-yellow, twigs dotted and velvety.

Leaves. Alternate, compound, 6 to 14 inches long with 11 to 23 linear-to-oblong leaflets, margins smooth, deep, shiny green on surfaces, thin wings along mid-rib. Autumn color: crimson.

Flowers. Inconspicuous, green, on loose panicles.

Fruits. Small drupes about ¼-inch in diameter form in dense crimson clusters. Not as persistent as staghorn sumac, but plants often retain them through winter.

Flowering period. July to September.

Fruiting period. Fall.

Habitat. Dry woods and upland clearings. Often forms hedgerows along fields and pastures. Tolerates many types of soils, in sun or partial shade.

Range. Southern Maine west to Michigan, south to Texas and Florida.

Hardiness zone. 5.

Landscape notes. This sumac is valued for its foliage in summer and colorful fruits in fall. It is good for naturalizing rocky, sterile soils, and should be planted in large areas where it can spread freely and form thickets. Young plants are dense and compact becoming more open, twisted, and picturesque with age. Old trunks and stems can be cut back to the ground in order to reestablish young stands. It transplants easily, is hardy, grows rapidly, needs little or no care, and prefers full sunlight.

Propagation. See Staghorn Sumac and Smooth Sumac.

Bird uses. See Sumacs.

SMOOTH SUMAC
Rhus glabra L.
ANACARDIACEAE

Description. Smooth sumac is a common invader of abandoned fields. Like flameleaf sumac (*R. copallina*), its wildlife value is as an emergency food source. Other common names are scarlet sumac, vinegar tree, and upland sumac.

Bark. Dark and smooth, twigs hairless.

Leaves. Alternate, compound, 12 to 24 inches long with 11 to 31 leaflets that are oblong to lanceolate and serrated, mature leaflets are pale below, deep green above. Autumn colors: red to orange.

Flowers. Small, green, form in dense clusters on tips of branches above the leaves.

Fruits. Small, red, one-seeded drupes, ¼-inch in diameter, covered with short hairs. Up to 700 seeds per fruiting head (Lovell 1964). Commonly remain on plants until the following summer.

Flowering period. June to August.

Fruiting period. August to October, persistent to the following summer.

Habitat. Typically found in well-drained soils along roadsides, borders of fields, and clear-cut areas. Common on abandoned farmland, and frequently found growing in association with eastern red cedar, blackberries, common juniper, and old field pioneer herbs (Smith 1974).

Range. Maine south to Florida, west to California.

Hardiness zone. 2.

Landscape notes. Smooth sumac is handsome when allowed to develop into a wide-spreading clone. It is a good species for dry soils and open slopes. Hardy and rapid growing, it needs little or no care, but it does need full sunlight for optimum growth.

Propagation. Seeds may be obtained from a commercial supplier, or collected from wild plants from September to December (Smith 1974). If collected from the wild, the seeds must be separated from their tough cases. This is accomplished by drying the fruits for three days at 110° F. and mechanically splitting the tough pericarps. If a large number of seeds is desired, the dried fruits may be placed in a cloth bag and pounded vigorously against a hard surface. The viable seeds can be separated from the others by placing the entire collection in a pan of water. Viable seeds will sink to the bottom and nonviable ones will rise to the surface where they can easily be removed (Smith 1970). Seeds may be air-dried and sealed in glass containers for storage. Before planting, they should be scarified by placing them in concentrated sulfuric acid for one to four hours, then washed and dried (Heit 1967b; Smith 1970). Seeds should be sown in fall or spring, ¼- to ½-inch deep in sandy loam. This species can be transplanted from a wild source if plants are 6 inches or less in height. It may also be propagated from root cuttings taken in December (Smith 1970; Edminster 1947; Doran 1957).

Birds That Use Smooth Sumac
(See Sumacs)

	Food	Cover[1]	Nesting
Turkey	F		
Ruffed grouse	F		
Bobwhite	F		
Ring-necked pheasant	F		
Common flicker	F		
Red-headed woodpecker	F		
Blue jay	F		
Common crow*	F		
Mockingbird*	F		
Gray catbird*	F		
Brown thrasher	F		
American robin	F		
Wood thrush*	F		
Hermit thrush	F		
Eastern bluebird*	F		
Starling	F		
Red-eyed vireo	F		
Yellow-rumped warbler	F		
Cardinal	F		
Pine grosbeak	F		
Purple finch	F		

Note: *preferred food; F, fruit; [1]provides good cover for birds and mammals in summer and emergency food in winter, but little or no fall and winter cover. Sources: Davison 1967; McKenny 1939.

STAGHORN SUMAC
Rhus typhina L.
ANACARDIACEAE

Description. Staghorn sumac is a shrub or small tree, and like smooth sumac (*R. glabra*), grows in a circular clone that spreads by root sprouts. Other common names are hairy sumac and velvet sumac.

Bark. Stems very hairy and sticky, twigs hairy, resembling velvet.

Leaves. Alternate, compound, 12 to 24 inches long with 11 to 31 oblong to lanceolate leaflets, margins toothed, surface bright green, undersides paler. Autumn color: orange-red.

Flowers. Yellow-green, forming in dense terminal panicles, inconspicuous, fragrant.

Fruits. Small drupes, ¼-inch in diameter, hairy, one-seeded, forming in compact clusters, bright red and persistent to spring. Clusters may contain up to 700 seeds (Lovell 1964).

Flowering period. May to July.

Fruiting period. August to September, persistent through winter.

Habitat. Usually forms clumps or hedgerows on well-drained soils of field margins, roadsides, and burned-over areas.

Range. Quebec west to Ontario and Minnesota, south to Tennessee and Georgia.

Hardiness zone. 4.

Landscape notes. Staghorn sumac grows well on steep banks and in low-nutrient soils where it has room to spread freely. The brilliant fruiting heads are highly ornamental in autumn. The flat-topped, dense stands are attractive during the entire growing season. A stand is particularly striking when surrounded by an expanse of low vegetation creating an island effect. When desired, suckers may be removed to encourage the formation of an attractive, twisted specimen. Plants are hardy, grow rapidly, and require little or no care. They will grow in sun or shade.

Propagation. Plants may be propagated from seeds, stem cuttings, and root cuttings. Seeds and stock are not readily obtained from commercial suppliers but can be gathered from plants growing wild. Seeds should be separated from the fruits in the following manner: place ripe fruits in a cloth bag and pound the bag against a hard surface for several minutes; dump contents of bag into a pan of water and stir; viable seeds will sink, while nonviable seeds and other debris will float to the surface where they can easily be skimmed off (Smith 1970). Air-dry viable seeds and store in sealed, glass containers.

Hard seed coats require scarification in concentrated sulfuric acid for one to four hours (Heit 1967b; Smith 1970) followed by washing and drying. Sow in fall or spring, 1/4- to 1/2-inch deep in moist sand or sandy loam. The germination period for properly treated seeds is about ten days (Smith 1970).

Root cuttings and stem cuttings can be taken in late fall. When transplanting young plants to dry ground, water well.

Birds That Use Staghorn Sumac
(See Sumacs)

	Food	Cover[1]	Nesting[2]
Turkey	F		
Ruffed grouse	F		
Bobwhite	F		
Ring-necked pheasant	F		
Common flicker	F		
Red-headed woodpecker	F		
Blue jay	F		
Common crow	F		
Black-capped chickadee	F		
Mockingbird	F		
Gray catbird	F		
Brown thrasher	F		
American robin	F		
Hermit thrush	F		
Eastern bluebird	F		
Cedar waxwing	F		
Starling	F		
Red-eyed vireo	F		
Cardinal	F		

Staghorn Sumac

	Food	Cover	Nesting[2]
Evening grosbeak	F		
Pine grosbeak	F		

Note: F, fruit; [1]provides cover in summer, but little in fall or winter; [2]not a common nest site.
Sources: McKenny 1939; Davison 1967.

Birds That Use Sumacs

	Food	Cover[1]	Nesting[2]
Turkey*	F		
Ruffed grouse*	F		
Bobwhite*	F		
Ring-necked pheasant*	F		
Common flicker	F		
Pileated woodpecker	F		
Downy woodpecker	F		
Eastern phoebe*	F		
Blue jay	F		
Gray jay	F		
Common crow*	F		
Fish crow	F		
Mockingbird*	F		
Gray catbird*	F		
Brown thrasher*	F		
American robin*	F		
Wood thrush*	F		
Hermit thrush*	F		
Swainson's thrush	F		
Veery	F		
Eastern bluebird*	F		
Starling*	F		
Red-eyed vireo	F		
Warbling vireo	F		
Yellow-rumped warbler	F		
Pine warbler	F		
Scarlet tanager	F		
Cardinal*	F		
Pine grosbeak	F		
Purple finch	F		
Northern junco	F		

Note: *preferred food; F, fruit; [1]because of their leggy growth, sumacs offer little winter cover for wildlife, but give protection in spring and summer when foliage is fully developed; [2]few birds are known to nest in the branches, but ground-nesting birds are known to nest at the base among the stems.
Sources: Martin et al. 1951; Davison 1967.

AMERICAN BLACK CURRANT
Ribes americanum Mill.
SAXIFRAGACEAE

Description. The fruits of black currants are choice foods of many birds, but shrubs of this genus are alternate hosts for white pine blister rust, a fungus disease. Attempts have been made to eradicate wild currant and gooseberry where white pine is an important timber tree. Another common name is wild black currant.

Leaves. Alternate or clustered, simple, ½- to 4 inches long, 3 to 5 lobes, margins double-toothed and hairy beneath. Autumn color: yellowish-green.

Flowers. Yellow or white, bell-shaped, ¼-inch long, clustered loosely on drooping racemes.

Fruits. Round, smooth, black berry ¼-inch in diameter, dotted with resin.

Flowering period. April to June.

Fruiting period. June to September.

Habitat. Commonly found in rich and poor soils on slopes and in lowlands.

Range. Nova Scotia south to Kentucky, west to Nebraska.

Hardiness zone. 5.

Landscape notes. American black currant grows to 5 feet and becomes a lovely spreading shrub under cultivation. It is particularly useful for naturalizing areas such as dry embankments that do not readily support growth. It is hardy and has a moderate growth rate.

Propagation. Seeds may be stratified in sand or peat for 200 days at 41°–45° F. to break embryo dormancy (U.S. Forest Service 1948). See Pasture Gooseberry.

Bird uses. See Gooseberries.

PASTURE GOOSEBERRY
Ribes cynosbati L.
SAXIFRAGACEAE

Description. Pasture gooseberry is a thorny shrub, 3 to 4 feet tall. It is a frequent nest site of several songbirds, and its fruits are relished by birds. Other common names are prickly wild gooseberry and dogberry.

Bark. Gray to dark brown, normally without bristles between thorns.

Leaves. Alternate, simple, ½- to 4 inches long, 3 to 5 lobes on each, teeth rounded, surfaces covered with small, white hairs, bright green above, paler beneath. Autumn colors: orange, yellow, or green.

Flowers. Small, green, bell-shaped blossoms forming alone, in pairs, or in groups of three.

Fruits. Round, purplish berries, ½-inch in diameter, covered with long spines, occasionally smooth, sweet.

Flowering period. April to June.

Fruiting period. July to September.

Habitat. Grows in a variety of soils in the open and in woodlands.

Range. New Brunswick south to North Carolina, Alabama, and Missouri.

Hardiness zone. 5.

Landscape notes. This is the most common gooseberry in the Northeast. Its ability to grow in shade and on poor soils makes it a good choice for such locations. It is useful in borders and hedges and as an understory shrub in woodlots. This shrub is an alternate host of the white pine blister rust, a fungus which destroys five-needled soft pines. It is therefore not recommended for plantings in areas where these trees are growing. Pasture gooseberry is not as widely cultivated as the European gooseberry.

Propagation. Pasture gooseberry may be propagated from seeds extracted from ripe fruits by maceration and sown in moist mineral soil with abundant humus. Fall-sown seeds usually germinate in the spring. Space 40 seeds per linear foot, and cover with ⅛- to ¼-inch of soil. Seeds may be stored for short periods

Pasture Gooseberry

[130]

in sealed containers at 41° F. or stratified in sand for ninety days or more at 41° F.

Plants may also be propagated from hardwood cuttings taken in autumn (U.S. Forest Service 1948).

Birds That Use Gooseberries

	Food	Cover	Nesting
Turkey	F		
Spruce grouse	F	X	
Ruffed grouse	F	X	
Bobwhite	F	X	
Ring-necked pheasant	F	X	
Mourning dove	F		
Common flicker	F		
Mockingbird*	F	X	X
Gray catbird*	F	X	X
Brown thrasher*	F		
American robin*	F	X	X
Hermit thrush	F	X	
Eastern bluebird*	F		
Cedar waxwing*	F		
Rufous-sided towhee	F	X	
Song sparrow	F	X	X

Note: *preferred food; F, fruit.
Sources: Davison 1967; Martin et al. 1951.

ROSES
Rosa spp.
ROSACEAE

Description. Roses are low, rounded, erect or climbing shrubs with long, spreading, usually thorny stems. Multiflora rose (*R. multiflora*), introduced from Asia, is a frequent nest site for many birds and a valuable winter food source for mockingbirds and cedar waxwings, among others.

Leaves. Alternate, compound, with 3 to 11 odd-pinnate leaflets.

Flowers. Occur singly or in loose clusters. Color varies from white to shades of pink and red.

Fruits. Thin-skinned, fleshy hips containing many small seeds.

Landscape notes. Roses are excellent shrubs for hedgerows and clumps. When planted close together, most form dense thickets that are excellent wildlife habitat. Although multiflora rose is a very valuable wildlife plant, it has been declared a noxious weed in several states. It spreads readily and can form an impenetrable mass. It also climbs readily when it reaches overhead branches, so it is best restricted to areas where it can be controlled.

Propagation. Roses can be grown from cuttings or seeds. Seed and stock of wild roses are generally not available from commercial suppliers. Seeds can easily be obtained by collecting ripe hips in the field. Seeds can be separated from the fruit by macerating the hips in water and floating off the pulp. They may be sown immediately without drying, stratified, or dried and stored for future use (U.S. Forest Service 1948).

Scarification in a sulfuric acid bath for one to two hours prior to stratification may speed germination of seeds having impermeable seed coats (U.S. Forest Service 1948). One method of stratification is to place seeds in damp peat moss for about two months at 35°–40° F., and then expose them to room tem-

Multiflora Rose

perature. When a few seeds germinate, refrigerate for six more weeks (Davis 1943). Sow stratified seed in early spring (Schumacher 1962). Seeds that are air-dried immediately following collection and placed in airtight containers at 34°–38° F. may be successfully stored for four to eight years (Heit 1967d).

Most species of roses can be propagated vegetatively from hardwood and softwood cuttings. Hardwood cuttings taken in fall or winter should be 6 to 8 inches long with tips cut just above a node and bases cut just below a node (Adriance 1939). Depending on winter cold, plant cuttings in cold frames or in the open in a mixture of peat and sand. Softwood cuttings should be 6 to 7 inches long and taken in spring or early summer. Remove only basal leaves. Treat stems with root-inducing hormone and insert them 3 inches deep in rooting medium. For best results, keep them shaded until rooting occurs, then gradually remove the shade. In April or May (south) or July or August (north), they can be planted in full sunlight in the field (Smithberg and Gill 1974).

Birds That Use Roses

	Food[1]	Cover	Nesting
Turkey	F	X	
Ruffed grouse	F, BD	X	
Bobwhite	F, BD	X	
Ring-necked pheasant	F, BD	X	
Mockingbird*	F	X	X[2]
Gray catbird	F	X	X[2]
Brown thrasher	F	X	X[2]
American robin	F		
Wood thrush	F		
Swainson's thrush*	F		
Eastern bluebird	F		
Cedar waxwing*	F		
Philadelphia vireo	F		
Cardinal	F	X	X[2]
Evening grosbeak	F		
American goldfinch	F		
Northern junco	F	X	
Tree sparrow	F	X	
Fox sparrow	F	X	
Song sparrow	F	X	X[2]

Note: *preferred food; [1]fruits are especially important to wildlife in winter; F, fruit; BD, buds; [2]preferred nest site is multiflora rose.
Sources: Martin et al. 1951; Van Dersal 1938; Davison 1967; McKenny 1939; DeGraaf et al. 1975.

[132]

Roses

| Species | Height | Flowering | | Fruiting | | Habitat and Range |
		Period	Color	Period	Color	
NATIVE						
Pasture Rose *Rosa carolina*	5'–7'	June to August	pink, 2"–2½" diameter	July to September, persistent	scarlet	Dry ground from Nova Scotia to Florida, W to Minnesota. Hardiness zone: 5.
Swamp Rose *Rosa palustris*	to 8'	June to August	pink	August to September, persistent	scarlet	Damp to saturated soils from Nova Scotia, S to Florida and Arkansas. Hardiness zone: 5.
Virginia Rose *Rosa virginiana*	to 6'	June to July	pink	July to August	scarlet	Common throughout E U.S. Most abundant rose in New England. Hardiness zone: 4.
Meadow Rose *Rosa blanda*	1'–4'	May to June	pink, 2½"–3" diameter	July to September, persistent	scarlet	Rocky soils from Newfoundland S through New England to New York, W to Illinois. Hardiness zone: 2.
INTRODUCED						
Rugosa Rose *Rosa rugosa*	to 6'	May to August	pink	June to September, persistent	scarlet	Intro. from E Asia. Widely planted and escaped in the NE U.S. Hardiness zone: 2.
Multiflora Rose *Rosa multiflora*	10'–12'	June to July	white	July to September, persistent	scarlet	Intro. from China, Korea, and Japan. Escaped from planted fence-rows, common throughout NE. Hardiness zone: 6.

Pasture Rose

[133] Shrubs

BRAMBLES
Rubus spp.
ROSACEAE

Description. These are open, straggling shrubs with slender upright or trailing, usually thorny, canes. Stems are short-lived, dying back after several years, but they are rapidly replaced by new shoots emerging from extensive root systems.

Leaves. Alternate, compound, with ovate leaflets in threes and fives, except *R. odoratus* which has simple, lobed leaves. Autumn colors: vary from shades of green to yellow and red depending on the species.

Flowers. Generally white, ½- to 1½ inches in diameter. *R. odoratus* bears showy purple blossoms up to 2 inches across.

Fruits. Aggregates of small red or black drupes, most of which are edible.

Habitat. Typically found in old fields, pastures, clearings, and hedgerows in a variety of soils and climates.

Landscape notes. All species listed are hardy and fast growing. Most are more attractive when pruned and fertilized for maximum fruit production. All are useful for naturalizing waste places where human presence is minimal.

Propagation. Stock can be obtained from local nurseries or directly from the field. Deep, sandy loam richly supplied with humus and adequate moisture is the ideal soil for cultivation. Transplanting suckers, root cuttings, and layering branch tips are common techniques of propagation. Plants should be dormant and cut back to ground level when transplanted.

Seed propagation is also common. Blackberries with extremely hard seed coats should be soaked in commercial grade sulfuric acid (specific gravity 1.84) for 50 to 60 minutes at 75°–80° F. (Heit 1967a and U.S. Forest Service

Common Northeastern Brambles

Species	Height	Leaves	Flower Period	Flower Color	Fruit Period	Fruit Color	Range
Fragrant Thimbleberry Purple-flowering Raspberry *Rubus odoratus*	3'–5'	simple 7"–9"	May to September	rose-purple	July to September	red, acid	Nova Scotia S to Georgia, W to Tennessee. Hardiness zone: 4.
Blackcap Raspberry Black Raspberry *Rubus occidentalis*	to 6'	cmpd., lflts. 2"–5"	May and June	white	July to August	black, sweet	Quebec W to Minnesota, S to southern states. Hardiness zone: 4.
Red Raspberry *Rubus idaeus*	3'–6'	cmpd., lflts. 2½"–3"	May and June	white	July	red, sweet	Newfoundland S to North Carolina. Hardiness zone: 4.
Allegany Blackberry American Blackberry *Rubus allegheniensis*	3'–8'	cmpd., lflts. 2"–4"	May and June	white	July to September	black, sweet	Quebec S to North Carolina, W to Minnesota and Indiana. Hardiness zone: 4.
Northern Dewberry American Dewberry *Rubus flagellaris*	1'–2'	cmpd., lflts. 2"–7"	May and June	white	June to August	black, sweet	Quebec W to Minnesota, S to southern states. Hardiness zone: 4.

1948) and rinsed thoroughly. They should be sown in late August or early September in mineral soil in the field or in peat moss in the nursery. Raspberry seeds germinate successfully after soaking for 10 to 30 minutes in sulfuric acid and sowing in late summer (Heit 1967b). Fragrant thimbleberry grows best in shade. The others cited here prefer full sunlight.

Birds That Use Brambles

	Food	Cover	Nesting
Turkey*	F		
Ruffed grouse*	F		
Bobwhite*	F		
Ring-necked pheasant*	F	X	
Common flicker	F		
Red-bellied woodpecker	F		
Red-headed woodpecker	F		
Hairy woodpecker	F		
Eastern kingbird	F		
Great crested flycatcher	F		
Eastern phoebe	F		
Willow flycatcher	F	X	X
Alder flycatcher	F	X	X
Blue jay*	F		
Common crow	F		
Fish crow*	F		
Tufted titmouse*	F		
Mockingbird*	F	X	X
Gray catbird*	F	X	X
Brown thrasher*	F	X	X
American robin*	F		
Wood thrush*	F		
Swainson's thrush	F		
Gray-cheeked thrush	F		
Veery*	F	X	
Eastern bluebird	F		
Cedar waxwing*	F		
White-eyed vireo	F	X	X
Red-eyed vireo	F		
Yellow-breasted chat*	F	X	X
Red-winged blackbird	F		
Rusty blackbird	F		
Common grackle*	F		
Orchard oriole*	F		

	Food	Cover	Nesting
Northern oriole*	F		
Scarlet tanager*	F		
Summer tanager*	F		
Cardinal*	F	X	X
Rose-breasted grosbeak*	F		
Evening grosbeak	F		
Blue grosbeak	F	X	X
Indigo bunting	F	X	X
Pine grosbeak*	F		
Rufous-sided towhee*	F		
Henslow's sparrow	F		
Field sparrow	F	X	X
White-throated sparrow	F		
Fox sparrow*	F	X	
Song sparrow	F	X	X

Note: *preferred food; F, fruit.
Sources: McKenny 1939; Davison 1967; Martin et al. 1951.

PUSSY WILLOW
Salix discolor Muhl.
SALICACEAE

Description. This native shrub is most familiar when in bud. The buds are eaten by ruffed grouse, and the upright twigs are a common nest site of the American goldfinch. Pussy willow grows 10 to 20 feet tall.
Bark. Smooth, dark brown or gray.
Leaves. Alternate, simple, 1¼ to 4 inches long, lanceolate to obovate or elliptic with slightly rounded teeth, bright green above, whitish beneath, with stipules. Autumn color: yellow.
Flowers. Male and female flowers occur on separate plants on catkins ¾- to 2¾ inches long.
Fruits. Capsules, ¼- to ⅜-inch long, containing seeds with long, silky down.
Flowering period. March to April.
Fruiting period. April to May.
Habitat. Grows in rich, damp soils of lowlands and along streams and lakes. Tolerates a variety of soils having sufficient moisture and a pH of 5.5 to 7.5 (Altman and Dittmer 1962; Spector 1956). Prefers full sunlight.
Range. Newfoundland south to the mountains of Tennessee, west to Idaho and Missouri.
Hardiness zone. 2.
Landscape notes. This is an excellent shrub for low, moist terrain. The fuzzy, staminate catkins, upon emerging from their scales, are decorative both on the bush and in the home. Plants are hardy and grow rapidly.
Propagation. Pussy willow reproduces naturally by seeds, suckers, sprouts, and root shoots. Commercial sources of seed are not available. Seeds may be collected when fruits ripen (turn yellowish-green) and sown immediately by broadcasting. Germination occurs rapidly and seedlings must be kept moist and shaded. In three to four weeks, they may be transplanted to prevent crowding and in one year or more, removed to their permanent locations (Rawson 1974; U.S. Forest Service 1948).

Cuttings 8 to 10 inches long may be taken from sprouts two years old or older and planted 6 to 8 inches deep in moist soil, taking care to leave two buds exposed. Take the cuttings in late winter or early spring before growth begins. If it is necessary to store the cuttings, bury them in an upright position in moist sand and keep them in a cool, dark place (Lamb 1915; Edminster and May 1951).
Bird uses. See Willows.

Pussy Willow

PRAIRIE WILLOW
Salix humilis var. *microphylla* (Anderss.) Fern.
SALICACEAE

Description. A low shrub with small leaves, prairie willow has twigs that are densely gray and hairy. It grows to 4 feet. Other common names are dwarf gray willow, sage willow, and dwarf prairie willow.

Bark. Gray, densely hairy.

Leaves. Alternate, simple, oblanceolate, ½- to 3 inches long, bases wedge-shaped with leaf stalks longer than side buds, thick when mature, gray-green above, gray with dense, woolly hairs beneath.

Flowers. Develop with the leaves on short, round, or oval catkins.

Fruits. Tiny capsules, ¼-inch long, containing small seeds.

Flowering period. March to April.

Fruiting period. April to May.

Habitat. Grows in dry soils of sandy plains and hillsides, in full or partial sunlight.

Range. Maine south through the mountains to northwest Florida, west to Minnesota and Oklahoma.

Hardiness zone. 5.

Landscape notes. Prairie willow is good for naturalistic plantings in dry soils where low, shrubby cover is desired. Plants are hardy and grow slowly.

Propagation. Seeds are probably not available from commercial sources. Propagation information is limited for this species because it is not in demand for landscape purposes. Transplanting is probably the most successful means of establishment.

Bird uses. See Willows.

PURPLEOSIER WILLOW
Salix purpurea L.
SALICACEAE

Description. Purpleosier willow is a tall shrub with purplish, hairless twigs. This willow was imported from Europe for making baskets. It grows 10 to 20 feet tall. Another common name is basket willow.

Bark. Purple when young, turning to gray or olive-gray with age, smooth.

Leaves. Alternate (often appearing opposite), simple, 2 to 4 inches long, oblanceolate, finely toothed at tips or teeth lacking, bluish-green above, pale green beneath.

Flowers. Appear on small, slender, cylindrical catkins before the leaves emerge, often paired.

Fruits. Small, whitish capsules containing small seeds.

Flowering period. April to early May.

Fruiting period. April to May.

Habitat. Grows in a variety of well-drained soils and poorly drained, infertile sites.

Range. Newfoundland south to Virginia, west to Wisconsin and Iowa. Imported from Europe and naturalized in the Northeast.

Hardiness zone. 5.

Landscape notes. This thicket-forming shrub spreads prolifically by layering of branches. It is useful in stabilizing banks of ponds and streams, particularly those subject to ice damage. Plants are hardy and grow rapidly, attaining a height of 2 to 3 feet in two years. They may reach maximum height in five years.

Propagation. This willow is easily propagated from fresh hardwood cuttings, ⅜- to ½-inch thick at the base and 12 to 15 inches long, made before the leaves emerge. Cuttings should be inserted vertically into moist ground to depths that allow only an inch or two of the cutting to protrude. When rooting takes place, plants may be transplanted to a hole large enough to accommodate the new root system (U.S. Soil Conservation Service 1960).

Bird uses. See Willows.

Birds That Use Willows

	Food	Cover	Nesting[1]
Mallard	CK	X	
Wood duck	CK	X	
Spruce grouse	BD, T	X	
Ruffed grouse*	BD, T	X	
Evening grosbeak	BD		
Pine grosbeak*	BD		
Common redpoll	BD		
American goldfinch		X	X[2]

Note: *preferred food; CK, catkins; BD, buds; T, twigs; [1]often used for nesting by songbirds; [2]pussy willow only.
Sources: Martin et al. 1951; McKenny 1939; Davison 1967.

AMERICAN ELDER
Sambucus canadensis L.
CAPRIFOLIACEAE

Description. American elder is a widespread, flowering shrub of wet areas. It grows 6 to 12 feet tall, and bears fruit that is readily eaten by many birds. Other common names are common elderberry, sweet elderberry, and blackberry elder.

Bark. Dark green when young, changing to yellow-brown with age, prominent lenticels, white pith.

Leaves. Opposite, pinnately compound, 4 to 11 inches long with 5 to 11 leaflets, each leaflet 4 to 6 inches long, oblong to ovate with margins finely toothed. Autumn color: greenish-yellow.

Flowers. Creamy white and fragrant, forming on showy, flat, compound cymes, 5 to 8 inches in diameter.

Fruits. Small, juicy berries, purple-black color and pleasant taste. The juice is often used for wines and jellies. Fruit production begins on two-year-old canes (Ritter and McKee 1964).

Flowering period. June to August.

Fruiting period. July to September.

Habitat. American elder tolerates a wide variety of open habitats throughout the Northeast, from wet bottomlands to 4,000-foot elevations in the Appalachian Mountains (Ritter and McKee 1964; Laurie and Chadwick 1931). Prefers moist, fertile soils.

Range. Nova Scotia west to Manitoba, south to Texas and Georgia.

Hardiness zone. 4

Landscape notes. American elder is useful for planting singly or in numbers to form thickets and hedges. It is hardy, transplants well, and tolerates severe pruning. Individual canes usually die between the third and fifth year (Deam 1932) and should be removed. Highly ornamental in bloom and attractive to birds in fruit, these plants are also useful as tall background plants in wet areas.

Propagation. Plants may be grown from rooted

cuttings or seeds, both of which are available commercially (Mahlstede and Haber 1957). Wild plants usually can be found with ease, their fruits removed, and cuttings taken without injuring the plant. Seeds should be removed as soon as the fruits ripen. Clean, dry, and store them in sealed, airtight containers at 41° F. until ready to plant. They will remain viable for at least two years (U.S. Forest Service 1948).

Prior to sowing in spring, seeds may be scarified in sulfuric acid for ten to twenty minutes, then washed and chilled at 36°–40° F. for two months (Heit 1967a). American elder seeds may be stratified by placing them in moist sand for 60 days at 68° F. (night) and 86° F. (day), followed by 120 days at 41° F. (Krefting and Roe 1949). Untreated seeds may be sown but will not germinate until the second year (Heit 1967a), and should be covered with mulch in winter to protect them from freezing (Davis 1927). Sow seeds ¼-inch deep (U.S. Forest Service 1948).

Stem cuttings may be taken in spring or fall. They should be 10 to 18 inches long and include three sets of opposite buds (Ritter and McKee 1964). Fall cuttings should be placed in peat moss, kept at 40° F. through the winter, and planted outside in the spring in sunny areas (Mahlstede and Haber 1957; Braun 1961).

Annual pruning of the canes improves fruit production. Dead wood should be removed along with all but five or six strong, one-year-old canes and one or two older canes per runner (Ritter and McKee 1964).

Birds That Use American Elder
(See Elders)

	Food	Cover	Nesting
Turkey	F	X	
Ring-necked pheasant	F	X	
Mourning dove	F		
Common flicker	F	X	
Red-bellied woodpecker*	F	X	
Red-headed woodpecker*	F	X	
Yellow-bellied sapsucker	F		
Eastern kingbird	F		
Great crested flycatcher	F		
Alder flycatcher	F	X	X
Blue jay*	F		
Mockingbird*	F	X	X
Gray catbird*	F	X	X
Brown thrasher*	F	X	
Eastern bluebird	F		
American robin*	F		
Wood thrush*	F	X	
Hermit thrush	F	X	
Swainson's thrush*	F	X	
Gray-cheeked thrush*	F	X	
Veery*	F		
Eastern bluebird*	F	X	
Cedar waxwing*	F	X	
Starling*	F		
Yellow warbler		X	X
Yellow-breasted chat*	F	X	
Common grackle	F	X	
Cardinal*	F	X	
Rose-breasted grosbeak*	F	X	
Indigo bunting	F	X	
American goldfinch		X	X
Rufous-sided towhee*	F	X	
White-throated sparrow*	F	X	
Chipping sparrow	F	X	
Song sparrow	F	X	

Note: *preferred food; F, fruit.
Sources: Petrides 1972; Davison 1967; Longenecker and Ellarson 1973.

SCARLET ELDER
Sambucus pubens Michx.
CAPRIFOLIACEAE

Description. Scarlet elder occurs somewhat farther north than does American elder, and is less likely to form thickets. It grows 2 to 12 feet tall. Other common names are red-berried elder and stinking elder.

Bark. Yellowish-gray with warty lenticels, twigs covered with fine hairs, pith brown.

Leaves. Opposite, pinnately compound with 5 to 7 leaflets, each 3 to 5 inches long, oblong to lanceolate or oval, finely toothed and covered with fine hairs. Autumn colors: yellowish-green to yellow.

Flowers. Small, cream or yellowish-white, strong-smelling, form early in spring on pyramidal panicles.

Fruits. Juicy, bright-red, round, small berries, forming closely in cone-shaped clusters, very showy, unpalatable.

Flowering period. April to July.

Fruiting period. June to September.

Habitat. Commonly found on rocky soils in dry woods and clearings, but will also grow on moist, rich soils.

Range. Newfoundland south to the mountains of Georgia, west to Oregon and Colorado.

Hardiness zone. 5.

Landscape notes. Scarlet elder is highly ornamental because of its clusters of bright-red berries. For most effective color, plants should be arranged in clumps or hedges in places where they can spread freely. Plants are easily transplanted and attain best growth in full sunlight. They are hardy and grow rapidly.

Propagation. Seed and stock are available from some nurseries. Propagation techniques are similar to those of American elder, but scarlet elder is more difficult to grow from seed. Germination may improve if seeds are scarified in acid for ten to fifteen minutes, stratified for three to four months at warm temperatures, and prechilled for two months (Heit 1967a).

Scarlet elder does better on drier sites than does American elder and can be successfully planted in a greater variety of soil and light conditions.

Birds That Use Scarlet Elder
(See Elders)

	Food	Cover	Nesting
Ruffed grouse*	F	X	
Bobwhite	F	X	
Ring-necked pheasant	F	X	
Common flicker	F	X	
Red-bellied woodpecker*	F	X	
Red-headed woodpecker*	F	X	
Eastern kingbird	F		
Alder flycatcher	F	X	
Mockingbird	F	X	
Gray catbird	F	X	
Brown thrasher	F	X	
American robin*	F	X	
Hermit thrush	F	X	
Swainson's thrush*	F	X	
Veery*	F	X	
Eastern bluebird	F	X	
Rose-breasted grosbeak*	F	X	

Note: *preferred food; F, fruit.

Birds That Use Elders

	Food	Cover	Nesting[1]
Turkey	F	X	
Ruffed grouse	F	X	
Ring-necked pheasant*	F	X	
Mourning dove	F	X	
Common flicker	F	X	
Pileated woodpecker*	F	X	
Red-bellied woodpecker	F	X	
Red-headed woodpecker	F	X	
Yellow-bellied sapsucker	F	X	
Eastern kingbird	F		
Great crested flycatcher	F		
Eastern phoebe	F		
Alder flycatcher	F	X	X
Blue jay	F	X	
Gray jay	F		
Tufted titmouse	F		
White-breasted nuthatch	F		
Red-breasted nuthatch	F		
Mockingbird*	F	X	X
Gray catbird*	F	X	X
Brown thrasher*	F	X	
Eastern bluebird	F	X	
American robin	F	X	
Wood thrush	F	X	
Hermit thrush	F	X	
Swainson's thrush*	F	X	
Gray-cheeked thrush	F	X	
Veery*	F	X	
Ruby-crowned kinglet	F		
Cedar waxwing	F		
Starling*	F		
White-eyed vireo	F	X	
Red-eyed vireo	F		
Warbling vireo	F		
Yellow warbler		X	X
Yellow-breasted chat*	F	X	
Common grackle	F	X	
Scarlet tanager	F		
Cardinal	F	X	
Rose-breasted grosbeak*	F	X	
Indigo bunting	F	X	
House finch	F		
American goldfinch		X	X
Rufous-sided towhee	F		
Chipping sparrow	F	X	
White-crowned sparrow	F	X	
White-throated sparrow	F	X	
Swamp sparrow	F	X	
Song sparrow	F	X	

Note: *preferred food; F, fruit; [1]American elder is more frequently used as a nest site than scarlet elder.
Sources: Martin et al. 1951; Davison 1967; McKenny 1939; Petrides 1972; Longenecker and Ellarson 1973.

NARROWLEAF MEADOWSWEET
Spiraea alba Du Roi
ROSACEAE

Description. Narrowleaf meadowsweet is a common northeastern spirea. All of the spireas listed are important as wildlife cover or nest sites; as food sources, they are unimportant. Other common names are Quaker lady, willow-leaved spirea, queen of the meadow, and pipestem. Grows 1 to 4 feet tall.
Bark. Stems yellowish-brown.
Leaves. Alternate, simple, 2 to 3 inches long, lanceolate to oblong, margins finely toothed. Autumn colors: dull yellow or red.
Flowers. Small, white or rose, ¼- to ⅜-inch in diameter, borne on dense, terminal panicles.
Fruits. Small, dry aggregates of follicles in dense terminal clusters.
Flowering period. June to September.
Fruiting period. Late summer to fall.
Habitat. Grows in wet meadows and damp soils of lowlands and mountains. Thrives on a variety of soil types but prefers neutral soil. Tends to form thickets.
Range. One of the most common northeastern spireas, and the most widespread, occurring from southwestern Quebec west to Saskatchewan, south to northern Missouri and North Carolina.
Hardiness zone. 4.
Landscape notes. Its thicket-forming tendencies make it an ideal choice for mass plantings and low borders. Best growth occurs in full sunlight. Plants are easily transplanted from field to garden and require very little care. They are hardy and grow rapidly.
Propagation. Narrowleaf meadowsweet thrives under cultivation. Roots spread laterally for several feet just below the surface and send up shoots which, if left to grow, will form dense thickets. Plants can be propagated from softwood and hardwood cuttings and from seeds (Mahlstede and Haber 1957).
Bird uses. See Spireas.

BROADLEAF MEADOWSWEET
Spiraea latifolia (Ait.) Borkh.
ROSACEAE

Description. Broadleaf meadowsweet has long, slender fruit and flower clusters like narrowleaf spirea (*S. alba*), but it is taller, has short, hairless buds, and is more common than narrowleaf spirea. Broadleaf meadowsweet grows to 6 feet with a spread of 4 feet.
Bark. Reddish or purplish-brown, hairless.
Leaves. Alternate, simple, 2 to 3 inches long, ¾- to ⅝-inch broad, elliptic, margins coarsely toothed.
Flowers. White or pale pink, small, forming on broad terminal panicles.
Fruits. Small, dry aggregates of follicles.
Flowering period. June to September.
Fruiting period. Late summer to fall.
Habitat. Frequently grows on dry, poor soils of abandoned fields and woodland borders. Prefers neutral soil.
Range. Newfoundland west to Michigan, south to North Carolina.
Hardiness zone. 2.
Landscape notes. Broadleaf meadowsweet is useful in borders along roadsides, gardens, and property boundaries, or as single shrubs where naturalizing is desired. Plants spread quite rapidly, are easily transplanted, hardy, require little or no care, and grow in sun or shade.
Propagation. This shrub can be propagated from seeds, hardwood cuttings, and softwood cuttings. If a small number of plants is desired, they may be transplanted successfully to similar habitats. Transplanted shrubs may be divided in three to four years or as soon as they become well established.
Bird uses. See Spireas.

HARDHACK
Spiraea tomentosa L.
ROSACEAE

Description. The only spirea with woolly twigs
and leaf undersides, the hardhack grows to 5
feet with a spread of 2 to 4 feet. Another
common name is steeplebush.
Bark. Stems covered with fine, brown hairs.
Leaves. Alternate, simple, 1 to 3 inches long,
egg-shaped to elliptic, margins with coarse
teeth, dark green above, brown and woolly
beneath. Autumn color: yellowish-green.
Flowers. Small, pink to pale purple or, less
commonly, white, borne on slender, pointed,
terminal clusters.
Fruits. Small, dry aggregates of follicles on
tall, narrow, pointed clusters.
Flowering period. July to September.
Fruiting period. Late summer, fall.
Habitat. Thrives in a variety of soils including
mountain swamps and wet meadows. A common species of old, unmown fields. Prefers
acid soil.
Range. Manitoba eastward, south to Georgia
and Arkansas.
Hardiness zone. 4.
Landscape notes. Hardhack is useful for naturalistic plantings in large areas where there is
room to spread freely. It is an excellent filler
for damp places. Attractive along roadsides,
these plants can be easily transplanted from
the wild. They are hardy, grow rapidly in sun
or shade, and need little or no care.
Propagation. Hardhack has a fibrous and suckering root system which, if allowed to grow,
will form a dense clump of stems. It is easily
transplanted and can be divided and re-
planted every three to four years (Robinson
1960). It can also be propagated by softwood
and hardwood cuttings. Cuttings should be
treated with root-inducing hormone before
insertion into rooting medium (Core 1974).
Bird uses. See Spireas.

Hardhack

Birds That Use Spireas

	Food	Cover	Nesting
Turkey		X	
Ruffed grouse	BD, L, S	X	
Bobwhite		X	
Ring-necked pheasant	S	X	
American woodcock		X	
Red-winged blackbird		X	X
American goldfinch			X
Field sparrow		X	X
Song sparrow		X	X
Dickcissel		X	
Northern junco		X	
Indigo bunting		X	X
Rufous-sided towhee		X	
Common redpoll		X	
Grasshopper sparrow		X	
Tree sparrow		X	
White-throated sparrow		X	

Note: BD, buds; L, leaves; S, seeds.
Sources: Core 1974; Petrides 1972; Martin et al. 1951.

COMMON SNOWBERRY
Symphoricarpos albus (L.) Blake
CAPRIFOLIACEAE

Description. Common snowberry was once commonly planted around homes but is less frequently seen today, probably due to the great variety of shrubs now available commercially. Snowberry is a valuable wildlife plant because it produces fruit in late fall and winter. It grows 3 to 4 feet with a spread of 3 to 6 feet. Another common name is belluaine.
Bark. Gray on older stems, light brown on younger branches.
Leaves. Opposite, simple, 1 to 2 inches long, oval, tips rounded or slightly pointed, margins smooth, blue-green above, paler beneath. Autumn color: bluish-green.
Flowers. Inconspicuous, white with shades of pink, ¼- to ⅜-inch long, bell-shaped, clustered in leaf axils and on tips of branches.
Fruits. Round, pure-white berry, ¼- to ⅝-inch in diameter, persistent.
Flowering period. May to July.
Fruiting period. August to May.
Habitat. Often seen in rocky places, fence-rows, and on river banks. Prefers limestone and clay soils but will grow almost anywhere. Grows well in sun and shade but sunlight encourages higher yields of fruit.
Range. Nova Scotia south to Pennsylvania (except the Atlantic coastal plain), and Kentucky, west to Wisconsin and Colorado.
Hardiness zone. 4.
Landscape notes. Snowberry is particularly attractive when cultivated. Its large, white, ornamental berries are enhanced when it is planted beside shrubs such as rugosa rose that simultaneously bear highly contrasting fruits. It is useful in clumps on lawns, in hedgerows, or scattered about as an understory shrub. Its ability to grow on steep banks makes it helpful in controlling soil erosion. It is hardy, rapid growing, and withstands city pollution.
Propagation. Common snowberry spreads naturally by seeds, suckering, and layering. Stock can be purchased locally, or propagated at home from stem and root cuttings. Wild plants can be removed with an ample soil ball and transplanted to a new area.

Seeds can be obtained by macerating ripe fruits in water. They may keep for two years or more if air-dried and refrigerated at 41° F. in sealed containers. Seeds may be stratified in sand or peat for 90 to 120 days at 68° F. (night) and 86° F. (day), followed by 180 days at 41° F. Seeds should be sown in spring, ¼-inch deep in beds, and covered with mulch until germination occurs the following spring (U.S. Forest Service 1948).

Softwood and hardwood stem cuttings should be made below a node and treated with potassium permanganate (Billard 1972).

2 Lines Short

	Food	Cover	Nesting
Ruffed grouse	F	X	
Ring-necked pheasant*	F	X	
Hermit thrush	F	X	
American robin	F		
Swainson's thrush	F	X	
Cedar waxwing	F		
Evening grosbeak	F	X	
Pine grosbeak*	F	X	

Note: *preferred food; F, fruit.
Source: McKenny 1939.

Common Snowberry

CORALBERRY

Symphoricarpos orbiculatus Moench
CAPRIFOLIACEAE

Description. This native shrub produces nectar that attracts ruby-throated hummingbirds (Davison 1967). It grows 2 to 5 feet tall. Other common names are buck-brush and Indian currant.
Bark. Gray and papery on older stems, twigs light brown.
Leaves. Opposite, simple, 1 to 1½ inches long, oval to nearly circular, without teeth, smooth, grayish-green above, downy and paler beneath. Autumn color: bluish-gray.
Flowers. Greenish-purple bells, less than 3/16-inch long, form in dense clusters in leaf axils.
Fruits. Round, purplish-red berries less than ⅜-inch long, persistent.
Flowering period. July to August.
Fruiting period. September to December, or longer.
Habitat. Grows in a variety of soils from dry to rocky to moist and rich, in sun or shade.
Range. New England south to Florida, west to Texas, Colorado, and South Dakota.
Hardiness zone. 2.
Landscape notes. The brightly colored fruits are highly decorative with or without the foliage. Shrubs form dense thickets excellent for bor-

Coralberry

ders, mass shrubberies, and low screens. Plants adapt well to rigorous conditions. Their usefulness in controlling erosion on steep banks has been proven along major highways. They are hardy, rapid growing, and tolerate city smoke (Gude 1973).

Propagation. See Common Snowberry.

Birds That Use Coralberry

	Food	Cover	Nesting
Turkey	F	X	
Ruffed grouse	F	X	
Bobwhite	F	X	
Ring-necked pheasant*	F	X	
Ruby-throated hummingbird*	N		
Brown thrasher	F		
American robin*	F		
Wood thrush	F	X	
Hermit thrush	F	X	
Cedar waxwing	F		
Warbling vireo	F		
Cardinal	F	X	
Evening grosbeak*	F	X	
Purple finch	F	X	
Pine grosbeak*	F	X	

Note: *preferred food; F, fruit; N, nectar.
Sources: McKenny 1939; Davison 1967; Martin et al. 1951.

CANADA YEW
Taxus canadensis Marsh.
TAXACEAE

Description. Canada yew is a prostrate evergreen shrub that was once common, but has been eradicated by deer in many areas. It grows to 3 feet, occasionally taller. Other common names are American yew and ground hemlock.

Bark. Brown on older stems, greenish-brown on young twigs.

Leaves. Alternate, linear needles, ³/₈- to 1 inch long, stalked, green on both sides.

Flowers. Small, forming in leaf axils in the spring, sexes occur on different plants.

Fruits. Round, fleshy red berries, ½-inch or less in diameter, containing one hard, nutlike seed.

Flowering period. April to May.

Fruiting period. July to September.

Habitat. Grows in cool, moist woodlands and bogs. Commonly found on cool, moist, well-drained soil that is rich in humus, in association with northern hardwoods, hemlock, and pine. Tolerates deep shade.

Range. Newfoundland south through the uplands to Virginia and northwestern North Carolina, west to Manitoba and Iowa.

Hardiness zone. 2.

Landscape notes. Canada yew is useful as a ground cover in places that are well shaded and moist. Fruiting is usually too sporadic to give plants ornamental value. Plants are hardy and grow at a moderate rate.

Propagation. Canada yew can be propagated by seeds or cuttings. Seeds may be collected from mature fruits by macerating them in sand or water. They may be stored in an airtight container at 32°–40° F. for a few years (Heit 1967c). Seeds sown before July of the following year will produce good stands the following spring. Fall-sown seeds take two years to germinate (Heit 1969).

Hardwood cuttings of one-, two-, or three-year-old wood root well in a sandy, peaty medium.

Transplanted shrubs should be removed with a large ball of soil intact to minimize root disturbance, and then planted in soils with a pH of 5.0 to 7.5 (Altman and Dittmer 1962; Spector 1956). They should be watered freely and fertilized.

The introduced Japanese yew (*Taxus cuspidata*) is widely used in open areas for formal and informal lawn and foundation plantings in the Northeast. It grows to 15 feet but may be kept small and shaped to desired form. This is a valuable plant for early nesting birds and for those species that prefer the dense cover of evergreen foliage. Many varieties of different sizes have been developed. Japanese yew grows vigorously in sun or shade and is hardy to zone 5.

Birds That Use Yews

	Food	Cover	Nesting
Ruffed grouse	F	X	
Mockingbird	F	X	X
American robin	F	X	X
Wood thrush	F	X	
White-throated sparrow	F	X	
Song sparrow	F	X	X
Chipping sparrow	F	X	X

Note: F, fruit.
Sources: McKenny 1939; Martin et al. 1951; Petrides 1972; Mason 1965.

Canada Yew

LOWBUSH BLUEBERRY
Vaccinium angustifolium Ait.
ERICACEAE

Description. Lowbush blueberry is a common species in the Northeast, and produces fruits favored by many birds. It grows ½- to 2 feet tall and is common in upland sites. Other common names are dwarf blueberry, sugar blueberry, and late low blueberry.

Bark. Reddish-purple on stems, light green on angular branches.

Leaves. Alternate, simple, ¼- to 1⅜ inches long, ovate to lanceolate and finely toothed, dull green above, lighter green beneath. Autumn colors: scarlet, crimson, and bronze.

Flowers. White, bell shaped, forming in loose racemes

Fruits. Round, bluish-white or shiny black berry, very sweet, edible.

Flowering period. April to June.

Fruiting period. July to September.

Habitat. Grows in dry, sandy, well-drained soils of open meadows and woodlands at all elevations. Does poorly on moist, rich soils. Often spreads profusely, forming thick carpets of green in summer, changing to brilliant red in autumn. Likes partial shade or full sunlight.

Range. Common in the Northeast from Newfoundland south to Virginia, west to Michigan.

Hardiness zone. 2.

Landscape notes. This shrub has little ornamental value except in autumn when its foliage turns red. It is useful as a ground cover in places where plants can spread rapidly and reach optimum growth. Plants are hardy and slow growing.

Propagation. Lowbush blueberry reproduces naturally from seeds, sprouts, underground stems, and suckers. Seed and stock are not usually available from nurseries so they must be collected in the wild. To collect seeds, gather fruits when ripe, and chill them at 50° F. for several days. Then place them in a blender partially filled with water for about 30 seconds to separate seed from pulp (Morrow et al. 1954). Sow seeds in a mixture of sand and peat and wait at least one month for germination to occur. Transplant six- to seven-week-old seedlings to another bed to permit uncrowded growth. Soils should be light and well drained with a pH of 4.3 to 4.8 for best results (Kender and Brightwell 1966).

Birds That Use Lowbush Blueberry
(See Blueberries)

	Food	Cover	Nesting
Ruffed grouse*	F, L	X	
Bobwhite	F	X	
Eastern kingbird*	F		
Tufted titmouse	F		
Gray catbird*	F		
Brown thrasher*	F		
American robin*	F		
Rufous-sided towhee	F	X	

Note: *preferred food; F, fruit; L, leaves.
Sources: McKenny 1939; Petrides 1972.

HIGHBUSH BLUEBERRY
Vaccinium corymbosum L.
ERICACEAE

Description. Highbush blueberry grows at low to medium elevations. Open-grown highbush blueberry forms a dense crown and is a common nest site. It is 6 to 15 feet tall. Other common names are tall blueberry and swamp blueberry.

Bark. Gray, copper, or bronze on older stems, yellowish-gray on younger stems and branches.

Leaves. Alternate, simple, 1⅝ to 3¼ inches long, elliptic, usually without teeth, dark green above, paler beneath. Autumn colors: bronze and crimson.

Flowers. Small, pale pink, bell-shaped blossoms borne on drooping racemes.

Fruits. Small, bluish-white or shiny black

berry, ¼-inch in diameter, sweet, edible.

Flowering period. May to June.

Fruiting period. June to September.

Habitat. Prefers moist, well-drained, slightly acidic soils bordering swamps, in open meadows, and woodland clearings. Highbush blueberry requires a minimum growing season of 160 days (Chandler 1943). This factor, coupled with its sensitivity to winter cold, restricts its growth to lower elevations north of the Canadian border.

Range. Along the east coast of North America from Nova Scotia and Quebec to Florida, and inland from New England west to Wisconsin.

Hardiness zone. 4.

Landscape notes. The flowers, fruits, and foliage of this shrub are highly ornamental. The branches become dense and compact when plants are cultivated and pruned. Plants are easily transplanted to any good garden soil having a slightly acid pH and a partially or totally sunny exposure. These hardy, slow-growing shrubs are useful in borders or in small clumps.

Propagation. Highbush blueberry usually bears fruit when eight to ten years old, but may occasionally fruit in as early as three years (Taylor 1962). The yield depends largely on honeybees, which are the main pollinating agents (Marucci 1966). Plants reproduce naturally from seeds, sprouts, underground stems and

Highbush Blueberry

suckers (Rogers 1974).

Seeds and small plants are available from nurseries. Plants can be propagated from one-year-old hardwood cuttings, 3 to 5 inches long, and ¼-inch in diameter or less if gathered in the spring just before the buds begin to grow (Doehlert 1953). Flower buds should be removed from the cuttings (Mainland 1966), and the cut ends treated with fungicide before inserting them into a mixture of sand and peat (Doehlert 1953). When rooting occurs, plants may be moved to nursery beds for further root development before winter (Rogers 1974).

Plants may also be propagated from seed. Fruits should be gathered when ripe, and chilled at 50° F. for several days. Seeds may easily be separated from the pulp with a food blender (Morrow et al. 1954) and sown in a mixture of sand and peat. When seedlings are seven weeks old, they should be transplanted to a roomier spot and remain there for one growing season before being removed to their final locations (Rogers 1974).

Birds That Use Highbush Blueberry
(See Blueberries)

	Food	Cover	Nesting
Ruffed grouse	F	X	
Ring-necked pheasant	F	X	
Mourning dove	F	X	
Eastern kingbird	F	X	X
Blue jay	F		
Black-capped chickadee	F		
Tufted titmouse*	F		
Gray catbird*	F	X	X
Brown thrasher*	F		
American robin*	F	X	X
Hermit thrush	F	X	
Eastern bluebird*	F		
Orchard oriole*	F		
Pine grosbeak	F		
Rufous-sided towhee*	F	X	

Note: *preferred food; F, fruit.
Sources: McKenny 1939; Petrides 1972.

Birds That Use Blueberries

	Food	Cover	Nesting
Canada goose*	F		
Turkey*	F	X	
Spruce grouse*	F, L	X	
Ruffed grouse*	F, L	X	
Bobwhite	F	X	
Ring-necked pheasant	F	X	
Mourning dove	F	X	
Ruby-throated hummingbird	N		
Common flicker*	F		
Red-bellied woodpecker*	F		
Red-headed woodpecker*	F		
Eastern kingbird*	F		
Great crested flycatcher	F		
Eastern phoebe	F		
Blue jay*	F		
Fish crow	F		
Black-capped chickadee	F		
Tufted titmouse	F		
Gray catbird*	F		X[1]
Brown thrasher*	F		
American robin*	F		
Wood thrush*	F	X	
Hermit thrush*	F	X	
Gray-cheeked thrush*	F	X	
Veery*	F	X	
Eastern bluebird*	F		
Cedar waxwing*	F		
Starling*	F		
Yellow-breasted chat*	F		
Orchard oriole*	F		
Northern oriole	F		
Scarlet tanager*	F		
Cardinal	F		
Pine grosbeak	F		
Rufous-sided towhee*	F	X	
Savannah sparrow	F		
Tree sparrow	F	X	
White-throated sparrow*	F	X	

Note: *preferred food; F, fruit; L, leaves; N, nectar; [1]preferred nest site.
Sources: McKenny 1939; Petrides 1972; Martin et al. 1951; Davison 1967.

MAPLELEAF VIBURNUM
Viburnum acerifolium L.
CAPRIFOLIACEAE

NOTE: Viburnums are notoriously difficult to classify. Those included here are common in the northeastern United States. Names used are from Gray's *Manual,* 8th ed. (Fernald 1950).

Description. Mapleleaf viburnum is an erect shrub, 3 to 6 feet tall. It is an understory shrub in dry woods. Another common name is dockmackie.

Bark. Reddish-brown, smooth.

Leaves. Opposite, simple, 3 to 5 inches long with 3 lobes resembling those of red maple, rounded or heart-shaped at the base, coarsely toothed. Autumn colors: yellow to shades of pink and purple.

Flowers. Creamy white, form at the tips of branchlets in attractive cymes that are 2 to 3 inches across.

Fruits. Small drupes, crimson at first turning deep purple-black upon ripening, persistent into winter.

Flowering period. May to early August.

Fruiting period. Late July to midwinter.

Habitat. Prefers dry and rocky woods but tolerates a wide range of conditions from arid, south-facing slopes to moist, north-facing slopes (Cantlon 1953; Harsberger 1919). Commonly grows along roadsides in the shade of larger trees and in partial and full sunlight.

Range. Quebec south to Georgia, west to Minnesota.

Hardiness zone. 4.

Landscape notes. This hardy, slow-growing plant is attractive as an understory shrub and along shady borders of woodlots where a natural appearance is desired.

Propagation. Mapleleaf viburnum may be propagated from seed, or vegetatively from root suckers, cuttings, and layers (U.S. Forest Service 1948). Seeds may be collected directly from fruits in the wild or purchased from commercial suppliers. If long-term storage of seeds is desired, they should be separated from the pulp by soaking and maceration. Then they should be dried, stored in sealed containers, and refrigerated at 34°–38° F. until sown. Seeds stored in this manner may remain viable for ten years (Heit 1967d). Seeds to be planted within two years of collection need not be separated from the fruits, but should be air-dried immediately after picking, sealed in airtight containers, and refrigerated at 41° F. (U.S. Forest Service 1948).

A two-stage stratification process is required to induce germination. Seeds require twelve to seventeen months exposure to temperatures of 68° F. (night) and 86° F. (day) for development of the radicle, and four months of 50° F. temperatures for growth of the plumule (Davis 1926; Giersback 1937). This process naturally takes approximately 1½ years. Seeds should be sown in spring or midsummer in drills 8 to 12 inches apart, ½-inch deep, in peat or sawdust. They should be mulched with straw, to be removed upon germination (U.S. Forest Service 1948).

Birds That Use Mapleleaf Viburnum
(See Viburnums)

	Food	Cover	Nesting
Ruffed grouse	F	X	
Bobwhite	F	X	
Common flicker	F		
American robin	F		
Hermit thrush	F	X	
Swainson's thrush	F	X	
Gray-cheeked thrush	F	X	
Eastern bluebird	F		
Cedar waxwing	F		
Purple finch	F		

Note: F, fruit.
Sources: McKenny 1939; Schutz 1974.

HOBBLEBUSH
Viburnum alnifolium Marsh.
CAPRIFOLIACEAE

Description. Hobblebush is a graceful, erect shrub or small tree that grows to 10 feet or more in moist, shady areas. Other common names are witch-hobble, trip-toe, American wayfaring-tree, and moosewood.
Leaves. Opposite, simple, 3 to 8 inches long, orbicular to ovate and deeply corrugated when fully developed. Autumn colors: brilliant red and orange.
Flowers. Showy, white, large-petaled, sterile flowers form along the margins of broad, flat cymes 3 to 5 inches across. Small, white, perfect flowers fill the central portion of the cyme and are less conspicuous.
Fruits. Fleshy drupes, ½-inch in diameter, dark purple when ripe.
Flowering period. May to July.
Fruiting period. July to October.
Habitat. Found in moist woodlands and cool ravines. Normally occurs as a shrub layer under taller vegetation.
Range. Grows throughout the Northeast, south to the Georgia uplands.
Hardiness zone. 4.
Landscape notes. This shrub has lovely flowers, foliage, and fruits. Its branches often bend to the ground and become rooted at the tips, hence the name "Trip-toe." This lateral growth can easily be controlled by pruning. Because hobblebush is hardy and rapid growing, it is useful as an understory shrub in moist woodlands where it can spread naturally and needs little care. Although capable of growing in the open, shade may be required for optimum development.
Propagation. Hobblebush may be planted from seed or from stock available at local nurseries. It can often be taken from woods and transplanted to areas with similar growing conditions. Branches that have layered naturally may be removed with their roots intact and relocated. Its growth is more manageable when grafted onto arrowwood (Keeler 1969).

Seeds in the wild usually germinate the second spring following fruit ripening due to a two-stage stratification process: during the warm days and cool nights of the first spring and summer, the radicle begins to grow; then, as colder temperatures of the second winter chill the seed, plumule dormancy breaks and, with the second spring's warmth, the plant begins to grow (Davis 1926; Giersbach 1937). Seeds of early fruits that are sown immediately upon ripening may germinate fully the following summer (Smith 1952). Seeds may be stratified in moist soil for ninety days at 68° F. (night) to 86° F. (day), followed by sixty days at 41° F. (U.S. Forest Service 1948).

Birds That Use Hobblebush
(See Viburnums)

	Food	Cover	Nesting
Ruffed grouse	F	X	
Brown thrasher	F		
Swainson's thrush	F	X	
Cedar waxwing	F		
Red-eyed vireo	F		
Pine grosbeak	F	X	

Note: F, fruit.
Sources: McKenny 1939; Holweg 1964.

WITHEROD

Viburnum cassinoides L.

CAPRIFOLIACEAE

Description. Like other viburnums, witherod is a characteristic understory shrub in northeastern forests. It prefers moist, shady sites, and grows 6 to 12 feet tall. Another common name is northern wild raisin.

Bark. Gray or brown covered with many lenticels.

Leaves. Opposite, simple, 2 to 5 inches long, egg-shaped, thick and leathery, margins finely toothed. Autumn color: vivid red.

Flowers. Small, white, borne on cymes 2 to 4 inches across, not fragrant.

Fruits. Small drupes, green at first ripening to blue-black, ¼-inch long, sweet and edible when ripe, persistent into winter.

Flowering period. May to July.

Fruiting period. September to midwinter.

Habitat. Grows on moist soils throughout its range. A common shrub of thickets, clearings, swamps, and forest margins.

Range. Newfoundland south to Tennessee, west to Alabama.

Hardiness zone. 2.

Landscape notes. This dense, compact, rounded shrub has spreading branches, and is attractive alone or in clumps in open areas and hedgerows. Its flowers and fruits are ornamental. It is hardy, tolerates pruning, grows at a moderate rate, and requires little care. Its tolerance for salt makes it suitable for coastal plantings (Allan 1973).

Propagation. Seed dormancy may be broken by sowing seeds in sand, maintaining temperatures of 68° F. (night) and 86° F. (day) for two months, and of 50° F. (day and night) for three months (U.S. Forest Service 1948). See Nannyberry.

Birds That Use Witherod
(See Viburnums)

	Food	Cover	Nesting
Ruffed grouse	F	X	
Bobwhite	F	X	
Ring-necked pheasant	F	X	
Pileated woodpecker	F		
Brown thrasher	F		
American robin	F		
Eastern bluebird	F		
Rose-breasted grosbeak	F		
Purple finch	F		

Note: F, fruit.
Sources: McKenny 1939; Petrides 1972.

SOUTHERN ARROWWOOD
Viburnum dentatum L.

NORTHERN ARROWWOOD
Viburnum recognitum Fern.
CAPRIFOLIACEAE

Description. Both arrowwoods occur in the northeastern United States. Their ranges overlap in southern New England. They are difficult to separate, and for wildlife value can be considered together. Northern arrowwood twigs are hairless. Both of these straight-stemmed, erect shrubs grow in clumps or thickets, so provide good cover and nest sites. They grow to 15 feet.

Bark. Gray to reddish-brown, smooth on stems.

Leaves. Opposite, simple, 1½ to 3 inches long, elliptic to round with coarse teeth and thick veins. Autumn colors: dark bronze to red.

Flowers. White, on cymes 2 to 3 inches in diameter.

Fruits. Small, oval to round, dark blue drupes.

Flowering period. June to August.

Fruiting period. Late August to November.

Habitat. Both species grow in sun or partial shade in moist, low ground. Commonly found along streams and ponds growing singly or in thickets.

Range. Southern arrowwood: southeastern Massachusetts south to Florida, west to Texas and Missouri. Northern arrowwood: New Brunswick south to South Carolina, west to Ohio and south Ontario.

Hardiness zone. Southern arrowwood: 5. Northern arrowwood: 2.

Landscape notes. These are excellent shrubs for clumps and borders wherever dense foliage is desired. A thick hedge of arrowwood is difficult to walk through because of its many upright stems. Both species will grow in sun or partial shade in any good garden soil. They transplant well, are hardy, grow at a moderate rate, and need little care. Arrowwood is a

Southern Arrowwood

good choice for urban areas because it tolerates city smoke (Terres 1968).

Propagation. To break seed dormancy of arrowwood, stratify seeds in moist peat at 68° F. (night) and 86° F. (day) for 12 to 17 months, and at 50° F. (day and night) for 2½ months (Giersbach 1937). See Nannyberry.

Birds That Use Arrowwood
(See Viburnums)

	Food[1]	Cover[2]	Nesting
Ruffed grouse	F	X	
Common flicker	F		
Eastern phoebe	F		
Gray catbird	F	X	X
Brown thrasher	F		
American robin	F		
Eastern bluebird	F		
White-eyed vireo	F		
Red-eyed vireo	F		
Rose-breasted grosbeak	F		

Note: [1]fruits are important food in fall for migrating birds; [2]thickets provide good cover for ground-nesting birds; F, fruit.
Sources: McKenny 1939; Petrides 1972.

NANNYBERRY
Viburnum lentago L.
CAPRIFOLIACEAE

Description. Nannyberry is one of the largest viburnums. In open sites, it occasionally grows as a small tree, 20 to 25 feet tall, with a dense, oval crown. It favors rich, moist sites. Its normal height is 10 to 20 feet tall, usually less. Other common names are sheepberry, sweet viburnum, and wild raisin.

Bark. Brown, twigs gray.

Leaves. Opposite, simple, 2 to 5 inches long, ovate to narrowly elliptic, finely toothed, leaf stalks winged. Autumn color: purplish-red.

Flowers. Small, white, slightly fragrant, forming on flat-topped, terminal cymes 2 to 5 inches across.

Fruits. Elliptic, blue-black drupes, raisinlike appearance, edible.

Flowering period. April to June.

Fruiting period. August to October.

Habitat. Grows in partial shade along forest edges and in the full shade of the forest interior in association with hardwoods and conifers. Also grows in full sunlight in hedgerows bordering fields and swamps. Dense stands form under optimal conditions.

Range. Quebec south to the mountains of Georgia, west to Manitoba and Colorado.

Hardiness zone. 2.

Landscape notes. This is a sturdy shrub or small tree for yard or woodland borders, and is handsome when planted singly or in clumps. These plants are excellent for background screens. They are hardy and grow rapidly.

Propagation. Nannyberry reproduces naturally by seed and root suckering. It is easily transplanted. Seeds and plant stock are available from nurseries, but high costs may make it more practical to propagate them by finding plants growing locally and making seed collections, taking softwood or hardwood cuttings, layering, or relocating entire plants.

Seeds planted the same season as collected

will normally germinate the second spring following sowing due to a two-stage stratification process. Seeds to be planted later should be cleaned of pulp, air-dried, and placed in sealed containers. These containers should be refrigerated at 34°–38° F. until ready for use (Heit 1967d). To speed up the process of breaking seed dormancy, stratify seeds in peat for five months at 68° F. (night) and 86° F. (day), and for three to four months at 41°–50° F. (Barton 1958; Giersback 1937). Seeds may be broadcast or sown in drills and mulched with sawdust to be removed upon germination. They may be transplanted after two seasons of growth.

Birds That Use Nannyberry
(See Viburnums)

	Food	Cover	Nesting
Ruffed grouse	F	X	
Bobwhite	F	X	
Ring-necked pheasant	F	X	
Common flicker	F		
Gray catbird	F	X	X
American robin	F		
Hermit thrush	F	X	
Eastern bluebird	F		
Cedar waxwing	F		
Rose-breasted grosbeak	F		
Purple finch	F		

Note: F, fruit.
Sources: McKenny 1939; Schutz 1974; Holweg 1964.

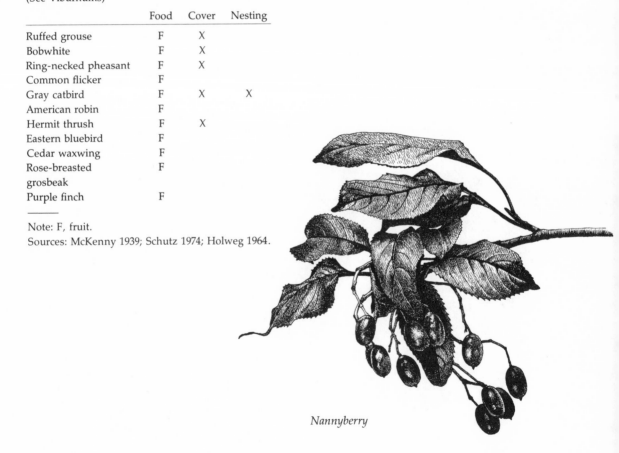

Nannyberry

AMERICAN CRANBERRYBUSH
Viburnum trilobum Marsh.
CAPRIFOLIACEAE

Description. American cranberrybush is a for-
est-edge viburnum of scattered distribution.
The fruits may not be preferred, but because
they persist through the winter, they serve as
an emergency food for many birds. This
shrub grows 6 to 15 feet tall. Other common
names are American highbush cranberry and
crampbark.

Bark. Tan to gray, smooth.

Leaves. Opposite, simple, 2 to 4 inches long, 3
long, pointed lobes per leaf with a few blunt
teeth at tips, none in sinuses, dark green in
summer, with or without fine hairs. Autumn
color: reddish.

Flowers. White, sterile flowers are larger than
fertile flowers and are borne on margins of
terminal cymes 2 to 4 inches in diameter.
Very showy.

Fruits. Globose or oval, bright red or orange
drupes, ⅜- to ½-inch long, very colorful
when leaves drop, remain on plant all winter,
edible.

Flowering period. May to July.

Fruiting period. August to October, persistent
throughout winter.

Habitat. A northern species of *Viburnum* found
naturally in low places in moist woods or
roadside ditches, but will grow when planted
in drier, more open sites.

Range. New Brunswick south to Pennsylvania,
west to British Columbia and Wyoming.

Hardiness zone. 2.

Landscape notes. This plant's year-round
beauty makes it a favorite shrub for landscape
use. It is attractive in hedgerows and clumps.
The low, dense variety *V. t. compactum,* is
useful for foundation plantings. American
cranberrybush is very hardy, grows rapidly,
and withstands heavy pruning. It is easily
transplanted.

Propagation. American cranberrybush can be
propagated from seed by forcing the breaking

American Cranberrybush

of dormancy. To force germination, stratify seeds in peat for two months, alternating temperatures from 50° F. (night) to 86° F. (day). Then reduce the temperatures for two more months to 41°–50° F., both day and night (Barton 1958; Giersback 1937). Seeds may be broadcast or sown in drills and mulched with sawdust. Seedlings can be transplanted after two seasons of growth. Seeds to be planted later may be cleaned, dried, and stored in airtight containers at 41° F. They should retain viability for up to 1½ years. Plants may also be propagated from hardwood and softwood cuttings and layers (U.S. Forest Service 1948).

Birds That Use American Cranberrybush
(See Viburnums)

	Food	Cover	Nesting
Turkey	F	X	
Spruce grouse	F	X	
Ruffed grouse	F	X	
Ring-necked pheasant	F	X	
Eastern bluebird	F		
Cedar waxwing	F		
Cardinal	F		

Note: F, fruit.
Sources: McKenny 1939; Davison 1967; Petrides 1972; Longenecker and Ellarson 1973; Holweg 1964.

Birds That Use Viburnums

	Food	Cover	Nesting
Turkey	F	X	
Spruce grouse	F	X	
Ruffed grouse*	F	X	
Bobwhite	F	X	
Ring-necked pheasant	F	X	
Common flicker	F		
Pileated woodpecker	F		
Great crested flycatcher	F		
Willow flycatcher		X	X
Gray jay	F		
Mockingbird	F		
Gray catbird	F		
Brown thrasher*	F		
American robin	F		
Wood thrush	F	X	X
Hermit thrush	F	X	
Swainson's thrush	F	X	
Gray-cheeked thrush	F	X	
Eastern bluebird	F		
Cedar waxwing*	F		
Starling	F		
Cardinal	F		
Rose-breasted grosbeak	F		
Purple finch	F		
Pine grosbeak	F		
White-throated sparrow	F	X	

Note: *preferred food; F, fruit.
Sources: Bump et al. 1947; Rollins 1974.

VINES

HEARTLEAF AMPELOPSIS
Ampelopsis cordata Michx.
VITACEAE

Description. This woody vine has heart-shaped leaves and a woody pith. The plants often have a bushy appearance. They do not climb as high in the Northeast as they do in the South. Tendrils are few and unbranched. Another common name is American ampelopsis.
Leaves. Cordate, 3 to 6 inches long with finely toothed edges.
Flowers. Inconspicuous, green, forming in clusters.
Fruits. Round, bluish, pea-sized berries, dry and inedible.
Flowering period. May to June.
Fruiting period. August to November.
Habitat. Fertile woods and bottomlands.
Range. Massachusetts (rare), Virginia to Nebraska, Texas and Mexico.
Hardiness zone. 5.
Landscape notes. Plants may be cultivated on a trellis and restrained by pruning, or located along property boundaries and allowed to spread freely. They provide good cover for low walls and fences.
Propagation. Plants may be propagated by layering in summer and by softwood and hardwood cuttings (Mahlstede and Haber 1957). Ripe seeds should be stratified at 40° F. for three months before sowing (Wyman 1977).

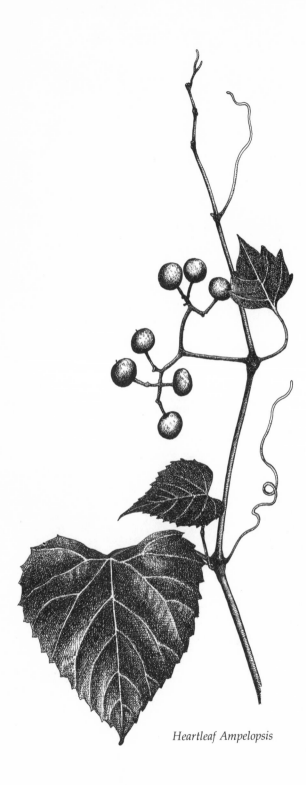

Heartleaf Ampelopsis

Birds That Use Ampelopsis

	Food	Cover	Nesting
Turkey	F		
Ruffed grouse	F		
Ring-necked pheasant	F		
Bobwhite	F		
Mourning dove	F		
Common flicker*	F		
Gray catbird	F		
Brown thrasher*	F		
Wood thrush*	F		
Eastern bluebird	F		

Note: *preferred food; F, fruit.
Sources: McKenny 1939; Davison 1967; Petrides 1972.

COMMON TRUMPETCREEPER
Campsis radicans (L.) Seem
BIGNONIACEAE

Description. This shrubby vine grows to 30 feet and clings by means of small, rootlike hold-fasts. Plants climb rapidly on stone, brick, and wood. They may become heavy with age and require the support of a trellis. Orange flowers attract ruby-throated hummingbirds.
Leaves. Compound with 7 to 11 elliptic, toothed leaflets, leaf length 3 to 12 inches. Autumn color: dark green.
Flowers. Tubular, orange-red, clustered blooms.
Fruits. Large, dry capsules, 4 to 8 inches long, containing many small, flat, winged seeds.
Flowering period. July to September.
Fruiting period. August to October.
Habitat. Grows in thickets in a variety of soils.
Range. Connecticut south to Florida, west to Iowa and Texas. Naturalized as far north as Massachusetts and Michigan.
Hardiness zone. 5.
Landscape notes. This attractive climber is useful on trellises and walls of buildings. The brilliant orange-red flowers contrast sharply with the deep-green foliage. Plants are valuable for controlling erosion on steep banks. If pruned severely, root sprouts occur in profusion.
Propagation. Trumpetcreeper is usually propagated from cuttings but may be grown from seed. Seeds should be collected from ripe fruits before the fruits split open and sown in fall, or stratified in moist sand for up to two months at 41°–50° F. (U.S. Forest Service 1948). Cuttings may be taken from softwood, hardwood, and roots. Layering is also practiced (U.S. Forest Service 1948; Hartman and Kester 1968). Plants north of 42° latitude should be protected from winter cold by placing them on the south side of buildings.

Birds That Use Common Trumpetcreeper

	Food	Cover	Nesting
Ruby-throated hummingbird	N		
American goldfinch	S		

Note: N, nectar; S, seeds.
Sources: Terres 1968; Longenecker and Ellarson 1973.

AMERICAN BITTERSWEET

Celastrus scandens L.

CELASTRACEAE

Description. This vigorous plant climbs to 60 feet by means of twining, thornless, brown stems.

Leaves. Elliptic to wedge-shaped, 2 to 5 inches long with fine, wavy teeth. Autumn color: yellow.

Flowers. Inconspicuous green blossoms, forming in clusters, with sexes on separate plants.

Fruits. Small, rounded, yellow to orange capsules with bright-red, fleshy seed coverings. Good crops are borne almost every year.

Flowering period. May to June.

Fruiting period. August to December, or longer.

Habitat. Grows in woods and along fencerows in a variety of soils, but may prefer drier sites. Grows in sun or partial shade.

Range. Quebec south to Georgia, west to Manitoba and Oklahoma.

Hardiness zone. 2.

Landscape notes. American bittersweet has
been cultivated for ornamental purposes since
1736 (U.S. Forest Service 1948). The red and
yellow fruits are decorative on the vine as
well as in the home. Male and female plants
should be located close together to facilitate
cross-pollination. If planted close to the house
or near trees and shrubs, they should be
pruned periodically to prevent rampant
growth. Plants are attractive on trellises,
fences, and low walls and are useful in stabilizing banks. They prefer sunny locations.

Propagation. Plants may be propagated from
seed, root cuttings, stem cuttings, and layers.
To propagate from seed, fruits should be collected when capsules open and expose the
small red globes. Seeds should be dried for
two to three weeks. It is not necessary to separate the seeds from the pulp before sowing
(U.S. Forest Service 1948). Seeds may be
sown in fall, or stratified in January in moist
sand or peat for three months at 41° F. and
sown in spring (U.S. Forest Service 1948).

Birds That Use American Bittersweet

	Food	Cover	Nesting
Turkey	F		
Ruffed grouse	F		
Bobwhite	F		
Ring-necked pheasant	F		
Mockingbird	F		
Gray catbird	F		
American robin	F		
Hermit thrush	F		
Eastern bluebird	F		
Cedar waxwing	F		
Starling	F		
Red-eyed vireo	F		
House sparrow	F		
Cardinal	F		
Pine grosbeak	F		

Note: F, fruit.
Sources: McKenny 1939; Davison 1967; Martin et al.
1951.

COMMON MOONSEED
Menispermum canadense L.
MENISPERMACEAE

Description. This dense, semiwoody vine
climbs up to 12 feet on trees, shrubs, and
fences. It usually dies back to the ground in
winter but quickly sprouts in spring (Wyman
1949). Another common name is Canada
moonseed.

Leaves. Large, 5 to 11 inches long with shallow lobes, leafstalk is attached to the inside
edge of the leaf on the underside. Autumn
color: yellow.

Flowers. White or yellowish, male and female
flowers form on separate plants.

Fruits. Inedible, black berries, ⅓-inch in diameter, covered with whitish powder, resembling small grapes, each containing one cres-
cent-shaped seed.

Flowering period. May to July.

Fruiting period. August to October.

Habitat. Damp soils of stream banks and river
banks.

Range. Western Quebec south to Georgia,
west to Manitoba and Oklahoma.

Hardiness zone. 6.

Landscape notes. Ivylike foliage is attractive on
a trellis when controlled by light annual
pruning. It is useful as a ground cover in
areas where plants can spread freely by underground stems.

Birds That Use Common Moonseed

	Food	Cover	Nesting
Turkey	F		
Brown thrasher	F		
American robin	F		
Cedar waxwing	F		
Rufous-sided towhee	F		

Note: F, fruit.
Source: Davison 1967.

VIRGINIA CREEPER

Parthenocissus quinquefolia (L.) Planch.
VITACEAE

Description. This high-climbing vine clings by means of long, slender tendrils. Its stems contain a white pith and are covered with tight, dotted bark. Other common names are American ivy and woodbine.
Leaves. Palmately compound with 5 (occasionally 3 or 7) toothed, oblong to obovate leaflets, leaf length varies from 3 to 8 inches. Autumn color: vivid scarlet.
Flowers. Inconspicuous, greenish, forming in clusters.
Fruits. Small, blue berries, 3/16- to 5/16-inch in diameter, lightly covered with white powder.
Flowering period. June to August.
Fruiting period. August to February.

Habitat. Woods and thickets, on many soil types.
Range. Southwestern Quebec south to Florida, west to Minnesota and Mexico.
Hardiness zone. 4.
Landscape notes. This vine grows well on trellises and other supports but will cling tightly to brick and stone. The deep-green leaves turn fiery red in autumn. Vines grow rapidly once they are established.
Propagation. Plants may be propagated from seeds, hardwood cuttings, and layering. Seeds may be separated from ripe fruits by maceration, then dried for storage or sowing. They may be sown in fall, or stratified in moist sand or peat for two months at 41° F. and sown in spring. Seeds should be sown in drills ⅜-inch deep in nursery soil (U.S. Forest Service 1948).

Birds That Use Virginia Creeper

	Food	Cover	Nesting
Turkey	F		
Bobwhite	F		
Common flicker	F		
Pileated woodpecker*	F		
Red-bellied woodpecker*	F		
Red-headed woodpecker	F		
Yellow-bellied sapsucker*	F		
Hairy woodpecker	F		
Downy woodpecker	F		
Eastern kingbird*	F		
Great crested flycatcher*	F		
Tree swallow	F		
Common crow	F		
Black-capped chickadee	F		
Tufted titmouse	F		
White-breasted nuthatch	F		
Mockingbird*	F		
Gray catbird	F		
Brown thrasher*	F		
American robin*	F		
Wood thrush*	F		
Hermit thrush	F		
Swainson's thrush	F		
Gray-cheeked thrush	F		
Veery	F		
Eastern bluebird*	F		
Starling	F		
White-eyed vireo	F		
Red-eyed vireo*	F		
Yellow-rumped warbler*	F		
Bay-breasted warbler*	F		
House sparrow	F	X	X[1]
Scarlet tanager	F		
Purple finch	F		
Fox sparrow*	F		

Note: *preferred food; F, fruit; [1]on buildings.
Sources: McKenny 1939; Davison 1967; Martin et al. 1951; Petrides 1972; Petit 1949.

CAT GREENBRIER
Smilax glauca Walt.
LILIACEAE

Description. This green-stemmed, high-climbing vine is similar to common greenbrier (*S. rotundifolia*), but has weak prickles. Another common name is sawbrier.
Leaves. Broadly oval, narrowing toward a more or less pointed tip, 2 to 5 inches long, undersides bluish-green and covered with fine, whitish powder. Autumn color: green.
Flowers. Inconspicuous, greenish-yellow, six-parted blossoms forming in small, rounded clusters.
Fruits. Small, blue-black berries with white powdery surfaces, containing one to several large seeds.
Flowering period. May to June.
Fruiting period. September to October, persistent through winter.
Habitat. Commonly found on low, wet ground bordering swamps and streams, and on drier soils of woodlands and hedgerows.
Range. New England south to Florida, west to Missouri and Texas.
Hardiness zone. 6.
Landscape notes. Plants form dense tangles and impenetrable thickets which are useful for naturalizing areas where there is little human activity. They provide excellent food and nesting cover for many songbirds.

Birds That Use Cat Greenbrier

	Food	Cover	Nesting
Turkey*	F	X	
Ruffed grouse*	F	X	
Ring-necked pheasant	F	X	
Common flicker	F		
Pileated woodpecker	F		
Red-bellied woodpecker	F		
Common crow	F		
Fish crow	F		
Mockingbird*	F	X	X
Gray catbird*	F	X	X
Brown thrasher	F	X	X
American robin*	F		
Hermit thrush	F	X	
Swainson's thrush*	F	X	
Gray-cheeked thrush	F	X	
Cedar waxwing	F		
Cardinal	F	X	X
White-throated sparrow	F	X	
Fox sparrow	F	X	

Note: *preferred food; F, fruit.
Sources: McKenny 1939; Davison 1967; Martin et al. 1951.

COMMON GREENBRIER
Smilax rotundifolia L.
LILIACEAE

Description. This is a vigorous, green-stemmed climbing vine with many strong thorns and long, thin tendrils. It climbs to 30 feet on trees and other supporting structures. Other common names are bullbrier and horsebrier.
Leaves. Broadly rounded or heart-shaped with prominent parallel veins, 2 to 5 inches long, shiny on both surfaces. Autumn color: green.
Flowers. Inconspicuous, greenish-yellow, with six-parted blossoms forming in small rounded clusters where the leaves and climbing stem join.
Fruits. Small, blue-black berries containing one to many large seeds, about ⅜-inch in diameter, sometimes covered with whitish powder.
Flowering period. April to August.
Fruiting period. September, persistent through winter.
Habitat. Prefers moist, low areas but will grow elsewhere. Common in woods and along fences and fields.
Range. Nova Scotia south to Florida, west to Michigan and Texas.
Hardiness zone. 5.
Landscape notes. This is an excellent plant for creating a dense, often impenetrable tangle in places where such growth should be appropriate. Some consider it a weed, but it provides excellent food and protection to wildlife.

Birds That Use Common Greenbrier

	Food	Cover	Nesting
Turkey*	F	X	
Ruffed grouse*	F	X	
Bobwhite	F	X	
Common flicker	F		
Pileated woodpecker	F		
Common crow	F		
Fish crow*	F		
Mockingbird*	F	X	X
Gray catbird*	F	X	X
Brown thrasher	F	X	X
American robin*	F		
Hermit thrush	F		
Swainson's thrush*	F	X	
Gray-cheeked thrush	F	X	
Eastern bluebird	F		
Cedar waxwing	F		
Common grackle	F		
Cardinal	F	X	X
White-throated sparrow	F	X	
Fox sparrow	F	X	

Note: *preferred food; F, fruit.
Sources: McKenny 1939; Davison 1967; Martin et al. 1951.

POISON IVY
Toxicodendron radicans L.
ANACARDIACEAE

Description. Plants may be shrublike, creeping, or climbing. Young stems are brown. Older stems and climbing stems are darker and covered with fine, aerial rootlets. This is a valuable food source for birds.

Leaves. Composed of three large, shiny leaflets, 2 to 4 inches long, margins smooth or bluntly toothed. Autumn colors: red to reddish-yellow.

Flowers. Small, green, in clusters 1 to 3 inches long.

Fruits. Small, white, rounded drupes, about ¼-inch in diameter, preferred by a great variety of birds.

Flowering period. May to July.

Fruiting period. August to November, persistent into winter.

Habitat. Open woods, fence-rows, and along stone walls.

Range. Quebec south to Florida, west to British Columbia and Arizona.

Hardiness zone. 4.

Landscape notes. Contact with all parts of the plant should be avoided because the plant produces an oil that irritates or blisters the skin of those who are susceptible. Poison ivy may be undesirable close to homes, but it is useful in creating a food source that is highly attractive to songbirds and gamebirds.

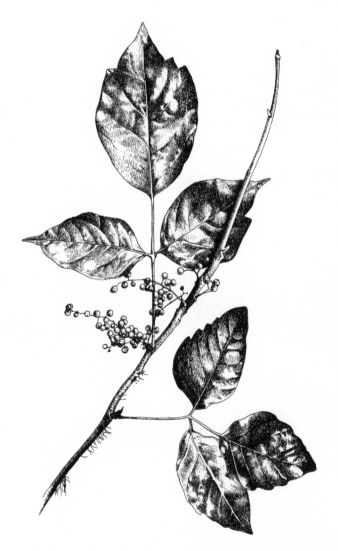

Birds That Use Poison Ivy

	Food	Cover	Nesting
Turkey*	F		
Ruffed grouse	F		
Bobwhite*	F		
Ring-necked pheasant	F		
Common flicker*	F		
Pileated woodpecker	F		
Red-bellied woodpecker*	F		
Yellow-bellied sapsucker*	F		
Hairy woodpecker*	F		
Downy woodpecker*	F		
Eastern phoebe	F		
Common crow	F		
Black-capped chickadee*	F		
Carolina chickadee*	F		
Tufted titmouse	F		
Carolina wren	F		
Mockingbird*	F		
Gray catbird*	F		
Brown thrasher	F		
Hermit thrush*	F		
Eastern bluebird	F		
Ruby-crowned kinglet*	F		
Cedar waxwing	F		
Starling*	F		
White-eyed vireo	F		
Warbling vireo	F		
Cape May warbler	F		
Yellow-rumped warbler*	F		
Purple finch	F		
Northern junco	F		
White-crowned sparrow	F		
White-throated sparrow*	F		
Fox sparrow	F		

Note: *preferred food; F, fruit.
Source: Martin et al. 1951.

GRAPES
Vitis spp.
VITACEAE

Description. These thornless, high-climbing vines cling by means of tendrils. The bark usually shreds in long strips. Vines that over-top small trees and shrubs create nest sites for many birds, especially cardinals and catbirds.
Leaves. Heart-shaped at base, often lobed, 2 to 9 inches long depending on species, margins toothed, surfaces hairy or smooth.
Flowers. Inconspicuous, green, forming in clusters, sexes form on same and on separate plants.
Fruits. Round, amber, blue, or black berries, 5/16- to 1 inch in diameter varying with species, sweet or sour. As a group, grapes are among the most valuable wildlife food plants.
Landscape notes. Grapes are often cultivated on arbors to serve as screens and allow easy access to fruits. Wandering branches may readily be pruned back without harming the plant. For best results, plant in sunny areas.
Propagation. (The following information applies to riverbank grape [*Vitis riparia*], but may work as well for other species.) Seeds may be separated from ripe fruits by macerating the pulp in water. They should be stratified for two months at 41° F. and sown in spring. Plants may also be propagated by layering and from cuttings (U.S. Forest Service 1948).

Fox Grapes

Some Recommended Native Grapes

Species	Height	Leaves	Flower Period	Flower Color	Fruit Period	Fruit Color	Habitat and Range
Fox Grape *Vitis labrusca*	high-climbing	3″–9″	May to July	green	August to October	½″–1″, black, purple, or amber, sweet	Fertile soils. Maine S to Georgia, W to Michigan and Tennessee. Hardiness zone: 6.
Riverbank Grape *Vitis riparia*	high-climbing	2″–9″	May to July	green	August to September	5/16″–½″, blue-black, usually sour	Streambanks. Quebec S to Tennessee, W to Manitoba and New Mexico. Hardiness zone: 3.
Summer Grape *Vitis aestivalis*	high-climbing	2″–9″	May to July	green	September to October	3/16″–½″, black, pleasant taste	Dry woods. Maine S to Georgia, W to Wisconsin and Texas. Hardiness zone: 4.
New England Grape *Vitis novae-angliae*	high-climbing	3″–9″	June to July	green	September	½″–¾″, shiny black, sweet	Fertile soils. New England, New Jersey, Pennsylvania, New York. Hardiness zone: 5.
Frost Grape *Vitis vulpina*	high-climbing	2″–9″	May to June	green	September to October	⅛″–⅜″, black, sweet aftertaste	Rich soils and bottomlands. New York S to Florida, W to Illinois and Texas. Hardiness zone: 6.

Birds That Use Grapes

	Food	Cover	Nesting
Turkey*	F		
Ruffed grouse*	F		
Bobwhite	F		
Ring-necked pheasant	F		
Mourning dove	F		
Yellow-billed cuckoo	F		
Common flicker	F		
Pileated woodpecker*	F		
Red-bellied woodpecker*	F		
Red-headed woodpecker*	F		
Yellow-bellied sapsucker	F		
Hairy woodpecker	F		
Eastern kingbird	F		X^1
Great crested flycatcher	F		
Blue jay	F		
Gray jay	F		
Common crow	F		
Fish crow	F		
Tufted titmouse	F		
Mockingbird*	F	X	$X^{1,2}$
Gray catbird*	F	X	$X^{1,2}$
Brown thrasher*	F	X	$X^{1,2}$
American robin*	F		
Wood thrush*	F		
Hermit thrush*	F		
Swainson's thrush*	F		
Gray-cheeked thrush*	F		
Veery	F	X	X^2
Eastern bluebird*	F		
Cedar waxwing*	F		X^2
Starling	F		
Red-eyed vireo*	F		
Philadelphia vireo	F		
Warbling vireo*	F		
Black-and-white warbler			X^2
Blue-winged warbler			X^2
Cape May warbler*	F		X^2
Black-throated blue warbler			X^2
Cerulean warbler			X^2
Chestnut-sided warbler			X^2

	Food	Cover	Nesting
Ovenbird*	F		
Yellow-breasted chat	F	X	X
Hooded warbler			X^2
American redstart*	F		X^2
House sparrow*	F		
Rusty blackbird	F		
Boat-tailed grackle	F		
Common grackle	F		
Orchard oriole	F		
Northern oriole	F		
Scarlet tanager*	F		
Summer tanager	F		
Cardinal*	F	X	X
Purple finch	F		
Pine warbler	F		X^2
American goldfinch			X^2
Rufous-sided towhee	F		X^2
Northern junco	F		
Fox sparrow*	F		

Note: *preferred food; F, fruit; [1]preferred nest site; [2]uses bark in nest.

Sources: McKenny 1939; Davison 1967; Martin et al. 1951; Petrides 1972; Langille 1884; Dugmore 1904; Headstrom 1970.

Appendix

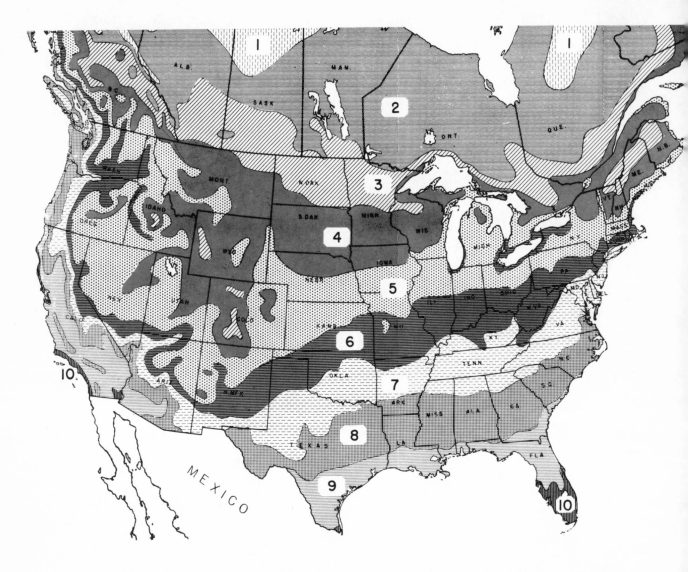

Plant Hardiness Zone Map prepared by U.S. National Arboretum and USDA in cooperation with the American Horticultural Society. Ag. Res. Serv. Misc. Pub. 814. May 1960.

Approximate range of average annual minimum temperatures for each zone

Zone 1	below −50°F
2	−50° to −40°
3	−40° to −30°
4	−30° to −20°
5	−20° to −10°
6	−10° to 0°
7	0° to 10°
8	10° to 20°
9	20° to 30°
10	30° to 40°

Flowering and Fruiting Periods of Low Trees (10–30 feet)[1]

Plant	Flower color	Fruit color	Jan.	Feb.	Mar.	Apr.	May	Jun.	Jul.	Aug.	Sept.	Oct.	Nov.	Dec.
Gray Birch	i	brown	o	o		*	*				o	o	o	o
American Holly	i	red	o	o	o	o	o*	o*		o	o	o	o	o
American Hop-hornbeam	i	brown				*	*	*		o	o	o	o	o
Bobwhite Crabapple	pnk/wte	yellow	o	o	o	o	*			o	o	o	o	o
Dorothea Crabapple	pnk/wte	yellow	o	o	o		*			o	o	o	o	o
Sargent Crabapple	white	red	o	o	o		*			o	o	o	o	o
Japanese Flowering Crabapple	white	red/yel	o	o	o		*			o	o	o	o	o
Tea Crabapple	white	yel/red	o	o			*			o	o	o	o	o
Common Apple	wte/pnk	red/grn				*	*	*			o	o	o	
Smooth Serviceberry	white	pur/blk			*	*	*	o*	o	o				
Shadblow Serviceberry	white	pur			*	*	*	o*	o	o				
Pin Cherry	white	red			*	*	*	*	o*	o	o	o	o	o
Common Chokecherry	white	pur/blk				*	*	*	o*	o	o	o		

[1]fruiting periods indicate when fruits and/or seeds are available to wildlife.
*flower; o, fruit; i, inconspicuous.

Flowering and Fruiting Periods of Medium Trees (30–60 feet)[1]

Plant	Flower color	Fruit color	Jan.	Feb.	Mar.	Apr.	May	Jun.	Jul.	Aug.	Sept.	Oct.	Nov.	Dec.
Eastern Red Cedar	i	blue	o	o	o*	*	*				o	o	o	o
Balsam Fir	i	brown	o	o	o		*	*		o	o	o	o	o
Pitch Pine	i	brown	o	o	o	o*	o*	o	o	o	o	o	o	o
Northern White Cedar	i	brown				*	*			o	o	o		
Bigtooth Aspen	i	brown				*	o*	o						
Quaking Aspen	i	brown				*	o*	o						
Black Willow	i	green		*	*	o*	o*	o*	o					
Butternut	i	green				*	*				o	o	o	o
Mockernut Hickory	i	brown				*	*				o	o	o	o
Sweet Birch	i	brown	o			*	*			o	o	o	o	o
American Hornbeam	i	brown				*	*	*		o	o	o		
Common Hackberry	i	red/pur	o	o		*	*				o	o	o	o
White Mulberry	green	wte/pnk					*		o	o				
Red Mulberry	green	red				*	*	o*	o	o				
Common Sassafras	grn/yel	blue				*	*	*		o	o	o		
American Mountain-ash	white	red/orng	o	o	o		*	*	*	o	o	o	o	o
Siberian Crabapple	white	red/yel	o	o	o		*			o	o	o	o	o
Downy Serviceberry	white	pur			*	*	*	o*	o	o				
Black Tupelo	grn/wte	blu/blk				*	*	*		o	o	o		
Flowering Dogwood	white	red			*	*	*	*		o	o	o	o	
Common Persimmon	white	orng/yel				*	*	*	*		o	o	o	
Green Ash	i	brown	o	o		*	*				o	o	o	o
Black Ash	i	brown	o	o	o	*	*	o	o	o	o	o	o	o

[1]fruiting periods indicate when fruits and/or seeds are available to wildlife.
*flower; o, fruit; i, inconspicuous.

Flowering and Fruiting Periods of Tall Trees (60–100+ feet) [1]

Plant	Flower color	Fruit color	Jan.	Feb.	Mar.	Apr.	May	Jun.	Jul.	Aug.	Sept.	Oct.	Nov.	Dec.
Eastern Hemlock	i	brown	o				*	*			o	o	o	o
Red Spruce	i	brown				*	*				o	o		
White Spruce	i	brown					*			o	o	o	o	
Colorado Spruce	i	brown	o	o		*	*				o	o	o	o
Eastern Larch	i	brown					*			o	o			
White Pine	i	brown				*	*	*			o	o		
Red Pine	i	brown	o	o	o	o*	o*	o*	o	o	o	o	o	o
Scotch Pine	i	brown	o	o	o	o	*	*			o	o	o	o
Eastern Poplar	i	brown		*	*	o*	o*	o						
Eastern Black Walnut	i	green				*	*	*			o	o	o	
Shagbark Hickory	i	brown				*	*				o	o	o	o
Pignut Hickory	i	brown				*	*	*			o	o	o	o
Yellow Birch	i	brown	o	o		*	*			o	o	o	o	o
Paper Birch	i	brown	o	o		*	*	*		o	o	o	o	o
American Beech	i	brown				*	*				o	o	o	
White Oak	i	brown			*	*	*				o	o	o	
Northern Red Oak	i	brown				*	*				o	o	o	o
Scarlet Oak	i	brown				*	*				o	o	o	
Pin Oak	i	brown				*	*				o	o	o	
Black Oak	i	brown				*	*				o	o	o	o
American Elm	i	brown		*	*	o*	o*	o						
Yellow-poplar	grn/orng	brown	o			*	*	*			o	o	o	o
American Sweetgum	i	yellow			*	*	*				o	o	o	
Black Cherry	white	pur/blk			*	*	*	o*	o	o	o	o		
Sugar Maple	yellow	brown				*	*	o*	o	o	o	o	o	o
Silver Maple	grn/red	brown		*	*	o*	o*	o						
Norway Maple	yellow	brown				*	*	*			o	o	o	
Boxelder	yel/grn	brown	o	o	o*	*	*			o	o	o	o	o
Red Maple	red	brown		*	o*	o*	o*	o	o					
White Ash	i	brown	o	o		*	*	*			o	o	o	o

[1]fruiting periods indicate when fruits and/or seeds are available for wildlife.
*flower; o, fruit; i, inconspicuous.

Flowering and Fruiting Periods of Low Shrubs (1–5 feet) [1]

Plant	Flower color	Fruit color	Jan.	Feb.	Mar.	Apr.	May	Jun.	Jul.	Aug.	Sept.	Oct.	Nov.	Dec.
Canada Yew	i	red				*	*		o	o	o			
Common Juniper	i	blue	o	o	o	o	o*	o	o	o	o	o	o	o
Prairie Willow	i	i			*	o*	o							
Sweetfern	i	i				*	*	*		o	o	o		
Japanese Barberry	yellow	red	o	o	o	*	*	*	o	o	o	o	o	o
Pasture Gooseberry	green	red				*	*	*	o	o	o			
American Black Currant	yel/wte	black				*	*	o*	o	o	o			
Broadleaf Meadowsweet	pnk/wte	brown						*	o*	o*	o*	o	o	
Narrowleaf Meadowsweet	wte/ros	brown						*	*	o*	o*	o	o	
Hardhack	pnk/pur	brown							*	o*	o*	o	o	
Fragrant Thimbleberry	ros/pur	red					*	*	o*	o*	o*			
Northern Dewberry	white	black					*	o*	o	o				
Common Snowberry	white	white	o	o	o	o	o*	*	*	o	o	o	o	o
Meadow Rose	pink	red					*	*	o	o	o	o	o	o
Alderleaf Buckthorn	i	black					*	*	*	o	o	o		
Shrubby St. Johnswort	yellow	brown	o						*	o*	o*	o	o	o
Black Huckleberry	green	black				*	*	o	o	o				
Box Huckleberry	pnk/wte	black				*	*	o	o					
Dwarf Huckleberry	pnk/wte	black				*	*	o*	o	o	o	o		
Common Bearberry	pnk/wte	red	o	o	o	*	*	*	o*	o	o	o	o	o
Lowbush Blueberry	white	blue				*	*	*	o	o	o			
Mapleleaf Viburnum	white	pur/blk	o				*	*	o*	o*	o	o	o	o
Coralberry	grn/pur	red	o						*	*	o	o	o	o
American Fly Honeysuckle	yel/grn	red				*	*	o*	o	o				
Swamp Fly Honeysuckle	grn/yel	red					*	*	o*	o	o			
Blackcap Raspberry	white	black					*	*	o	o				
Red Raspberry	white	red					*	*	o					

[1] fruiting periods indicate when fruits and/or seeds are available for wildlife.

*flower; o, fruit; i, inconspicuous.

Flowering and Fruiting Periods of Medium Shrubs (6–10 feet) [1]

Plant	Flower color	Fruit color	Jan.	Feb.	Mar.	Apr.	May	Jun.	Jul.	Aug.	Sept.	Oct.	Nov.	Dec.
American Hazel	i	brown	o	o	*	*			o	o	o	o	o	o
Beaked Filbert	i	brown	o	o		*	*		o	o	o	o	o	o
Speckled Alder	i	brown			*	*	*			o	o	o	o	o
Smooth Alder	i	brown				*	*			o	o	o	o	o
European Barberry	yellow	red	o	o	o	o*	*	*	o	o	o	o	o	o
Allegany Blackberry	white	black					*	*	o	o	o			
Pasture Rose	pink	red						*	o*	o*	o	o	o	o
Swamp Rose	pink	red						*	*	o*	o	o	o	o
Virginia Rose	pink	red						*	o*	o				
Rugosa Rose	pink	red					*	*	o	o*	o			
Red Chokeberry	white	red				*	*	*	*	o	o	o	o	o
Black Chokeberry	white	black	o	o		*	*	*	*	o	o	o	o	o
Bartram Serviceberry	wte/pnk	pur/blk					*	o*	o*	o*	o			
Flameleaf Sumac	i	red	o	o	o				*	o*	o*	o	o	o
Inkberry	i	black	o	o	o*	*	*	*	o	o	o	o	o	o
Devil's Walkingstick	white	black							*	*	o	o		
Silky Dogwood	white	blue						*	*	o	o	o		
Red-osier Dogwood	white	white					*	*	o*	o*	o	o		
Gray Dogwood	white	white					*	*	o*	o	o	o	o	o
Dangleberry	grn/pnk	black					*	o*	o	o	o			
Highbush Blueberry	pink	blue					*	o*	o	o	o			
Common Buttonbush	white	grn/brn	o	o	o			*	*	*	o*	o	o	o
American Elder	white	pur/blk						*	o*	o*	o			
Scarlet Elder	white	red				*	*	o*	o*	o	o			
Glossy Buckthorn	i	black					*	o*	o*	o	o			
Scarlet Firethorn	white	orange	o	o	o	o	*	*			o	o	o	o
Hobblebush	white	purple					*	*	o*	o	o	o		
American Cranberrybush	white	red	o	o	o	o	*	*	*	o	o	o	o	o
Witherod	white	pur/blk	o				*	*	*		o	o	o	o
Tatarian Honeysuckle	pnk/wte	red					*	o*	o	o	o	o	o	
Standish Honeysuckle	white	red				*		o	o	o				
Morrow Honeysuckle	wte/yel	red/yel					*	o*	o	o				
Northern Bayberry	i	gray	o	o	o	o	o*	o*	o*	o	o	o	o	o

[1]fruiting periods indicate when fruits and/or seeds are available for wildlife.

*flower; o, fruit; i, inconspicuous.

Flowering and Fruiting Periods of Tall Shrubs (11–20+ feet)[1]

Plant	Flower color	Fruit color	Jan.	Feb.	Mar.	Apr.	May	Jun.	Jul.	Aug.	Sept.	Oct.	Nov.	Dec.
Pussy Willow	i	i			*	o*	o							
Purpleosier Willow	i	i				o*	o*							
Allegany Chinkapin	i	brown						*	*	o	o			
Common Spicebush	grn/yel	red			*	*	*			o	o	o		
Witch-hazel	yellow	brown	o	o	o	o	o	o	o	o	*	*	*	o
Multiflora Rose	white	red	o	o	o	o		*	o*	o	o	o	o	o
Cockspur Hawthorn	white	red	o	o				*		o	o	o	o	o
Washington Hawthorn	white	orng/red	o					*			o	o	o	o
Paul's Scarlet Hawthorn	pnk/red	red						*			o	o		
Smooth Sumac	green	red	o	o	o			*	*	o*	o	o	o	o
Staghorn Sumac	green	red	o	o	o		*	*	*	o	o	o	o	o
Common Winterberry	grn/wte	red	o	o	o	*	*	*	*	o	o	o	o	o
Smooth Winterberry	i	red					*	*		o	o	o	o	o
Common Buckthorn	i	black	o			*	*	o*	o*	o	o	o	o	o
Autumn Olive	yellow	red	o				*	*		o	o	o	o	o
Russian Olive	sil/yel	sil/wte	o	o	o	o	*	*	*	o	o	o	o	o
Alternate-leaf Dogwood	white	blu/blk						*	*	o	o	o		
Northern and Southern Arrowwood	white	blue						*	*	o*	o	o	o	
Nannyberry	white	blu/blk			*	*	*			o	o	o		
Amur Honeysuckle	white	red					*	*	o*	o	o	o	o	

[1]fruiting periods indicate when fruits and/or seeds are available for wildlife.

*flower; o, fruit; i, inconspicuous.

Flowering and Fruiting Periods of Vines[1]

Plant	Flower color	Fruit color	Jan.	Feb.	Mar.	Apr.	May	Jun.	Jul.	Aug.	Sept.	Oct.	Nov.	Dec.
Fox Grape	i	pur/blk					*	*	*	o	o	o		
Riverbank Grape	i	blu/blk					*	*	*	o	o			
Summer Grape	i	black					*	*	*		o	o		
New England Grape	i	black						*	*		o			
Frost Grape	i	black					*	*			o	o		
American Bittersweet	i	yel/orng					*	*		o	o	o	o	o
Common Greenbriar	i	blu/blk	o	o	o	*	*	*	*	*	o	o	o	o
Cat Greenbriar	i	blu/blk	o	o	o		*	*			o	o	o	o
Heartleaf Ampelopsis	i	blue					*	*		o	o	o	o	
Virginia Creeper	i	blue	o	o				*	*	o*	o	o	o	o
Common Trumpetcreeper	orng/red	brown							*	o*	o*	o		
Common Moonseed	i	black					*	*	*	o	o	o		
Poison Ivy	i	white	o	o			*	*	*	o	o	o	o	o

[1]fruiting periods indicate when fruits and/or seeds are available to wildlife.

*flower; o, fruit; i, inconspicuous.

Street Trees That Are Valuable for Birds

Shade trees for street planting should show six characteristics:

Hardiness to city conditions
Straightness of growth
Insect resistance
Shade production
Cleanliness—lack of litter
Longevity

Some trees that meet these criteria, and are also valuable to birds in the Northeast are given below:

Wide Streets (more than 50 feet wide)

Sugar maple (*Acer saccharum*)*
Common hackberry (*Celtis occidentalis*)
White ash (*Fraxinus americana*)
Green ash (*Fraxinus pennsylvanica*)
Yellow-poplar (*Liriodendron tulipifera*)
White oak (*Quercus alba*)

Medium Streets (40–50 feet wide)

Norway maple (*Acer platanoides*)
Red maple (*Acer rubrum*)
American sweetgum (*Liquidambar styraciflua*)
Northern red oak (*Quercus rubra*)
Scarlet oak (*Quercus coccinea*)
Pin oak (*Quercus palustris*)

Narrow Streets (less than 40 feet wide)

Flowering dogwood (*Cornus florida*)
Cockspur hawthorn (*Crataegus crus-galli*)
Paul's scarlet hawthorn (*Crataegus oxycantha pauli*)
Washington hawthorn (*Crataegus phaenopyrum*)

*Not recommended for streets salted in winter.
Sources:
Bush-Brown, J. and L. 1965. *America's garden book.* New York: Charles Scribner's Sons.
Fenska, R. R. 1956. *The complete modern tree expert's manual.* New York: Dodd, Mead and Co.

Plants That Will Grow in Dry, Sandy Soils

Trees

EVERGREEN

Eastern red cedar (*Juniperus virginiana*)
White spruce (*Picea glauca*)
Red pine (*Pinus resinosa*)
Pitch pine (*Pinus rigida*)
White pine (*Pinus strobus*)
Scotch pine (*Pinus sylvestris*)

DECIDUOUS

Boxelder (*Acer negundo*)
Gray birch (*Betula populifolia*)
Pignut hickory (*Carya glabra*)
Bigtooth aspen (*Populus grandidentata*)
Quaking aspen (*Populus tremuloides*)
Black cherry (*Prunus serotina*)
Scarlet oak (*Quercus coccinea*)
Common sassafras (*Sassafras albidum*)

Shrubs

EVERGREEN

Common bearberry (*Arctostaphylos uva-ursi*)
Inkberry (*Ilex glabra*)
Common juniper (*Juniperus communis*)

DECIDUOUS

Japanese barberry (*Berberis Thunbergii*)
European barberry (*Berberis vulgaris*)
Sweetfern (*Comptonia peregrina*)
Russian olive (*Elaeagnus angustifolia*)
Black huckleberry (*Gaylussacia baccata*)
Shrubby St. Johnswort (*Hypericum spathulatum*)
Morrow honeysuckle (*Lonicera Morrowi*)
Northern bayberry (*Myrica pensylvanica*)
Common buckthorn (*Rhamnus cathartica*)
Glossy buckthorn (*Rhamnus frangula*)
Flameleaf sumac (*Rhus copallina*)

Smooth sumac (*Rhus glabra*)
Staghorn sumac (*Rhus typhina*)
Pasture gooseberry (*Ribes cynosbati*)
Meadow rose (*Rosa blanda*)
Pasture rose (*Rosa carolina*)
Rugosa rose (*Rosa rugosa*)
Virginia rose (*Rosa virginiana*)
Coralberry (*Symphoricarpos orbiculatus*)
Lowbush blueberry (*Vaccinium angustifolium*)

Plants That Withstand City Conditions

Trees

Norway maple (*Acer platanoides*)
Common hackberry (*Celtis occidentalis*)
Flowering dogwood (*Cornus florida*)
Hawthorns (*Crataegus* spp.)
American sweetgum (*Liquidambar styraciflua*)
Yellow-poplar (*Liriodendron tulipifera*)
Colorado spruce (*Picea pungens*)
Pin oak (*Quercus palustris*)

Shrubs

Serviceberries (*Amelanchier* spp.)
Devil's walkingstick (*Aralia spinosa*)
Red chokeberry (*Aronia arbutifolia*)
Japanese barberry (*Berberis Thunbergii*)
Gray dogwood (*Cornus racemosa*)
Autumn olive (*Elaeagnus umbellata*)
Witch-hazel (*Hamamelis virginiana*)
Inkberry (*Ilex glabra*)
Common spicebush (*Lindera benzoin*)
Honeysuckles (*Lonicera* spp.)
Scarlet firethorn (*Pyracantha coccinea*)
Common buckthorn (*Rhamnus cathartica*)
Roses (*Rosa* spp.)
American elder (*Sambucus canadensis*)
Common snowberry (*Symphoricarpos albus*)
Coralberry (*Symphoricarpos orbiculatus*)
Japanese yew (*Taxus cuspidata*)
Viburnums (*Viburnum* spp.)

Vines

Heartleaf ampelopsis (*Ampelopsis cordata*)
Common trumpetcreeper (*Campsis radicans*)
American bittersweet (*Celastris scandens*)

Some Salt-Tolerant Plants

Trees

EVERGREEN

American holly (*Ilex opaca*)
Eastern red cedar (*Juniperus virginiana*)
White spruce (*Picea glauca*)
Colorado spruce (*Picea pungens*)
Pitch pine (*Pinus rigida*)
Northern white cedar (*Thuja occidentalis*)

DECIDUOUS

Paper birch (*Betula papyrifera*)
Paul's scarlet hawthorn (*Crataegus oxycantha pauli*)
American hornbeam (*Carpinus caroliniana*)
Common persimmon (*Diospyros virginiana*)
American sweetgum (*Liquidambar styraciflua*)
White mulberry (*Morus alba*)
Red mulberry (*Morus rubra*)
Quaking aspen (*Populus tremuloides*)
Black cherry (*Prunus serotina*)
White oak (*Quercus alba*)
Northern red oak (*Quercus rubra*)
Common sassafras (*Sassafras albidum*)

Shrubs

EVERGREEN

Common bearberry (*Arctostaphylos uva-ursi*)
Inkberry (*Ilex glabra*)
Common juniper (*Juniperus communis*)

DECIDUOUS

Red chokeberry (*Aronia arbutifolia*)
Sweetfern (*Comptonia peregrina*)
Russian olive (*Elaeagnus angustifolia*)
Autumn olive (*Elaeagnus umbellata*)
Tatarian honeysuckle (*Lonicera tatarica*)
Northern bayberry (*Myrica pensylvanica*)
Flameleaf sumac (*Rhus copallina*)

Meadow rose (*Rosa blanda*)
Rugosa rose (*Rosa rugosa*)
Virginia rose (*Rosa virginiana*)
Witherod (*Viburnum cassinoides*)

Some of the plants listed above have not undergone experimental testing for salt tolerance, but are known to withstand moderate to heavy amounts of salt by their presence in coastal areas.

SOURCES:
Bush-Brown, J. and L. 1965. *America's garden book.* New York: Charles Scribner's Sons.
Roberts, E. A., and Rehmann, E. 1929. *American plants for American gardens.* New York: Macmillan Co.
U.S. Soil Conservation Service. 1975. *Guidelines for soil and water conservation in urbanizing areas of Massachusetts.* Soil Conservation Service. Amherst, Massachusetts.
U.S. Soil Conservation Service. 1975. *Annual technical report.* Cape May Plant Materials Center. Cape May, New Jersey.

Sources

Adriance, G. W., and Brison, F. R. 1939. *Propagation of horticultural plants.* New York: McGraw-Hill Co.

Allan, D. N. 1973. *Native viburnums.* U.S. Soil Conserv. Serv. Info. Sheet MA-64. Amherst, Ma.

Allan, P. F., and Steiner, W. W. 1965. *Autumn olive.* USDA Leaflet No. 458.

Allen, A. A. 1934. *American bird biographies.* Ithaca, New York: Comstock Pub. Co.

Altman, P. L., and Dittmer, D. D., eds. 1962. *Growth, including reproduction and morphological development.* Fed. Am. Soc. for Exp. Biol. Biol. Handb. Serv. Washington, D.C.

Barnes, I. R. 1973. "Planting for birds." *Landscaping for Birds,* edited by S. A. Briggs, pp. 2–10. Washington, D.C.: Aud. Nat. Soc.

Barton, L. V. 1958. Germination and seedling production of species of *Viburnum. Plant Prop. Soc.* 8:126–35.

Billard, R. S. 1972. *Birdscaping your yard.* Hartford, Conn.: Conn. Dept. Envir. Protection.

Borell, A. E. 1962. *Russian olive.* USDA Leaflet No. 517. Washington, D.C.

Braun, E. L.
1950. *Deciduous forests of eastern North America.* New York: Hafner Pub. Co.
1961. *The woody plants of Ohio.* Columbus: Ohio State Univ. Press.

Bump, G.; Darrow, R. W.; Edminster, F. C.; and Crissey, W. F. 1947. *The ruffed grouse: life history, propagation, management.* N.Y. State Conserv. Dept.

Cantlon, J. E. 1953. Vegetation and microclimates on north and south slopes of Cushetunk Mountain, N.J. *Ecol. Monogr.* 23(3):241–70.

Chandler, F. B. 1943. Lowbush blueberries. *Maine Agr. Exp. Sta. Bull.* 423:105–31.

Coggeshall, R. G. 1960. Whip and tongue graft for dogwoods. *Am. Nurseryman* 111(2):9, 56–59.

Collins, H. H., and Boyajian, N. R. 1965. *Familiar garden birds of America.* New York: Harper and Row.

Conway, V. M. 1949. The bogs of central Minnesota. *Ecol. Monogr.* 19:175–206.

Core, E. L. 1974. "Spireas." In *Shrubs and Vines for Northeastern Wildlife,* edited by J. D. Gill and W. M. Healy, pp. 132–33. NE For. Exp. Sta., Upper Darby, Pa. (USDA For. Serv. Gen. Tech. Rep. NE-9).

Curtis, J. T. 1959. *The vegetation of Wisconsin.* Madison: Univ. of Wisconsin Press.

Davis, C. A. 1943. Methods of germinating rose seeds. *Am. Rose Magazine* 5(4):68–69.

Davis, O. H.
1926. Germination of seeds of certain horticultural plants. *Florist and Nursery Exch.* 63:917–22.
1927. Germination and early growth of *Cornus florida, Sambucus canadensis,* and *Berberis Thungergii. Bot. Gaz.* 84:225–63.

Davison, V. E. 1967. *Attracting birds: from the prairies to the Atlantic.* New York: Thomas Y. Crowell Co.

Deam, C. C. 1932. *Shrubs of Indiana.* Ind. Dept. Conserv. Publ. 44.

DeGraaf, R. M.; Thomas, J. W.; and Pywell, H. R. 1975. *Relationships between songbird nest height, vegetation, and housing density in New England suburbs.* Trans. 32nd Northeast Wildl. Conf. pp. 130–50.

Doehlert, C. A. 1953. *Propagating blueberries from hardwood cuttings.* N.H. Agr. Exp. Sta. Circ. 551.

Doran, W. L. 1957. *Propagation of woody plants by cuttings.* Univ. of Mass. Exp. Sta. Bull. 491.

Dugmore, A. R. 1904. *Bird homes.* New York: Doubleday, Page and Co.

Edminster, F. C. 1947. *The ruffed grouse: its life story, ecology, and management.* New York: Macmillan Co.

Edminster, F. C., and May, R. M. 1951. *Shrub*

plantings for soil conservation and wildlife cover in the Northeast. USDA Circ. 887. Washington, D.C.

Fernald, M. L. 1950. *Gray's manual of botany.* 8th ed. New York: American Book Co.

Flemion, F. 1938. Breaking the dormancy of seeds of *Crataegus* species. *Boyce Thompson Inst. Contrib.* 9:409–23.

Forbush, E. H., and May, J. B. 1939. *Natural history of the birds of eastern and central North America.* Boston: Houghton Mifflin Co.

Fordham, A. J. 1967. Seed dispersal by birds and animals in the Arnold Arboretum. *Arnoldia* 27(10–11):73–84.

Free, M. 1957. *Plant propagation in pictures.* New York: Am. Garden Guild and Doubleday and Co.

Giersbach, J. 1937. Germination and seedling production of species of Viburnum. *Boyce Thompson Inst. Contrib.* 4:27–37.

Grimm, W. C. 1952. *The shrubs of Pennsylvania.* Harrisburg, Pa.: Stackpole Co.

Gude, G. 1973. "Shrubs attractive to birds." *Landscaping for Birds,* edited by S. A. Briggs, pp. 26–32. Washington, D.C.: Aud. Nat. Soc.

Harlow, W. M., and Harrar, E. S. 1969. *Textbook of dendrology.* 5th ed. New York: McGraw-Hill.

Harris, R. E. 1961. The vegetative propagation of *Amelanchier alnifolia. Can. J. Plant Sci.* 41:728–31.

Harrison, H. H. 1975. *A field guide to birds' nests.* Boston: Houghton Mifflin Co.

Harsberger, J. W. 1919. Slope exposure and the distribution of plants in eastern Pennsylvania. *Geogr. Soc. Phila. Bull.* 17:53–61.

Hartmann, H. T., and Kester, D. E. 1968. *Plant propagation: Principles and practices.* 2nd ed. Englewood Cliffs, N.J.: Prentice-Hall.

Headstrom, R. 1970. *A complete field guide to nests in the United States.* New York: Ives Washburn, Inc.

Heit, C. E.
1967a. Propagation from seed. Part 6: Hardiness—a critical factor. *Am. Nurseryman* 125(10):10–12, 88–96.
1967b. Propagation from seed. Part 7: Germinating six hardseeded groups. *Am. Nurseryman* 125(12):10–12, 37–45.
1967c. Propagation from seed. Part 10: Storage methods for conifer seeds. *Am. Nurseryman* 126(8):14–15, 38–54.
1967d. Propagation from seed. Part 11: Storage of deciduous tree and shrub seeds. *Am. Nurseryman* 126(10):12–13, 86–94.
1968. Propagation from seed. Part 15: Fall planting of shrub seeds for successful seedling production. *Am. Nurseryman* 128(4):8–10, 70–80.
1969. Propagation from seed. Part 18: Testing and growing seeds of popular taxus forms. *Am. Nurseryman* 129(2):10–11, 118–28.

Holweg, A. W.
1964. Some shrubs and vines for wildlife food and cover. *N.Y. Conserv.* 19(2):22–27.
1974. "Common winterberry." In *Shrubs and Vines for Northeastern Wildlife,* edited by J. D. Gill and W. M. Healy, pp. 150–53. NE For. Exp. Sta., Upper Darby, Pa. (USDA For. Serv. Gen. Tech. Rep. NE-9).

Hottes, A. C. 1931. *The book of shrubs.* New York: A. T. De La Mare Co.

Jewell, M. E., and Brown, H. W. 1929. Studies on northern Michigan bog lakes. *Ecology* 10(4):427–75.

Kains, M. G., and McQuesten, L. M. 1938. *Propagation of plants.* New York: Orange Judd Pub. Co.

Kammerer, E. L. 1934. What deciduous shrubs will endure shade? *Morton Arbor. Bull. Pop. Inf.* 9:9–12.

Keeler, H. L. 1969. *Our northern shrubs and how to identify them.* New York: Dover Pub. Inc.

Kelsey, H. P., and Dayton, W. A. 1942. *Standardized plant names.* 2nd ed. Harrisburg, Pa.: J. Horace McFarland Co.

Kender, W. J., and Brightwell, W. T. 1966. "Environmental relationships." In *Blueberry Culture,* edited by P. Eck. New Brunswick, N.J.: Rutgers University Press.

Krefting, L. W., and Roe, I. E. 1949. The role of some birds and mammals in seed germination. *Ecol. Monogr.* 19:269–86.

Lamb, G. N. 1915. *Willows: Their growth, use, and importance.* USDA Bull. 316. Washington, D.C.

Langille, J. H. 1884. *Our birds in their haunts.* New York: S. E. Cassino and Co.

Laurie, A., and Chadwick, L. C. 1931. *The modern nursery: a guide to plant propagation, culture, and handling.* New York: Macmillan Co.

Lemmon, R. S. 1952. *The best loved trees of North America: intimate close-ups of their year-round traits.* Garden City, N.Y.: Am. Garden Guild and Doubleday and Co.

Link, C. B. 1945. The Christmas hollies. *Plants and Gard.* 1(4):203-6.

Liscinsky, S. A.
1960. *The American woodcock in Pennsylvania.* Final Rep. P-R WSOR.
1972. *The Pennsylvania woodcock management study.* Pa. Game Comm. Res. Bull. 171.
1974. "Gray dogwood." In *Shrubs and Vines for Northeastern Wildlife,* edited by J. D. Gill and W. M. Healy, pp. 42-43. NE For. Exp. Sta., Upper Darby, Pa. (USDA For. Serv. Gen. Tech. Rep. NE-9).

Livingston, R. B. 1972. Influence of birds, stones and soil on the establishment of pasture juniper (*Juniperus communis*) and red cedar (*Juniperus virginiana*) in New England pastures. *Ecology* 53:1141-47.

Longenecker, G. W., and Ellarson, R. 1973. *Landscape plants that attract birds.* Univ. of Wis. Ext. Bull. G1609.

Lovell, J. F. 1964. "An ecological study of *Rhus glabra.*" Ph.D. diss., Kansas State Univ.

Mahlstede, J. P., and Haber, E. S. 1957. *Plant propagation.* New York: John Wiley and Sons.

Mainland, C. M. 1966. "Propagation and planting." In *Blueberry Culture,* edited by P. Eck. New Brunswick, N.J.: Rutgers Univ. Press.

Martin, A. C.; Zim, H. S.; and Nelson, A. L. 1951. *American wildlife and plants.* New York: Dover Pub., Inc.

Marucci, P. E. 1966. Blueberry pollination. *Am. Bee J.* 106(7):250-51, 264.

Mason, E. A. 1965. *One, two, three.* Lincoln, Ma.: Mass. Aud. Soc.

McAtee, W. L. 1942. *Local bird refuges.* Cons. Bull. 17. USDI Fish and Wildl. Serv. Washington, D.C.

McKenny, M. 1939. *Birds in the garden and how to attract them.* New York: Reynal and Hitchcock.

Miller, W. J. 1959. The flowering dogwood on Long Island, New York. *Nat. Hort. Mag.* 38:83-91.

Morrow, E. B.; Darrow, G. M.; and Scott, D. H. 1954. A quick method for cleaning berry seed for breeders. *Am. Soc. Hort. Sci. Proc.* 63:265.

National Wildlife Federation. 1974. *Gardening with wildlife.* Washington, D.C.

Osborn, A. 1933. *Shrubs and trees for the garden.* London: Ward, Lock, and Co.

Pease, R. W. 1953. Growing flowering dogwood from softwood cuttings. *Nat. Hort. Mag.* 32:71-73.

Petit, T. S. 1949. *Birds in your backyard.* New York: Avenel Book Co.

Petrides, G. A. 1972. *A field guide to trees and shrubs.* Boston: Houghton Mifflin Co.

Pogge, F. L. 1975. Sassafras. *Pa. Game News.* 46(7):17-19.

Rawson, J. W. 1974. "Willows." In *Shrubs and Vines for Northeastern Wildlife,* edited by J. D. Gill and W. M. Healy, pp. 147-49. NE For. Exp. Sta., Upper Darby, Pa. (USDA For. Serv. Gen. Tech. Rep. NE-9).

Ritter, C. M., and McKee, G. W. 1964. The elderberry, history, classification and culture. *Pa. Agr. Exp. Sta. Bull.* 709:21.

Robinson, F. B. 1960. *Useful trees and shrubs.* Champaign, Ill.: Garrard Pub. Co.

Rogers, R. 1974. "Blueberries." In *Shrubs and Vines for Northeastern Wildlife,* edited by J. D. Gill and W. M. Healy, pp. 12-15. NE For. Exp. Sta., Upper Darby, Pa. (USDA For. Serv. Gen. Tech. Rep. NE-9).

Rollins, J. A. 1974. "Viburnums." In *Shrubs and Vines for Northeastern Wildlife,* edited by J. D. Gill and W. M. Healy, pp. 140-46. NE For. Exp. Sta., Upper Darby, Pa. (USDA For. Serv. Gen. Tech. Rep. NE-9).

Rushmore, F. M. 1969. *Sapsucker damage varies with tree species and seasons.* NE For. Exp. Sta., Upper Darby, Pa. (USDA For. Serv. Res. Pap. NE-136).

Schumacher, F. W. 1962. *How to grow seedlings of trees and shrubs.* Privately pub. Sandwich, Ma.

Schutz, W. E. 1974. *How to attract, house, and feed birds.* New York: Collier Books, Macmillan Co.

Sharp, W. M. 1974. "Hawthorns." In *Shrubs and Vines for Northeastern Wildlife,* edited by J. D. Gill and W. M. Healy, pp. 59–64. NE For. Exp. Sta., Upper Darby, Pa. (USDA For. Serv. Gen. Tech. Rep. NE-9).

Smith, B. C. 1952. Nursery research at Ohio State. *Am. Nurseryman* 95:15, 94–96.

Smith, H. K.
1970. "The biology, wildlife use and management of sumac in a study area in northern lower Michigan." Ph.D. diss., Michigan State Univ.
1974. "Sumacs." In *Shrubs and Vines for Northeastern Wildlife,* edited by J. D. Gill and W. M. Healy, pp. 134–37. NE For. Exp. Sta., Upper Darby, Pa. (USDA For. Serv. Gen. Tech. Rep. NE-9).

Smith, R. H. 1973. Crabapples for wildlife food. *N.Y. Fish and Game J.* 20(1):1–24.

Smithberg, M. A. 1964. "Patterns of variation among some climatic races of red-osier dogwood." M.S. thesis, Univ. of Minnesota.

Smithberg, M. A., and Gill, J. D. 1974. "Roses." In *Shrubs and Vines for Northeastern Wildlife,* edited by J. D. Gill and W. M. Healy, pp. 116–21. NE For. Exp. Sta., Upper Darby, Pa. (USDA For. Serv. Gen. Tech. Rep. NE-9).

Spector, W. S., ed. 1956. *Handbook of biological data.* Philadelphia: W. B. Saunders Co.

Spinner, G. P., and Ostrom, G. F. 1945. First fruiting of woody plants in Connecticut. *J. Wildl. Mgmt.* 9(1):79.

Spurway, C. H. 1941. *Soil reaction pH preferences of plants.* Mich. St. Col. Agr. Exp. Sta. Spec. Bull. 306.

Stearns, F. W. 1974. "Hazels." In *Shrubs and Vines for Northeastern Wildlife,* edited by J. D. Gill and W. M. Healy, pp. 65–70. NE For. Exp. Sta., Upper Darby, Pa. (USDA For. Serv. Gen. Tech. Rep. NE-9).

Swingle, C. F. 1939. *Seed propagation of trees, shrubs, and forbs for conservation planting.* U.S. Soil Conserv. Serv. Tech. Publ. 27. Washington, D.C.

Taylor, N. 1962. *Taylor's garden guide.* New York: Dell Pub. Co.

Terres, J. K. 1968. *Songbirds in your garden.* New York: Thomas Y. Crowell Co.

U.S. Forest Service. 1948. *Woody-plant seed manual.* USDA Misc. Publ. 654. Washington, D.C.

U.S. Forest Service. 1965. Fowells, H. A., ed. *Silvics of forest trees of the United States.* USDA Handbk. No. 271. Washington, D.C.

U.S. Soil Conservation Service.
1960. *Purpleosier willow.* Info. Sheet MA-26. Amherst, Ma.
1960. *Bayberry.* Info. Sheet MA-27. Amherst, Ma.
1966. *Tatarian honeysuckle.* Info. Sheet MA-42. Amherst, Ma.
1969. *Autumn olive.* Info. Sheet MA-29. Reg. Tech. Serv. Ctr., Upper Darby, Pa.

Van Dersal, W. K. 1938. *Native woody plants of the United States, their erosion control and wildlife values.* USDA Misc. Publ. 303. Washington, D.C.

Vines, R. A. 1960. *Trees, shrubs, and woody vines of the Southwest.* Austin: Univ. of Texas Press.

Wilde, S. A. 1946. Soil-fertility standards for game food plants. *J. Wildl. Mgmt.* 10(2):77–81.

Wood, G. W.
1974a. "Common spicebush." In *Shrubs and Vines for Northeastern Wildlife,* edited by J. D. Gill and W. M. Healy, pp. 129–31. NE For. Exp. Sta., Upper Darby, Pa. (USDA For. Serv. Gen. Tech. Rep. NE-9).
1974b. "Witch-hazel." In *Shrubs and Vines for Northeastern Wildlife,* edited by J. D. Gill

and W. M. Healy, pp. 154–57. NE For. Exp.
Sta., Upper Darby, Pa. (USDA For. Serv.
Gen. Tech. Rep. NE-9).

Wyman, D.
1949. *Shrubs and vines for American gardens.*
New York: Macmillan Co.
1951. *Trees for American gardens.* New York:
Macmillan Co.
1977. *Wyman's gardening encyclopedia.* New
York: Macmillan Co.

Zak, J. M.; Troll, J.; Havis, J. R.; Hyde, L. C.;
Kaskeski, P. A.; and Hamilton, W. M. 1972.
*A handbook for the selection of some adaptable
plant species for Massachusetts roadsides.* Univ.
of Mass. Roadside Dev. Report 24-R5-2656.

Glossary

Achene—a dry, nonsplitting fruit containing one seed closely surrounded by its case.

Acorn—the nut of the oak, usually partially enclosed by a hard, woody cup.

Acuminate—gradually tapering to an elongate tip.

Annual plant—one that completes its life cycle in a single growing season.

Axil—the angle between a leaf and stem.

Berry—a fleshy fruit that contains one or many small seeds.

Biennial plant—one that lives for two years, growing vegetatively during the first year and dying after flowering during the second.

Bipinnate—twice pinnate (*see* pinnately compound).

Bract—a modified leaf, usually occurring at the base of a flower, fruit, or leaf.

Branchlet—the smallest division of a branch representing the last season's growth.

Cambium—a thin layer of tissue—in the stems of most vascular plants—which produces new cells and is responsible for secondary growth.

Cane—a slender, woody stem, usually short-lived.

Capsule—a dry, usually many-seeded fruit with more than one cavity; fruit splits open at maturity.

Catkin—a spike of either male or female flowers, often caterpillarlike and drooping.

Clone—a group of plants produced by asexual means from a single plant, thus possessing characteristics of the original plant.

Compound leaf—a leaf that is divided into separate leaflets.

Cone—usually a woody structure with overlapping scales containing seeds of gymnosperms.

Cordate—heart-shaped.

Corymb—a rounded, flat-topped flower cluster in which the outer flowers usually open first.

Cyme—a flat-topped flower cluster in which the central flowers usually open first.

Deciduous—not persistent, dropping off at the end of the growing season.

Dehiscent—opening regularly by valves, slits, etc., as a capsule or anther.

Dioecious—having male and female flowers (unisexual) on separate plants.

Drupe—a simple, one-seeded fruit with a fleshy outer wall and a bony inner wall.

Elliptic—having the outline of an ellipse, being widest in the middle and tapering at both ends.

Follicle—a dry, dehiscent pericarp, opening only along one suture.

Inflorescence—the flowering portion of a plant.

Lanceolate—lance-shaped, longer than broad, tapering toward the tip.

Lenticel—a circular or striped corky mark on bark originating as a breathing pore.

Linear—long and narrow with parallel margins.

Monoecious—having male and female (unisexual) flowers on the same plant.

Naturalized—spreading without cultivation to areas outside the native habitat.

Node—location on stem where leaves or branches originate.

Nut—a hard, indehiscent, usually one-seeded fruit.

Nutlet—a small nut.

Oblanceolate—lanceolate, with tip tapering toward base of leaf.

Oblong—longer than broad with margins nearly parallel.

Obovate—ovate, with tip tapering toward base of leaf.

Obovoid—*see* obovate.

Ovate—egg-shaped, oval.

Palmately compound—a leaf with three or more leaflets radiating like a fan from a common point.

Panicle—a freely branched, conical inflorescence.

Perennial plant—one that lives year after year.

Perfect flower—one with both male (staminate) and female (pistilate) parts.

Pericarp—the wall of a mature ovary.

Petiole—the stalk or stem of a leaf.

pH—a scale of numbers from 1 to 14 representing a range of acidity and alkalinity; numbers below 7.0 indicate acidity; those above 7.0 indicate alkalinity.

Pinnately compound—a leaf that has leaflets arranged along one central rachis.

Pith—the spongy, central portion of a stem.

Plumule—the bud or growing part of the embryo which develops into stems and leaves.

Pome—a fleshy fruit (i.e., apple, pear) with a central core containing seeds.

Raceme—a cluster of stalked flowers on an elongated axis.

Rachis—the axis of an inflorescence or compound leaf.

Radicle—the part of the embryo that develops into roots.

Rhizome—a prostrate underground stem, usually rooting at the nodes and becoming upturned at the apex.

Samara—a nonsplitting, winged fruit.

Scarification—a treatment applied to hard, impervious seed coats—usually by acid or mechanical means—to render the coat permeable to water and hasten germination.

Schizocarp—a fruit that splits into one-seeded portions.

Scion—a short piece of living shoot containing dormant buds that is grafted onto another plant.

Serrate—small, sharp, marginal teeth that point forward.

Sessile—without a stalk, attached directly to the stem.

Simple leaf—a single leaf, not divided into leaflets.

Sinus—the indentation between two lobes of a leaf.

Spike—an unbranched, elongated cluster of unstalked flowers.

Sporophyll—a specialized organ for the production of spores.

Stipule—a small appendage that occurs at the base of a leaf petiole.

Stolon—a stem that runs along the surface of the soil and commonly roots at the joints.

Stratification—a moist-chilling treatment applied to seeds imbedded in sand or peat to overcome seed dormancy and bring about uniform germination.

Taproot—primary descending root.

Tendril—a slender outgrowth of stem or leaf that clings to a support.

Umbel—a convex or flat-topped flower cluster in which the flower stalks originate from the same point.

Index of Plant Species

Abies balsamea, 2, 3
Acer
  negundo, xii, 3, 4, 178
  platanoides, 4, 5, 178, 179
  rubrum, 5, 178
  saccharinum, 6
  saccharum, xii, 6–8, 178
alder
  black, 113
  common, 81
  hazel, 81
  smooth, 81
  snapping, 109
  speckled, 80
allspice bush, 116
Alnus
  rugosa, 80
  serrulata, 81
Amelanchier
  arborea, xi, 9
  bartramiana, 82
  canadensis, 10, 11
  laevis, 11
Ampelopsis cordata, 160, 179
ampelopsis
  American, 160
  heartleaf, 160, 179
angelica-tree, 83
apple, common, 42
Aralia spinosa, 83, 84, 179
arbor-vitae, eastern, 74
Arctostaphylos uva-ursi, 84, 85, 178, 180
Aronia
  arbutifolia, 85, 86, 179, 180
  melanocarpa, 86, 87
arrowwood
  northern, xiv, 154, 155
  southern, xiv, 154, 155
ash
  black, 30
  darlington, 31
  green, 31, 178

  red, 31
  white, 29, 30, 178
aspen
  bigtooth, 60, 61, 178
  largetooth, 60
  quaking, 61, 178, 180
  trembling, 61

barberry
  common, 88
  European, 88, 178
  Japanese, 87, 178, 179
bayberry, northern, 121, 122, 178, 180
bearberry
  common, 84, 85, 178, 180
  red, 84
bear's grape, 84
beech
  American, 28, 29
  water, 18
belluaine, 144
Berberis
  Thunbergii, 87, 178, 179
  vulgaris, 88, 178
Betula
  alleghreniensis, 12, 13
  lenta, 12
  papyrifera, 14, 15, 180
  populifolia, 16, 17, 178
bilberry, 84
birch
  black, 12
  canoe, 15
  cherry, 12
  fire, 16
  gray, 16, 17, 178
  old-field, 16
  paper, 14, 15, 180
  poverty, 16
  sweet, 12
  white, 15
  yellow, 12, 13

bittersweet, American, 162, 163, 179
blackberry
    Allegany, 134
    American, 134
blackgum, 48
bluebeech, 18
blueberry
    dwarf, 148
    highbush, xiv, 148-50
    late low, 148
    lowbush, 148, 179
    sugar, 148
    swamp, 148
    tall, 148
bluetangle, 108
boxelder, xii, 3, 4, 178
brambles, 134, 135
buck-brush, 145
buckthorn
    alderleaf, 123, 124
    common, 124, 178, 179
    European, 124
    glossy, 124, 125, 178
bullbrier, 166
bunchberry, 94
butternut, 34
buttonbush, common, 90
buttonwillow, 90

Campsis radicans, 161, 179
candleberry, 121
Carpinus caroliniana, 18, 19, 180
Carya
    glabra, 19, 178
    ovata, 20, 21
    tomentosa, 22
Castanea pumila, 88, 89
cedar
    eastern red, 36-38, 178
    northern white, 74, 75, 180
    swamp, 74
Celastrus scandens, 162, 163, 179
Celtis occidentalis, 23, 178, 179
Cephalanthus occidentalis, 90
cherry
    bird, 62
    black, 63, 64, 178, 180
    cabinet, 65
    choke, 65, 66
    fire, 62
    pin, xii, 62, 63

rum, 63
wild red, 62
chinkapin
    Allegany, 88
    eastern, 88, 89
chokeberry
    black, 86, 87
    red, 85, 86, 179, 180
Comptonia peregrina, 91, 178, 180
coralberry, 145, 146, 179
cornel
    dwarf, 94
    red-stemmed, 96
    silky, 93
Cornus
    alternifolia, xiv, 91, 92
    amomum, xi, 93
    canadensis, 94
    florida, xi, 24-26, 178, 179
    racemosa, xiv, 95, 179
    stolonifera, xiv, 96, 97
Corylus
    americana, 98, 99
    cornuta, 100
cottonwood, eastern, 59, 60
crabapple, 42-44
    'Bobwhite,' 44
    'Dorothea,' 44
    Japanese, 44
    Sargent, 44
    Siberian, 44
    tea, 44
crampbark, 157
cranberry, American highbush, 157
cranberrybush, American, xi, xiv, 157, 158
Crataegus, 100-102, 179
    crus-galli, 102, 178
    oxycantha pauli, 102, 178, 180
    phaenopyrum, xii, 102, 178
creeper, Virginia, 164, 165
currant
    American black, 129
    wild black, 129

dangleberry, 108, 109
devil's walkingstick, 83, 84, 179
dewberry
    American, 134
    northern, 134
Diospyros virginiana, 26-28, 180
dockmackie, 151

dogberry, 130
dogwood
    alternate-leaf, xiv, 91, 92
    American, 24
    blue, 91
    bunchberry, 94
    flowering, xi, 24–26, 178, 179
    gray, xiv, 95, 179
    gray-stemmed, 95
    green osier, 91
    pagoda, 91
    panicled, 95
    red-osier, xiv, 96, 97
    silky, xi, 93
    white, 24

Elaeagnus
    angustifolia, xiv, 103, 178, 180
    umbellata, xi, 104, 105, 179, 180
elaeagnus, autumn, 104
elder
    American, 138–40, 179
    blackberry, 138
    red-berried, 140
    scarlet, 140, 141
    stinking, 140
    sweet, 138
elderberry, common, 138
elm
    American, 77, 78
    false, 23

Fagus grandifolia, 28, 29
feverbush, 116
filbert
    American, 98
    beaked, 100
fir, balsam, 2, 3
firethorn, scarlet, 122, 123, 179
Fraxinus
    americana, 29, 30, 178
    nigra, 30
    pennsylvanica, 31, 178

gallberry, bitter, 111
Gaylussacia
    baccata, 106, 178
    brachycera, 106, 107
    dumosa, 107
    frondosa, 108, 109
globeflower, 90

gooseberry
    pasture, 130, 131, 179
    prickly wild, 130
grape, 168–70
    fox, 169
    frost, 169
    New England, 169
    riverbank, 169
    summer, 169
greenbrier
    cat, 165, 166
    common, 166
gum
    red, 39
    sour, 48
    starleaf, 39

hackberry, common, 23, 178, 179
hackmatack, 38
Hamamelis virginiana, 109, 110, 179
hardhack, 143
hawthorn, 100–102, 179
    cockspur, 102, 178
    Paul's scarlet, 102, 178, 180
    Washington, xii, 102, 178
hazel
    American, 98, 99
    beaked, 100
hazelnut, 98
he-balsam, 52
hemlock
    eastern, xii, 76, 77
    ground, 146
Hercules-club, 83
hickory
    mockernut, 22
    pignut, 19, 178
    shagbark, 20, 21
hobblebush, 152
holly
    American, 32, 33, 180
    Christmas, 32, 33
    low gallberry, 111
    northern, 113
    swamp, 113
honeyballs, 90
honeysuckle, 118–20, 179
    American fly, 120
    Amur, xiv, 120
    Morrow, 120, 178
    Standish, 120

Honeysuckle (*cont.*)
  swamp fly, 120
  Tatarian, xiv, 120, 180
hop-hornbeam
  American, 49, 50
  eastern, 49
hornbeam, American, 18, 19, 180
horsebrier, 166
huckleberry
  black, 106, 178
  box, 106, 107
  dwarf, 107
  high-bush, 106
  tall, 108
Hypericum spathulatum, 110, 111, 178

Ilex
  glabra, 111, 112, 178, 179, 180
  laevigata, 112
  opaca, 32, 33, 180
  verticillata, xi, 113, 114
Indian-currant, 145
inkberry, 111, 112, 178, 179, 180
ironwood, 18, 49
ivy
  American, 164
  poison, 167, 168

Juglans
  cinerea, 34
  nigra, 34–36
juneberry
  mountain, 82
  oblongleaf, 10
juniper
  common, 115, 116, 178, 180
  dwarf, 115
  old field, 115
  pasture, 115
Juniperus
  communis, 115, 116, 178, 180
  virginiana, 36–38, 178

kinnikinic, 84

larch, eastern, 38, 39
Larix laricina, 38, 39
Lindera benzoin, 116, 117, 179
Liquidambar styraciflua, 39, 40, 178, 179, 180
Liriodendron tulipifera, 41, 178, 179

Lonicera, 118–20, 179
  canadensis, 120
  maacki, xiv, 120
  Morrowi, 120, 178
  oblongifolia, 118, 120
  standishi, 120
  Tatarica, xiv, 118, 120, 180

mahogany, mountain, 12
Malus, 42–44
  baccata, 44
  'Bobwhite,' 44
  'Dorothea,' 44
  floribunda, 44
  hupehensis, 44
  pumila, 42
  sargentii, 44
maple
  ashleaf, 3
  hard, 6
  Norway, 4, 5, 178, 179
  river, 6
  red, 5, 178
  rock, 6
  silver, 6
  soft, 6
  sugar, xii, 6–8, 178
  swamp, 5
  white, 6
meadowsweet
  broadleaf, 142
  narrowleaf, 142
Menispermum canadense, 163
moonseed
  Canada, 163
  common, 163
moosewood, 152
Morus
  alba, xi, xii, 45, 180
  rubra, 46, 47, 180
mountain-ash, American, xi, 73
mulberry
  red, 46, 47, 180
  Russian, 45
  white, xi, xii, 45, 180
musclewood, 18
Myrica pensylvanica, 121, 122, 178, 180
myrtle, barren, 84

nannyberry, 155, 156
Nyssa sylvatica, 48, 49

oak
  black, 70
  northern red, 69, 70, 178, 180
  pin, 69, 178, 179
  ridge white, 66
  scarlet, 68, 178
  stave, 66
  white, 66, 67, 178, 180
oilnut, 34
oleaster, 103
olive
  autumn, xi, 104, 105, 179, 180
  Russian, xiv, 103, 178, 180
  wild, 103
Ostrya virginiana, 49, 50

Parthenocissus quinquefolia, 164, 165
persimmon, common, 26-28, 180
Picea
  glauca, xii, 50, 51, 178, 180
  pungens, xii, 51, 52, 179, 180
  rubens, 52
pine
  eastern white, xii, 56, 57, 178
  Norway, 53
  pitch, 54-56, 178, 180
  red, 53, 178
  Scotch, 58, 59, 178
Pinus
  resinosa, 53, 178
  rigida, 54-56, 178, 180
  strobus, xii, 56, 57, 178
  sylvestris, 58, 59, 178
pipestem, 142
poison ivy, 167, 168
poplar
  eastern, 59
  yellow, 41, 178, 179
popple, 60, 61
Populus
  deltoides, 59, 60
  grandidentata, 60, 61, 178
  tremuloides, 61, 178, 180
Prunus
  pensylvanica, xii, 62, 63
  serotina, 63, 64, 178, 180
  virginiana, 65, 66
pyracantha, 122
Pyracantha coccinea, 122, 123, 179

Quaker lady, 142

queen of the meadow, 142
Quercus
  alba, 66, 67, 178, 180
  coccinea, 68, 178
  palustris, 69, 178, 179
  rubra, 69, 70, 178, 180
  velutina, 70

raisin
  northern wild, 153
  wild, 155
raspberry
  black, 134
  black cap, 134
  purple-flowering, 134
  red, 134
Rhamnus
  alnifolia, 123, 124
  cathartica, 124, 178, 179
  frangula, 124, 125, 178
Rhus
  copallina, 125, 178, 180
  glabra, 126, 127, 179
  typhina, 127-29, 179
Ribes
  americanum, 129
  cynosbati, 130, 131, 179
Rosa
  blanda, 133, 179, 180
  carolina, 133, 179
  multiflora, xiv, 131, 133
  palustris, 133
  rugosa, 133, 179, 180
  virginiana, 133, 179, 180
rose
  meadow, 133, 179, 180
  multiflora, xiv, 131, 133
  pasture, 133, 179
  rugosa, 133, 179, 180
  swamp, 133
  Virginia, 133, 179, 180
Rubus, 134-35
  allegheniensis, 134
  flagellaris, 134
  idaeus, 134
  occidentalis, 134
  odoratus, 134

Salix
  discolor, 136
  humilis, 137

Salix (*cont.*)
  nigra, 71
  purpurea, 137, 138
Sambucus
  canadensis, 138–40, 179
  pubens, 140, 141
Sassafras albidum, 72, 178, 180
sassafras, common, 72, 178, 180
sawbrier, 165
serviceberry, 179
  Allegany, 11
  Bartram, 82
  downy, xi, 9
  shadblow, 10, 11
  smooth, 11
shadbush, 9, 82
sheepberry, 155
silverberry, Japanese, 104
Smilax
  glauca, 165, 166
  rotundifolia, 166
snapping-alder, 109
snowberry, common, 144, 145, 179
Sorbus americana, 73
spicebush, common, 116, 117, 179
Spiraea
  alba, 142
  latifolia, 143
  tomentosa, 143
spirea
  willow-leaved, 142
spruce
  blue, 51
  Canadian, 50
  cat, 50
  Colorado, xii, 51, 52, 179, 180
  eastern, 52
  prickly, 51
  red, 52
  white, xii, 50, 51, 178, 180
  yellow, 52
squawbush, 93, 96
steeplebush, 143
St. Johnswort, shrubby, 110, 111, 178
sugarberry, 23
sumac
  dwarf, 125
  flameleaf, 125, 178, 180
  hairy, 127
  mountain, 125
  scarlet, 126

  shining, 125
  smooth, 126, 127, 179
  staghorn, 127–29, 179
  upland, 126
  velvet, 127
  wing-rib, 125
sweetfern, 91, 178, 180
sweetgum, American, 39, 40, 178, 179, 180
Symphoricarpus
  albus, 144, 145, 179
  orbiculatus, 145, 146, 179

tamarack, 38
tangleberry, 108
Taxus
  canadensis, 146, 147
  cuspidata, 147, 179
thimbleberry, fragrant, 134
thorn, evergreen, 122
Thuja occidentalis, 74, 75, 180
Toxicodendron radicans, xii, 167, 168
trip-toe, 152
trumpet creeper, common, 161, 179
Tsuga canadensis, xii, 76, 77
tuliptree, 41
tupelo, black, 48, 49

Ulmus americana, 77, 78

Vaccinium
  angustifolium, 148, 179
  corymbosum, xiv, 148–50
Viburnum
  acerifolium, 151
  alnifolium, 152
  cassinoides, 153, 180
  dentatum, xiv, 154, 155
  lentago, 155, 156
  recognitum, xiv, 154, 155
  trilobum, xi, xiv, 157, 158
viburnum
  mapleleaf, 151
  sweet, 155
vinegar tree, 126
Vitis, 168–70
  aestivalis, 169
  labrusca, 169
  novae-angliae, 169
  riparia, 168, 169
  vulpina, 169

walnut
  eastern black, 34–36
  white, 34
wayfaring-tree, American, 152
whitewood, 41
willow
  basket, 137
  black, 71
  dwarf gray, 137
  dwarf prairie, 137
  Jerusalem, 103
  prairie, 137
  purpleosier, 137, 138
  pussy, 136
  red, 93
  sage, 137

winterberry
  common, xi, 113, 114
  evergreen, 111
  smooth, 112
winter-bloom, 109
witch-hazel, common, 109, 110, 179
witch-hobble, 152
witherod, 153, 180
woodbine, 164

yew
  American, 146
  Canada, 146, 147
  Japanese, 147, 179